POWER

POWER

THE ULTIMATE APHRODISIAC

Dr. Ruth K. Westheimer
with Dr. Steven Kaplan

MADISON BOOKS
Lanham • *New York* • *Oxford*

Published by Madison Books
4720 Boston Way
Lanham, Maryland 20706

12 Hid's Copse Road
Cumnor Hill, Oxford OX2 9JJ, England

Distributed by National Book Network

Library of Congress Cataloging-in-Publication Data

Westheimer, Ruth K. (Ruth Karola), 1928–
    Power : the ultimate aphrodisiac / Ruth K. Westheimer.
      p. cm.
    Includes bibliographical references and index.
    ISBN 1-56833-230-0 (cloth : alk. paper)
    1. Sex—History. 2. Power (Social sciences)—History. 3. Statesmen—Sexual
behavior—History. 4. Kings and rulers—Sexual behavior—History. 5. Queens—
Sexual behavior—History. 6. Mistresses—History. I. Kaplan, Steven. II. Title.

HQ12 .W49 2001
306.7'09—dc21

                                                              2001037015

∞™ The paper used in this publication meets the minimum requirements of
American National Standard for Information Sciences—Permanence of
Paper for Printed Library Materials, ANSI/NISO Z39.48-1992.
Manufactured in the United States of America.

Who is powerful?
He who conquers his passion.

—Pirke Avot 4:1

To the memory of my entire family who perished during the Holocaust. I am thankful that they had the opportunity to instill in me the much cherished values of the Jewish tradition before they were lost to me. To the memory of my late husband, Fred, who encouraged me in all my endeavors.

To the family of now: daughter, Miriam Westheimer, Ed.D.; son-in-law, Joel Einleger, M.B.A.; their children, Ari and Leora; my son, Joel Westheimer, Ph.D.; daughter-in-law, Barbara Leckie, Ph.D.; and their daughter Michal.

—R. Westheimer

I dedicate this book, which discusses sex and power from King *David* to Camp *David*, to Dr. *David* Satran, in gratitude for more than twenty years of unwavering support and friendship.

—S. Kaplan

CONTENTS

acknowledgments

DR. RUTH WESTHEIMER

Pierre Lehu, MBA, and I are now entering our twenty-first year of working together. A special toast to my "Minister of Communications" and to many more years of cooperation.

I have so many people to thank that it would require an additional chapter, so let me just mention a few:

Rep. Gary Ackerman, Ruth Bachrach, Peter Banks, M.D., Frank Bennack, Peter Berger, M.D., Mem Bernstein, Rabbi Stephen Berkowitz, Mark Bleschner, Ph.D., Richard Brown, Susan Brown, Hersh Cohen, Richard Collins, Esther Coopersmith, Thierry Chaunu, Carlita C. de Chavez, Mayor David Dinkins, Brian Dubin, Martin Englisher, Cynthia Fuchs Epstein, Ph.D., Howard Epstein, Gabe Eram, Ricardo Fernandez, Ph.D., Edith Frankel, Yosh Gafni, Josh Gaspero, John Gerlach, Rachel Gilon, Ellen Goldberg, Stephen Goodman, DDS, David Goslin, Ph.D., Amos Grunebaum, M.D., Werner Gundersheimer, Ph.D. and Karen Gundersheimer,

ACKNOWLEDGMENTS

John Harding, Richard and Elaine Heffner, Christie Hefner and Bill Maravitz, Elliot Horowitz, Fred Howard, John Jacobs, Vera Jelinek, Al Kaplan, Michael and Ronnie Kassan, Amy Kassiola and Joel Kassiola, Ph.D., Bonnie Kaye, Richard and Barbara Kendall, John Kilcullen, Rep. Jack Kingston, Larry Kirshbaum, Mayor Ed Koch, Robert Krasner, M.D. and Leslie Krasner, Nathan Kravetz, Ph.D. and Evelyn Kravetz, Cantor Michael Kruk, Marga and Bill Kunreuther, Marsha Lebby, Rabbi and Mrs. William Lebeau, Robin and Rosemary Leckie, Joanne Seminara Lehu, Esq., Arthur Levine, Ph.D., Lou Lieberman, Ph.D. and Mary Cuadrado, Ph.D., John and Ginger Lollos, Sanford Lopater, Ph.D., Frank Luntz, Jonathan Mark, Stanley and Molly Michels, Vernon Mosheim, Robert and Nicky Nachamie, Dale Ordes, Frank Osborne, Bruce Paisner, Niko Pfund, Robert Pinto, Dan Present, M.D., Fred and Ann Rosenberg, Cliff Rubin, Larry Ruvo, Jonathan Sacks, Tim Satterfield, Rose and Simeon Schreiber, Daniel Schwartz, Romie and Blanche Shapiro, Amir Shaviv, John Silberman, Esq., Jerome Singerman, John and Marianne Slade, Richard Stein, Hannah Strauss, Charles Sullivan, Malcolm and Barbara Thomson, Gary Tinterow, Stephen Weltzen, Michael Weiss, M.D., Greg Willenborg, Mildred Witkin, Ph.D., Ben Yagoda, and Ed Zolla.

A special thank-you to Henry Kissinger, from whom I heard the words of the title.

Bravo to the hardworking, competent group at Madison Books—Jed Lyons, Rich Freese, Michael Dorr, Michael Messina, Alyssa Theodore, Ross Plotkin, and Ginger Strader. What a pleasure working with you!

And to my coauthor, Steve Kaplan, what an honor and pleasure to work with you again!

Thank you all!

DR. STEVE KAPLAN

This book could not have been written without the encouragement of my friends David Satran, Mindy Milberg, Linda Aronson, Kay K. Shelemay, Hagar Salamon, Monica Devens, Sally Zanger, Eyal Ben-Ari, Reuven Amitai, Wayne Horowitz and Gabriel Motzkin, and Ruth Butler; the patience of my children Booshun, Yona, and Denise; the understanding of my mother Ruth and my sisters Eva and Judy; the efficiency of Pierre Lehu; the editorial judgment of Colin Jones, Heidi Freund, Alyssa Theodore, and Ginger Strader; the support, trust, and generosity of Ruth K. Westheimer; and the friendship and love of Albert Owens. My deepest thanks to all of them.

introduction

It happened late one afternoon when the king rose up from his bed and was walking on the roof of the palace that he saw a woman bathing and the woman was very beautiful. And David sent someone to inquire about the woman.

—2 SAMUEL 11:2–3

We can only speculate how the popular newspapers from 1000 B.C.E. would have reported on King David's affair with Bathsheba. For the time being, all we have is the biblical record and it tells us quite a bit. A powerful king sees a beautiful woman bathing. Even after he learns that she's married, he has her brought to him and has sex with her. When she becomes pregnant, the king tries to cover it up by bringing her soldier-husband back from the front so that he'll sleep with her and think the child is his. When this fails, the king has him killed! No sooner has the woman finished her period of official mourning than the king has her brought to the palace and marries her. High crimes and misdemeanors indeed!

If your only sources of information are tabloid newspapers or chat radio programs, you might think that sex scandals (and even sex itself) were invented in twentieth-century America. To many modern observers we appear unique in our fascination with the private lives of the rich and powerful. Yet, as the story of David and Bathsheba and many others like it teach us, there has always been an intimate link between power and sex. In fact, their son, King Solomon, probably got it right when he noted, "There is nothing new under the sun!"

And Solomon (who himself had 700 wives and 300 concubines) certainly knew what he was talking about when it came to the connection between sex and power.

THIS IS NOT A BOOK ABOUT *THAT* SCANDAL!

Since the Monica Lewinsky story broke in January 1998, I must have been asked at least a thousand times to give my opinion about her accusations, the president's behavior, and every other aspect of the episode. And I have consistently refused. In fact, I may be the only sex expert in the world who hasn't talked or written about the subject! I certainly don't have any regrets about that. Given the speed with which events and people's version of those events changed, I was happy to hold my tongue. All too often "instant experts" were caught (pardon the expression) with their pants down. I was happy to avoid embarrassing myself and others.

Now that things have begun to calm down a little, I'm still not going to comment on "Monica and Bill." And I have an even better reason. So many books and articles have been written about that episode and other escapades of celebrities and current political and religious leaders, why should I try to compete with them and add yet one more? (King Solomon also wrote, "Of the making of books there is no end.") But no one has attempted to place these episodes in a broader perspective by looking at their historical and cultural backgrounds. And that's why I decided to write this book. People have been so busy looking over every detail of the current scandals with a microscope that no one has stood back to see the larger picture. In an era of "kiss-and-tell" memoirs, I thought it was about time for a "kiss-and-reflect" approach.

By looking into the past and surveying different cultures, we're able to step outside our own narrow cultural certainties and consider the ways in which others have understood sexual norms. I can still remember when it was almost impossible for someone who was divorced (in a perfectly legal and above-the-board procedure) to pursue a political career in the United States. Common wisdom taught that marital instability disqualified a person from public service. At the same time the codes that governed television programming dictated that only couples who were married in real life, like Ozzie and Harriet Nelson or Richard Benjamin and Paula Prentice, could be shown sharing a double bed. All other couples were put in twin beds. Today, of course, many of our leading politicians have been divorced, and television routinely shows married couples, adulterers, single heterosexuals, gays, and lesbians sharing a bed and more.

If such different norms prevailed in our own society only a generation or two ago, it's hardly surprising to discover that in the more distant past and in other cultures, leaders and rulers were judged by standards very different from our own. One of the purposes of this book is to examine these standards, look at the expectations that people have had of the rich and powerful, and see how they reacted when these expectations weren't met. Although I'm a firm believer in a code of morality, one thing I'm not going to do in this book is judge the people I write about by our standards today.

POWER AND SEX—SEX AND POWER

During the early 1970s when Dr. Henry Kissinger served as the American secretary of state, he was often found in the company of beautiful women. Asked to explain the unlikely pairing of a portly middle-aged diplomat with heavily accented English[1] and starlets such as Jill St. John and Marlo Thomas, Kissinger quipped, "Power is the ultimate aphrodisiac."[2]

Actually, things are a bit more complicated than Dr. Kissinger might make us think. First of all it's probably more accurate to say that male power is an aphrodisiac. Women in power have often had a much different experience. While the power Aristotle Onassis derived from his great wealth gave him access to some of the most beautiful and desirable women in the world, Queen Elizabeth I's political office made it almost impossible for her to find a suitable partner. Indeed, Eleanor Roosevelt, whose story is discussed in chapter 16, is known to have said, "(How) men despise women

---

1. This was, of course, before my own heavily accented English became all the rage!

2. Kissinger was, in fact, paraphrasing Napoleon, who is said to have commented bitterly that women "belong to the highest bidder. Power is what they like—it is the greatest of all aphrodisiacs."

who have real power." This is only one example of the way in which the double standard has operated and continues to operate.

There's yet another way in which Kissinger's aphorism needs to be qualified. While some people (like John Kennedy and Catherine the Great) used power to get sex, others (like Eva Perón, Madame de Pompadour, and the biblical Delilah) have used sex to get power. How, when, and why they do it is what I'd like to discuss in this book.

Although I've tried to bring as wide a variety of examples as possible, there's at least one unavoidably arbitrary aspect about the cases I've selected for this book. The only powerful figures you'll find discussed below are those whose private foibles and failures, achievements and exploits have become public knowledge. Even if we assume that people under intense scrutiny such as the rich and royalty are more likely to have their sexual behavior exposed to the light of day, most have probably taken their secrets with them to their graves. Of course, sometimes the truth only comes out years later. Indeed, it seems like every year at least one new biography challenges our assumptions about our leaders and the lives they led. A few years ago, Thomas Jefferson might not have been included in this kind of book, and the chapter on Eleanor Roosevelt would have been very different. Who's next? Whatever we may say about Dwight Eisenhower and Kay Summersby or Queen Victoria's association with John Brown (neither of which I've been able to discuss here), we can't say that they are unique or even exceptional. What we can say is that for a variety of reasons these private episodes became public knowledge.

COMING ATTRACTIONS

Here are a couple of the things you can read about below.

Chapters 1 and 2   The More the Merrier . . . or at Least the
                    More Powerful

Throughout history powerful men have displayed their vigor by surrounding themselves with women. While some biologists trace this phenomenon back to evolutionary drives that dictated that dominant males sought to pass on their genes by having children with as many women as possible, it survives in many cultural forms. The first two chapters look at the public role played by the conspicuous display of polygamy, including its most institutionalized form: the harem. Examples are presented from both China and the Muslim world. One of the things I'm going to try to understand is how harems, intended as arenas for the exhibition of male power, sometimes became a major focus of female power. I'll also be looking at a Chinese concubine who almost destroyed a dynasty and a Turkish woman who ruled her country's empire for more than twenty years.

Chapter 3   Trophy Wives

Rich and powerful men often end up marrying beautiful women who are younger, poorer, and less powerful. Labeled in recent years as the "trophy wife" phenomenon, such marriages have become particularly noticeable among senior businessmen in the second half of the twentieth century. They are often seen as a confirmation of the man's potency in all senses of the word. One of the personalities I'm going to examine in some detail is Aristotle Onassis, who was not only a notorious womanizer, but eventually married a woman whom many Americans viewed as almost royalty, Jacqueline Kennedy.

Chapter 4   Sleeping Your Way to the Top

In some ways, this chapter is the flip side of the previous chapter on trophy wives. It examines instances in which sexual favors are offered or provided in exchange for economic and political influence and power. I discuss why this particular behavior has historically been found most frequently among women and examine in detail the fascinating case of Eva (Evita) Perón, who rose from the stigma of illegitimacy in a small town in Argentina to become the First Lady of that country.

Chapter 5   The Power to Destroy

No book has contributed as much to the Judeo-Christian understanding of gender roles as the Bible. Among the most powerful images found there are a series of stories in which women use their sexual attractiveness to bring about the downfall of their personal and national enemies. Although the stories of Esther and Haman, Samson and Delilah, Judith and Holofernes profess to depict specific historic events, their themes and rich symbolism transcend history. Part folktale, part historical novel, and part nightmare, these stories seem to be as much about collective male fears as about individual female triumphs.

Chapter 6   Political Marriages

Although our modern romantic perception of marriage tends to depict it as a union of two people joined by a combination of love and sexual attraction, in the past it was common to build alliances between ruling families and noble houses through unions between their members. Via such arrangements families preserved and expanded their wealth and political power. Both men and women, but especially the women, were expected to sacrifice their individual interests for the good of their families and countries. Sometimes these arrangements ended in personal disaster, sometimes in farce. In this chapter, I've decided to focus on the strange case of Queen Caroline of England, whose husband George IV, a known adulterer, tried to divorce her, claiming she had betrayed him. Not only does this episode show just how unsuccessful such arrangements can be, but it offers a particularly interesting glance into the way in which the media dealt with scandals in high places before the days of radio, television, and the Internet.

Chapter 7   Mistresses

Although in modern America being caught with a mistress could spell the end of a politician's career, this has not always been the case. In many societies men of power were not only allowed to have a mistress, but even *expected* to have one. While formally demanding monogamy, they accepted the right of rulers to have concubines, mistresses, and other forms of extramarital liaisons. This was their way of dealing with what one columnist has called "the insatiable need of powerful men to be adored by women other than their wives." In this chapter, I'll consider the role of a mistress. Why did some women pursue this role? Why were some families, even husbands, not merely willing to have their women become mistresses of powerful men, but eager to promote this kind of bond? What were the "qualifications" that made it possible for a woman to not only become a mistress, but, even more importantly, stay a mistress? I'll try to answer these questions by considering the life of Madame de Pompadour, who was Louis XV's mistress for more than twenty years.

Chapter 8   Master, Slave, and the Peculiar Institution

At about the same time as William Jefferson Clinton's DNA was getting him in trouble, a similar form of evidence was being used to clarify questions about a long-rumored liaison of his predecessor and namesake: Thomas Jefferson. In the late eighteenth and early nineteenth centuries, it was not unusual for a Virginia slaveowner to have sexual relations with one or more of his slaves. But when one of the United States' foremost thinkers and diplomats maintained a long-term relationship with his slave, Sally Hemings, during which she bore him several children, eyebrows were raised and controversy raged. This chapter looks at this episode, puts it in the context of the time, and attempts to clarify the meaning of modern scientific evidence.

Chapters 9 and 10   Forsaking All Others?

While the societies discussed at the beginning of the book permitted and even encouraged polygamy, others, especially in recent times, have expected their leaders—including presidents, prime ministers, and kings—to be monogamous and faithful. These chapters look at these different expectations and the successes and failures of those in leadership. I've chosen to focus on the Irish American President John Kennedy and an Irish politician who lived in the late nineteenth century, Charles Stewart Parnell. I'm going to try to understand why the womanizing Kennedy was unscathed by his numerous extramarital affairs, while in contrast, Parnell's long-term romance with a married woman, Mrs. Katharine (Kitty) O'Shea, contributed to his political demise. Ultimately, I will look at the ways that changes in laws and the nature of media have changed the rules of the game for politicians.

Chapters 11–14   Women on Top

In contrast to the previous chapters, which focus primarily on male power, I'm also going to devote several chapters to women in power. Given the fact that for most of history and in most societies women in power were rare and unusual, it's hardly surprising to find that their situations and sex lives have often been the subject of speculation and rumor. I'll be looking at the legendary Egyptian Queen Cleopatra; the strange case of the cross-dressing Queen Christina of Sweden; the rise to power of the Virgin Queen, Elizabeth I; and the lurid tales about Catherine the Great. Each of these women found a different way to deal with her position of authority: One sought to expand her power; one surrendered power; one abandoned (at least publicly) her sexuality; and one lived her life pretty much like male rulers of her time.

Chapter 15   Gay and Lesbian Politicians

In recent years in most countries any politician involved in a homosexual relationship put his career at grave risk. However stable and loving the relationship might have been, the mere fact of such a relationship was more or less tantamount to political suicide. Things haven't always been that way. For one thing, the idea that a person can be defined solely on the basis of his or her sexuality is comparatively new. Moreover, attitudes toward same-sex marriages or gays in the military have not always been what they are today. In this chapter, I'm going to look at the "moral panic" that purged large numbers of homosexuals from the entourage of Kaiser Wilhelm in early twentieth-century Germany. In particular, I'll look at the rise and fall of the man who was one of the Kaiser's closest friends: Phillip Eulenburg.

Chapter 16   The Many Worlds of Eleanor and Franklin

As may be apparent from the list above, I've decided to organize this book thematically. One result of this is that the placement of the historical examples has been pretty arbitrary. Human relationships don't usually break down into neat, clear-cut categories. In fact, most of the stories I examine contain several themes at once. Both Queen Caroline of England and Catherine the Great suffered the indignity of a not very successful (arranged) political marriage, but I thought Catherine's special problems as a sexually active female ruler were more interesting, so that's where I put the focus in her case. Most of Catherine's lovers were probably trying to sleep their way to power, but since this is much more common among women than men, I decided to look at Evita Perón, who is a bit more "typical" of such behavior. The story of Franklin and Eleanor Roosevelt allows me to bring together many of the themes I've previously discussed (political marriages, fidelity, homosexuality) and examine the way they play themselves out in a single episode.

Conclusion

The final chapter looks at what we learned in this book; explores the reasons why a particular set of circumstances has developed in the last years of the twentieth century, which has led to our particular fascination with sex and power; and considers how things may develop in the twenty-first.

PUTTING SEX IN ITS PLACE

One of the unfortunate consequences of our fascination with the sex lives of the rich and famous is that we often lose sight of the manner in which they became rich or the reason why they became famous. At least part of the confusion in such matters is the modern tendency to confuse celebrities with heroes. We, in the words of Daniel J. Boorstein, "lose sight of the men and women who do not simply seem great because they are famous, but who are famous because they are great."[3] Recent biographies of famous authors and composers seem to be more concerned with pigeonholing their sexual preferences than analyzing the literary works or musical compositions that brought them renown.[4] Business tycoons and generals have become better known for their conquests in the bedroom than their achievements in the boardroom or on the battlefield.

Although the two phenomena have usually not been connected, I believe that there is an intimate link between our current fascination with the sex lives of the rich and powerful and the willingness of so many ordinary people to expose the most intimate details of their lives to studio, television, and Internet audiences. There is, however, a crucial difference. The sex lives of the famous interest us because they have achieved fame in some *other* area of their lives. The "stars" of *Jerry Springer* and other such shows are seeking to achieve fame *through* their sex lives! While initially the mass media tended to devote itself to mass phenomena—wars, elections, sports, etc.—there is an increasing tendency to turn the private into the public; to engage in small-town gossip on a national and even a global level.

---

3. *Psychology Today,* July/August 1992, 52.

4. The same day that I wrote this section, a British researcher announced that, based on his analysis of the earliest versions of the Robin Hood legend, he had concluded that Robin was homosexual! I wasn't sure whether to feel sorry for Marian or to wonder if we shouldn't rename his Merry Men his Gay Men. Of course, the real issue is whether our own rather rigid notions of sexual preference are applicable to Robin's time at all. See my discussion of this issue in chapter 15.

While some would claim that "the private life of a great man is public property," I'm not sure I accept this idea. It certainly carries with it many dangers. As the late John F. Kennedy Jr. commented in an editorial in his magazine, *George*, we have become so obsessed with the private weaknesses of our leaders that we lose sight of their public achievements.

Edward Shils of the University of Chicago, one of the most brilliant sociological minds of the twentieth century, probably said it best in his 1967 article "Privacy and Power."

> A civil society is not a society of complete mutual transparency or visibility. Everyone needs to be allowed to live somewhat in the shade—both rulers and ruled—in order to "keep" what belongs to them. Intrusions on privacy are baneful because they interfere with an individual in his control of what belongs to him. The "social space" around an individual, the recollection of his past, his conversation, his body, and its image, all belong to him. He does not acquire them through purchase or inheritance. He possesses them and is entitled to possess them by virtue of his charisma, which is inherent in his existence as an individual soul—as we say nowadays, in his individuality—and which is inherent in his membership in the civil community. They belong to him by virtue of his humanity and civility—his membership in the human species and his membership in his own society. A society that claims to be both humane and civil is committed to their respect. When its practice departs from that respect for what belongs to the private sphere, it also departs to that degree from humanity and civility.

One of my fears is that this book will contribute further to this collapse of civility. Although it's far more concerned with history than any of the other books I've written, I haven't tried to write complete biographies of any of the figures I've discussed. Although Aristotle Onassis's shipping empire, Catherine the Great's political successes, and Evita Perón's activities on behalf of workers are all crucial parts of their stories, they're just not the parts that I'm most interested in here. But nor do I want readers to think that I'm reducing these people to one-dimensional characters. What I've tried to do is focus on one aspect of their lives in order to deepen our understanding of a wide variety of issues about sex in general and particularly the interrelationship between power and sex. To this end, I've tried to frame these stories both by placing them in the broader context of contemporary social norms and practices and by seeking to explore the lessons we can learn from each case. I've included a list of references at the end of each chapter, so readers will not only know from where I got my information, but where to look for more detailed discussions of the people and issues I've discussed.

Since I'm already on the topic of sources and access to information, I need to make a little confession. Although I have my own website and there's a CD-ROM version of *Dr. Ruth's Encyclopedia of Sex*, I'm a computer illiterate. I barely know how to turn a computer on, much less use one. Now given the fact that the World Wide Web is loaded with sites dealing with sex, I realize that this is rather old-fashioned. Nevertheless, I've managed to keep up to date in other ways, and I've plenty of other sources of information for most of the topics I deal with.

I was rather startled, however, to discover how valuable the Internet was in preparing this book. It seems that our current fascination with the sex lives of the rich and powerful is not limited to the present or confined to conventional sources such as books and encyclopedias. There seems to be no inherent conflict between the use of modern media and a fascination with historical figures. Often the first indications as to just how interesting some of these figures were came through a website, and I've also included many of these among the references. It is interesting to note that this new technology has led not only to a far greater scrutiny of the lives of modern leaders, but also to a much wider distribution of information about those of the past.

The manner in which different media treat people's private lives is yet another theme that runs through this book. Although some American observers have claimed that it's only in recent years that the sex lives of politicians and other famous people have become the subject of public scrutiny, this is only partially true. It's true that for much of this century the American media exercised a great deal more self-censorship—on all matters. FDR was never pictured getting in and out of his wheelchair, so it's not terribly surprising that neither his nor Eleanor's extramarital relationships were publicly discussed. JFK's numerous affairs were the subject of many rumors, but treated as off-limits by the press. However, I was surprised when I started working on this book to discover just how much discussion there was of such matters in earlier centuries. The British chortled when the young Queen Victoria spent her honeymoon at a town called "Maidenhead," and George IV's attempt to divorce Queen Caroline had all the trappings of a modern media circus. The sexual practices and preferences of both Catherine the

Great and Queen Christina of Sweden were the subject of rumor and speculation throughout their lifetimes and for many years after. In fact, the sexual behavior of the powerful has always provoked curiosity and commentary, and this too is part of the story I'm trying to tell in this book.

HERE WE GO AGAIN!

This is the third book on which I've collaborated with Dr. Steven Kaplan of the Hebrew University of Jerusalem. Each book has been a little bit different, and actually this is the first one that has anything to do with sex!

Steve and I first met in 1991 when I traveled to Israel as the producer of a documentary entitled *Surviving Salvation*, which looked at the experience of Ethiopian Jewish immigrants in Israel. Since Steve is a world-renowned authority on the Ethiopians and my Doctorate of Education was in the Interdisciplinary Study of the Family, it was only natural that we should join forces and produce a book, also called *Surviving Salvation* (New York University Press, 1992) that focused on Ethiopian Jewish families in Israel.

Steve and I both immensely enjoyed collaborating on that project, and throughout the intervening years I kept my eyes open for another opportunity to work together. This came about in 1998 when the people at Routledge Press invited us to produce *Grandparenthood*, which combined information, advice, and a guide to resources for the almost 100 million grandparents in America today. In this case, it was not our fields of study that were complementary, but our places in the life cycle. All too often books about grandparents have been written by grandparents for grandparents and have ignored the parents' generation. By working with Steve, I was able to write a book that emphasized intergenerational communication and balanced the needs of grandchildren, parents, and grandparents.

No sooner had Steve and I completed that manuscript than we began thinking about our next project. In the spring of 1998, during a chat over coffee at the King David Hotel in Jerusalem, I casually mentioned how often I had been asked to comment on the Monica Lewinsky affair and how steadfastly I'd refused. Steve observed that no one had yet tried to place that scandal in a wider perspective, and a lightbulb went off in my head! Why shouldn't we write just that kind of book?

Once again we had to decide on an effective way to organize our work. The first rule I insisted upon was that we would not discuss any persons who are still living. I know that this will be disappointing to some readers, but I felt it would be unfair to intrude into the lives and relationships of living people. So while I've been able to include some pretty juicy stories in this book, you won't be reading about the foibles of current politicians, the exploits of movie stars or media moguls, the excesses of famous athletes or rock musicians, or the falls from grace of well-known preachers. Fortunately (or perhaps unfortunately), given human nature, even with this self-imposed limitation, I still have a few thousand years' worth of stories to tell and examine.

Once Steve and I had agreed about what incidents to discuss, we set out to scour the libraries for information. Given his background in comparative history this was pretty easy, and in what seemed like no time at all we had a preliminary list of people we wanted to write about. The next step was taking the life stories of people who in most cases had been the subject of not one but numerous lengthy biographies and condensing them into manageable narratives focused on one of the book's themes. Gradually, a pattern began to develop. As each case became clearer, we also had to go behind the story to find its deeper relevance and interest for today's readers.

Basically I've tried to consider each of these stories as if the principal characters had called or written to me, and I've tried to consider each case on its merits. I need to stress that the situation here is much more like a phone-in than sitting with a patient in the privacy of my office. It always has to be kept in mind that in this book I'm evaluating the situation of a public figure, usually from a distant time and place, whom I've never met. This is not, therefore, an attempt to write a detailed psychohistory of any of the characters.

One of the things that have constantly surprised me is the tremendous differences that exist in different biographies of a person. The woman who one author portrays as sexually insatiable was according to another source barely interested in sex; one writer's indefatigable philanderer is another's loyal husband. Except in those rare instances when people have left very detailed letters or diaries, we usually can only speculate about their most intimate relationships, especially if these were viewed as illicit or irregular at the time. (Indeed, in several cases we know that the protagonists or their heirs destroyed material to protect their reputations or to avoid legal troubles.) In cases when both people confirm a relationship, we can probably assume this to be the case. But most of what's been written about the "Virgin Queen" Elizabeth's affairs is based on gossip and speculation, and much of what we "know" about Catherine the Great is patent exaggeration. In every case I've read the books and made my best judgment of the facts.

Anyone who has followed today's stories of sex and politics knows that it's often hard to distinguish between the image and the reality. A daily barrage of newspaper stories and television specials tells us not necessarily what happened, but what people think happened and what "experts" think we should believe and be shocked by. There's nothing new about this. To the extent that this book is concerned as much with perceptions as facts, I'm also going to consider the portrayal of these figures as much as the reality. In many cases the stories told about certain people both during their lifetimes and after their deaths are as interesting as what they actually did.

Another of the things I found surprising in researching the stories of so many fascinating people is how many of them have been the subject not only of books and plays, but, in recent years, films. By this I mean not only excellent documentaries such as the one about Eleanor Roosevelt shown on many PBS stations in January 2000, but also historical dramas prepared for both commercial television and the movie houses. Of course, I had already seen *Evita* (both the play and the movie), but as part of my research I also set out to see as many of these films as possible. These included Greta Garbo's depiction of her countrywoman Christina and Catherine Zeta-Jones's portrayal of her namesake Catherine the Great. I've managed to see several versions of the life of Cleopatra and at least two films that touched upon Jefferson's relationship with Sally Hemings. Of course, we have to remember that recent films and plays about figures like Delilah, Evita Perón, or Thomas Jefferson usually tell us as much about *our* notions of power and sex as they do about theirs. But this doesn't make them any less interesting.

In most of the books I've written, I've started out with a fairly large body of knowledge about the subject (birth control, pregnancy, relationships) and the challenge has been how best to pass it on to my audience. In this book, part of the fun has been learning about so many fascinating people. I've certainly had fun exploring the lives of these fantastic people, and I hope you enjoy reading about them just as much!

many wives, many powers: The politics of polygyny

Men have more than one wife and the number of these wives varies with their station in life. It is quite remarkable that whereas our wives are keen to prevent us from acquiring the friendship and the favors of other women, their wives are anxious to enable them to acquire such favors and friendships. Their women place the honor of their husbands above anything else and seek to have as many co-wives as possible, for this testifies to the good reputation of their husbands.

—Montaigne, *The Essays*[1]

There are lots of ways in which I could have begun this book. I chose the subject of polygamy for a variety of reasons. OK, I admit that it's a pretty racy topic and one I don't get to say much about in my regular work as a sex therapist. However, there are several other factors that justify giving this topic a prominent place in this book.

First of all, as foreign as the subject may seem to most of us, it still strikes a deep chord in the present day. Second, although most casual observers are more fascinated by the sexual than the political aspects of polygamy (and who can blame them), I will attempt to demonstrate that it is always a political phenomenon. Third and last, it's a marvelous way of showing right off the bat just how complicated the relationship between sex and politics really is.

---

1. Quoted in Clignet, *Many Wives, Many Powers.*

One of the most conspicuous ways in which power and sex are linked is through the display (usually by men) of the number and/or the quality (beauty and youth) of their sexual partners. Whether it was the emperor of China with thousands of wives and concubines or King Solomon with his "mere" hundreds, powerful men throughout history seem to have been inordinately proud of not so much the quality but the quantity of their sexual relations. Despite the echoes of such behavior in our own time, no aspect of distant societies (whether the distance is measured in years or miles) has provoked as much comment as the institution of polygyny (multiple wives). Missionaries and women's rights activists have condemned it, male travelers and writers have fantasized over it, and anthropologists and historians have pondered it. In the late nineteenth century, scholars with preconceived notions, assisted by explorers with overactive imaginations (or perhaps active fantasy lives), speculated that "in the beginning" no marriages existed and all women were possessed in common either by one or several dominant males.

In order to even begin to understand the relationship between power and polygyny we need to begin by dispelling some of the myths that surround it and putting it in its correct cultural and historical perspective. Discussions with modern practitioners of polygyny (mainly men, but also women) usually elicit amused and skeptical reactions to our fascination/horror with the institution. Isn't (they ask) the serial monogamy of marriage, divorce, and remarriage so common in the West just another form of polygamy? Which is better and healthier (they challenge), the institutionalized existence of co-wives, or the phenomenon of clandestine affairs and mistresses? There may be more than a little truth to these arguments. Sultans and emperors don't appear to be the only ones who take pride in their sexual prowess. After all, not all that long ago author Graham Greene claimed to have slept with 10,000 women, and basketball player Wilt Chamberlain doubled this by claiming 20,000.[2]

There are lots of theories as to why men seem to have this tendency to have multiple partners. In many traditional societies,

---

2. I'm not sure if these claims should be taken literally. Twenty thousand partners works out to more than a woman a day over a period of fifty years! What's as interesting as the number is that men as successful as Greene and Chamberlain should have felt the need to publicize the number.

the existence of polygyny appears to be related to other practices associated with sex and childbearing. In many polygynous societies, for example, there are extensive taboos concerning sexual relations during late pregnancy and while the mother is nursing (usually a period of one to two years). In a monogamous couple this would mean that both members of the couple would not have intercourse for several years! Doubtless this would result in numerous affairs and, perhaps inevitably, divorces. It's hard enough to keep the romance alive after children even without this sort of taboo.[3] Polygyny means that a husband has an alternative sexual partner when one or more of his wives are pregnant. I cannot say that I envy the wives, however. Nevertheless, there is some compensation for them. Several studies indicate that while men with several wives have more offspring, the individual wives tend to have fewer children and spend more time nursing and generally rearing each of them. So perhaps these long periods of sexual abstinence are balanced by a more fulfilling mothering experience.

Yet another explanation tries to put polygyny in a broader evolutionary perspective. According to the evolutionary biologists, men who had multiple sexual partners had the best chance of passing their genes along to the next generation. Thus natural selection would tend to favor males who had the means and desire to mate with as many women as possible. In contrast, women seeking to pass on their genes to the next generation had no need for multiple partners—one fertile male was enough. The insurance they needed and sought came more in the form of stability and protection, which could better be provided by a single loyal partner who stuck around, rather than a one-night stand.

I've always been a little bit skeptical of such bioevolutionary explanations. Their supporters seem to use them rather selectively, and all too often they tend to reduce human beings to the level of animals or at least to little more than a collection of genetically programmed behaviors. In the realm of sexuality, I've always found it hard to understand in terms of evolution why men go through a refractory period after orgasm, during which they lose their sexual excitement and cannot have an erection or reach orgasm, while women generally don't. This would seem to lead to an argument for polyandry, women having two or more husbands. When the

---

3. See the last chapter of *Dr. Ruth's Pregnancy Guide for Couples* (Routledge, 1999), which I coauthored with Dr. Amos Grunebaum.

first reaches orgasm and needs a rest, number two would just move in! I'm only joking, but it shows where such arguments can lead.

In any event, the issue that interests me here is not whether evolution or some other factor encourages men to have multiple wives or partners, but rather the political and social roles played by the public display of these relationships. In other words, it's not the fact of multiple partners as such that interests me in this chapter, but the manner in which they are used to make a political statement.[4]

Whatever the origins of polygyny as a social phenomenon may have been, this much appears clear: Its survival depends on either a constant shortage of men or a clear imbalance of power, or both. In other words, the only way polygyny can exist as an institution is if there are too few men (too many women) and/or certain men have the power to gain access to women and deny it to other men. One possible scenario is a war in which many men were killed, leaving an overabundance of women. Another is a massive depletion of the male population as happened during the transatlantic slave trade.[5]

However, almost inevitably, whatever the underlying circumstances, the prevalence of polygyny depended on an unequal division of power. Certain individuals or societies were able to acquire "extra" women at the expense of their less powerful rivals. Just how many wives or concubines they acquired depended on just how much power they had at their disposal. Thus as Montaigne noted in the quote at the beginning of this chapter, the number of wives a man had served as an indication of his status in society. The higher his status the more wives he had, or perhaps more accurately the more wives he had the higher his status was perceived to be. Thus, on a very important level the accumulation of wives went beyond the personal needs of any one man. Marriages were arranged to cement political alliances (see chapter 6), and women were acquired as a demonstration of power and wealth.

It's important at this point to make a distinction between two basic configurations. In certain polygynous societies wives worked

---

4. For cases in which powerful figures chose to keep such multiple relationships private, see chapters 10 and 16.

5. Slave traders sought to take two-thirds men and only one-third women. The loss of so many men between the ages of fifteen and twenty-five led to a rise in polygyny among those left behind. For more on the sexual aspects of the slave trade, see chapter 8.

and children were considered an economic resource. In these instances, the male head of household received immediate economic rewards and benefits as a consequence of having a large household. Each marriage was carefully considered as an investment with a keen eye to the eventual return.

However, for my purposes it is even more interesting to look at those cases in which wives and children were not an asset, but an economic burden: cases in which not only did they not contribute to the household economy, but they were a considerable drain upon it. Such wives didn't work, rather they were cared for by servants and other retainers. Only a wealthy and powerful man could afford the luxury of multiple wives under such circumstances. Indeed, his ability to support his wives and children was a testimony to the resources he commanded. The more numerous these were, the more powerful and potent he was. Imperial China offers an excellent example of this phenomenon.

THE CONCUBINES OF CHINA

From earliest recorded times, the rulers of China displayed their political power and wealth by accumulating lovely young women as handmaidens. A minor ruler might have anywhere from a dozen to more than a hundred such women. At least one early emperor is said to have had over ten thousand maids and concubines, and many of his successors had more than a thousand. Throughout the imperial period, rich men acquired young women as a form of conspicuous consumption and proof of virility. There were even texts that provided an index as to the number of concubines deemed appropriate to each political rank! While no one seems to have been bound by the standards set in these texts, they represent a striking example of the linking of political power and sex.

The acquisition of concubines was by no means limited to political figures. Wealthy men typically acquired concubines when they reached middle age, and some continued to do so into their seventies and eighties. Concubines, it must be pointed out, were not prostitutes. These also existed in imperial China, as they have in every society. However, a wealthy or powerful man usually preferred the services of one of his concubines to a visit to the quarters where prostitutes or other entertainers thrived.

There was also a clear division between wives and concubines. A concubine could never become a wife, even if her master's wife died. A maid, however, who was seduced by her master and bore him a child could be "promoted" to the position of concubine.

Typically, concubines came from less well-to-do families that had fallen upon hard times. Desperate parents in need of cash sold their daughters to brokers or even directly to their masters. Some, however, trained their daughters from birth in the skills expected of a concubine in order to raise their asking prices. The demand for such girls always exceeded the supply, and brokers resorted to deceit and even kidnapping to acquire girls. Thus, although there was no great stigma attached to being a concubine, the women who found themselves in this profession came disproportionately from poorer and less fortunate families. It would not be an exaggeration to say the Chinese system, as with so many others, resulted in older men from powerful families obtaining the sexual services of young, attractive women from not very powerful families. In this case, power was not an aphrodisiac, but more a resource for the acquisition of sexual partners.[6]

IT'S NOT OVER UNTIL THE FAT LADY SINGS

Nevertheless, this is only part of the story. While most concubines lived out their days in quiet anonymity, a select few achieved not only fame, but power and influence. One of the most fascinating stories from among countless told in China about imperial concubines concerns a woman named Yang Guifei. I first heard of her when I visited the Los Angeles Antiques Show in 1999. As I was admiring a pottery figure of a "Fat Lady" from the Tang dynasty (618–906), Edith Frankel, an expert on Oriental art, began to explain its background. The model for the figure, she told me, was almost certainly a concubine named Yang Guifei. Although the precise facts of her life and death remain unclear, for more than a millennium she has served as an inspiration for writers, poets, and artists. Once you've heard her story, you'll understand why.

Yang was a concubine of the emperor Xuan Zong (r. 713–755), also known as Ming Xuan (the Brilliant Emperor). During the first part of his reign (713–742), there was a period of peace and pros-

---

6. In a story published in the *New York Times* in mid-August 2000, a situation remarkably similar to that described above is depicted regarding relations between wealthy men from Hong Kong and poor women in mainland China.

perity. He was a model of Confucian ethics and wisdom, ruling justly and introducing road and farming improvements as well as numerous other civil projects. He restored order after a period of administrative chaos and took vigorous measures against the corruption of his predecessors. The second half of his reign was dramatically different and was characterized by massive corruption, wasteful expenditure, and, very nearly, the collapse of the dynasty. This dramatic change in his conduct and in the fortunes of the Chinese people is, more often than not, attributed to his infatuation with the woman who became his beloved concubine.

According to tradition, Yang Guifei was originally the concubine of the eighteenth son of the emperor. One day the emperor saw her bathing (shades of David and Bathsheba!) and was captivated by her beauty. The chief court eunuch, always eager to please his master, arranged for the sixty-year-old emperor to meet the teenaged girl in private.[7] The emperor fell hopelessly in love with her, took her away from his son, and made her his concubine. (In an act of incredible cynicism he justified his behavior on the grounds of the Confucian value of filial piety, the rules of which he had engraved on stone pillars!)

In the words of the Chinese poet Po Chu-I, who commemorated the couple in his "Lament Everlasting":

> *Heaven endowed her with a beauty impossible to ignore;*
> *It led one day to her being selected to the King's side.*
> *Such a wealth of seductive art came forth with her smiling glance.*
> *That every harem occupant seemed colorless in comparison. . . .*
> *She was a fixed object of royal pleasure,*
> *Inseparable attendant at feasts unending,*
> *As day's joy merged with night's ecstasy,*
> *The king, owner of three thousand harem beauties*
> *Loved only one, Maiden Yang, with exclusive devotion.*

Tradition tells us that Yang Guifei was not only beautiful (although a bit heavy by today's standards), but also vivacious and an excellent *raconteur*. She was a fine singer and dancer. She, like the emperor, was a composer and patron of the arts. She also had a tremendous love for giving and receiving gifts. At one point she gave so many gold inlaid boxes as gifts that it threatened to dry up

---

7. Small wonder that a book on Chinese eunuchs was subtitled *The Structure of Intimate Politics*.

the imperial coffers. Laws were passed forbidding the manufacture of such boxes so she could no longer give them as gifts!

She was an avid equestrienne, polo player, and art collector. Not surprisingly, given her hobbies, she particularly loved the horse motif in the arts. The style of horse depictions that she preferred set the standard for the art of the period. Even more strikingly, she transformed the entire Chinese ideal of beauty, with the depiction of corpulent court ladies based on her own figure becoming the norm. (It was just such a depiction that caught my interest at the exhibit.)

To appease Yang Guifei's nearly insatiable taste for luxuries, the emperor would have ice brought to her daily by runners who collected it on the top of mountains and then passed it on to other runners until the "anchor" of the relay reached her palace. Her taste for peaches was met by the finest fruit from the distant central Asian kingdom of Samarkand, and lichees were brought by special couriers from South China. Special roads were built to speed the messengers on their way. The emperor also had baths built for her at the hot springs in Shaanxi province. He also saw to it that her family was appropriately honored. Three of her sisters joined the nobility, and one of her cousins, Yang Kuo-chung, became prime minister.

Ming and Yang are said to have loved each other deeply.[8] In 751, on the seventh day of the seventh month, the emperor and Yang Guifei prayed to the stars at the Palace of Eternal Youth and vowed to love each other forever:

> *The time is right to whisper to you of love*
> *And vow to be true for ever*
> *May the twin stars in heaven be our witness*
> *[we] love each other so dearly that we wish*
> *to be husband and wife in every*
> *incarnation and never be parted.*
> *May the twin stars witness our vow.*

This fairy tale love story might have continued indefinitely had not the Tang dynasty fallen upon hard times. Although there were obviously numerous causes, including corrupt officials and

---

8. I should point out that not all versions depict the love story so ideally. According to some versions, Yang had an affair with one of the emperor's important generals and was caught having oral sex with his brother. Although the emperor initially banished her for this betrayal, he later forgave her.

high military expenditures, the extravagances of Yang and her entourage were blamed. When a general from one of the provinces led his troops in rebellion and conquered the imperial capital, Ming Xuan was forced to abdicate in favor of the same son from whom he had taken Yang. (Revenge indeed!) Faced by a mutiny from his troops, who killed both Yang's sister and her cousin, the prime minister, the emperor was forced to let Yang Guifei commit suicide. According to official records she was escorted to the border, where she took her own life. But some traditional sources record that a look-alike committed suicide in her place, while she was secretly sent to a Japanese nunnery. In support of this version, tradition records that her body is said to have vanished from her tomb, and for the next three years until the emperor's death, a gift arrived on his birthday, sent from the Japanese nunnery!

Another no less romantic version says that the emperor was so depressed by her death that he finally consulted a necromancer who found her in the heavenly realm. There she repented for her excesses, but not for her love:

> Before heaven and earth, the moon and the stars
> In all sincerity I review my past;
> For all my sins I deserved this punishment
> But tonight, repentant, I confess my crimes;
> May heaven pardon me and be my witness!
> Only my love I can never repent,
> For I am still drowning in a sea of love;
> And even if I cannot be reborn,
> I will go on loving the emperor even in hell.

The emperor is said to have missed her so much that he eventually refused to eat or drink and died at the age of seventy-eight. Finally, he and his beloved Yang were reunited.

> Here on this wonderful night,
> The lovers are reunited,
> And the moon shines full upon them.
> They have passed through life and death
> And existed as spirit and fairy
> To be reunited at last in paradise
> Like two lotus flowers on a single stem
> Their former pledge fulfilled.

For hundreds of years, the story of Yang and her emperor inspired Chinese artists, dramatists, and poets. For some authors, including those I've quoted from above, it was depicted as the ultimate tragic love story. Two lovers, pledged to each other for eternity, separated by death and their enemies, and ultimately reunited in the world to come.

CONCLUSIONS

As interesting as the stories I'm discussing may be in and of themselves, I've chosen them not merely for themselves, but also for the lessons they teach us. I don't want to get too far ahead of myself and build too much on this one example, but there are several themes in this case that are worthy of comment and will recur in other parts of this book.

First of all, it's important that we understand just how culturally and historically bound sexual norms are. While we might be concerned with the immorality of a man keeping a concubine or with the gap between the senior man and his younger lover, this was not what troubled Ming Xuan, his contemporaries, or most Chinese commentators. For many of them, it represented the ultimate tale of the man who became too preoccupied with his concubine and neglected his real duties and responsibilities. For in traditional China, there was no shame in having a concubine or even several. Scandal derived not from the concubine's presence, but from her exaggerated prominence. A prominent man risked ridicule and, in the case of a leader, unrest if he followed his heart (or his penis) and not his head. This certainly seems to be the case for Emperor Ming Xuan.

Unlike our own times, no one seems to have been terribly concerned with the age gap between the elderly emperor and his teenaged concubine. What concerned them was that the emperor fell in love. Under the Confucian values of T'ang China, love was an incredibly dangerous emotion. The emperor stood to be condemned not for the exploitation of a young girl by a powerful older man, but for trying to make it into a meaningful relationship.

The second point that needs to be stressed here, however, is that the relationship between the emperor and Yang Guifei quickly went from being a private affair to a public matter of state. While it may be a bit of a stretch to say that Emperor Ming's decline was a direct result of his infatuation with Yang, there seems to be little question that it had a powerful and direct influence on his decisions and policies. Not only did indulging her consume funds and resources, but it may also have clouded the emperor in choosing her cousin for the important office of prime minister. This seems to be a case in which even the most generous of interpreters would have to agree that what went on in the bedroom was relevant as not merely an affair, but as an affair of state.

Finally, this story provides us with an excellent demonstration of the complex dynamics of the relationship between sex and power. While it may initially have been Ming Xuan's power that made his relationship with Yang possible, it was her relationship with him that gave her access to power. He used power to get sex; she used sex to get power. We shall have a chance to revisit this phenomenon in the next chapter as we explore the fascinating story of life in a harem.

SUGGESTIONS FOR FURTHER READING

Clignet, Remi. *Many Wives, Many Powers: Authority and Power in Polygynous Families*. Evanston, Ill.: Northwestern University Press, 1970.

Ebrey, Patricia Buckley. *The Inner Quarters: Marriage and the Lives of Chinese Women in the Sung Period*. Berkeley: University of California Press, 1993.

Frankel, Edith. Personal communication. May 10, 1999.

Herbert, P. A. *Under the Brilliant Emperor: Imperial Authority in T'ang China as Seen in the Writings of Chang Chiu-ling*. Canberra: Faculty of Asian Studies in association with Australian National University Press, 1978.

Levy, Howard S. *Lament Everlasting (The Death of Yang Kuei-fei)*. n.p., 1962.

Mitamura, Taisuke. *Chinese Eunuchs: The Structure of Intimate Politics*. Rutland, Vt.: C. E. Tuttle, 1970.

Sheng, Hung. *The Palace of Eternal Youth*. Peking: Foreign Languages Press, 1955.

The sultanate of women: sex and power in the ottoman Harem

A man's wife has more power over him than the state has.

—Ralph Waldo Emerson

The harem is probably one of the most misunderstood institutions in human history. Just say the word and it conjures up an image of a large group of women, wives, and concubines whose sole purpose was to meet the sexual needs of their master. They are as beautiful and sensuous as they are anonymous. Women reduced to nothing but sexual objects to be looked at (should you succeed in getting behind the walls, barred windows, and veils) and used.

This picture is, to a considerable degree, the product of the misunderstandings and fantasies of Western observers and travelers.[1] The reality was far more complex, and for many of the women (at least as far as the sexual side was concerned), radically different. The word *harem* comes from an Arabic root, which generally is used to refer to things that are forbidden, sacred, or taboo. The holy

---

1. For a fascinating book that both documents and, to a considerable extent, perpetuates this tradition, see Malek Alloula, *The Colonial Harem* (Minneapolis: University of Minnesota, 1995).

cities of Islam, Mecca and Medina are, for example, referred to as
haremeyn-i-sherifeyn (the noble sanctuaries or harems), while the Islam holy sites in Jerusalem are called *harem-i-sherif* (the noble sanctuary). The term, far from having sexual connotations, carries with
it associations of respect, religious purity, and honor. In fact, as
some astute observers have noted, for the great majority of
women, the harem—with its isolation from the world, hierarchical
organization, and enforced chastity—resembled a nunnery more
than a house of ill repute! To quote Sophia Lane Poole, one of the
first European women to visit a harem:

> The ideas entertained by many in Europe of the immorality of the
> harem are, I believe erroneous. . . . The discipline which is exercised
> over the young women in the Eastern harem can only be compared
> with that which is established in the convent.[2]

For a male head of household and master of a harem, the seclu-
sion of women, and particularly a large number of women, sent
several messages to the surrounding society. As in any polygamous
society, the ability to acquire and provide for a large number of
women was an expression of his power and potency. This was usually also conveyed by the existence of a large number of sons and
daughters, the fruit of his loins.

The harem not only demonstrated the master's control over the
women of his household, but also protected men at large from what
was perceived to be the threat of female sexual power. There is a
saying in Morocco, for example, that women are Satan's leash (*libel
al-shitan*), which means that they are capable of dragging men away
from virtue and tying them up (which is also a euphemism for impotence)! This image of women as the bearers of powerful and even
menacing sexual passions is, of course, not limited to the Muslim
world and has roots in many cultures.[3] However, in the Muslim
case the ability to seclude his women from the public gaze was also
an index of his and his family's status.[4] Among the common folk in

---

2. Quoted by Graham-Brown, *Images of Women*, 78.

3. One need only think of such biblical figures as Delilah and Judith,
discussed in chapter 5.

4. It is interesting to note that even the method of *executing* women of
the harem seems to have preserved their modesty. In most cases, they
were drowned by being placed in burlap sacks that were dropped into the
ocean. In some cases, sultans replaced their entire harem, drowning
dozens at one time.

the poorer parts of town, men and women mingled freely on the streets and in the bazaars. One of the clear dividing lines between the elites and the masses was that the former possessed the means to segregate their women. Since Islamic law mandated such segregation, the ability to enforce a separation between the sexes was not only an expression of means, but also an act of piety.

Within a typical harem one would find not only the wife or wives and concubines of the patriarchal head of the household, but also his children, and perhaps his widowed mother, his unmarried or divorced sisters, and female slaves. While the harem of a household of means might hold a dozen or so women, the imperial harems of the Ottoman Empire were often much larger and far more complex institutions. Although Western travelers tended to exaggerate the numbers involved, between the mid-sixteenth and the mid-seventeenth centuries reliable sources indicate that 150 to 400 women resided in the sultans' harems. When eunuchs, slaves, and other servants were included, the number could rise to almost a thousand.

Now while this would seem to be a sufficient number for both the sexual and political needs of any man, this does not appear to have been the case for some of history's more erratic rulers. Several sultans are said to have killed all their concubines and replaced them with new women in fits of anger, out of revenge, or from sheer boredom. Like the apocryphal multimillionaire who is said to have bought a new car whenever the ashtray filled up, they replaced their entire harems with a whole new batch of girls.

THE SECRETS OF THE HAREM

One of the questions I've always had about the harem or any other polygynous household with a large number of women is: What did the women do to relieve their boredom? Obviously many of them were occupied with their children and, as we shall see in the final section of this chapter, others served in important political positions. However, at any given time there was a large number of sexually active women under a single roof with vast amounts of free time on their hands. Since they weren't allowed out of the harem, they had to find their entertainment from within.

It seems that I'm not the only one who wondered how the women of the harem entertained themselves. For hundreds of years books that told tales of life in the harem circulated in both

Western and Middle Eastern countries. I can't vouch for the truth behind any of these stories, but I offer a couple for consideration.

One of the most common themes concerned illicit relations between the women of the harem and the eunuchs or other men admitted to their presence. Although castration usually kills both potency and desire, this is not always the case, and rumors of intimate affairs between the women and their keepers were a constant source of anxiety to men and amusement to women. One author familiar with life in the palace claimed that his partners were forced to divorce their wives who were former harem girls when the women informed them that (even) the eunuchs were better lovers than they!

Other women are said to have risked their lives through relationships with slave boys. Letters that have been preserved from the "golden cage" (as the harem was sometimes called) offer clear evidence of lesbian relationships between its residents as well. The women of the Ottoman Empire were, moreover, familiar with the use of a *zibik* (a wooden dildo), as is evidenced by both artwork and stories of the production, sale, and acquisition of such objects.

The attitudes of men toward the women in their harems varied significantly. Some were insatiable and never tired of acquiring new girls. Others, as surprising as it may seem, viewed the harem more as a burden than an asset. One eighteenth-century sultan is said to have worn gold and silver nails on his shoes, so that his wives and all other women would hear him approaching and go into hiding. One of his successors is said to have fallen so deeply in love with one of his slave girls that he viewed himself as *her* slave. As he wrote in one of his letters to her:

> Please grant me the pleasure of your company, that will be my joy. Tonight is the night of the new moon. I am in your hands. Please do me a kindness; do not let me suffer anymore. Last night I could hardly restrain myself. I am your humble slave at your feet.[5]

This lucky slave girl appears to have judged her man well. Other sultans would have had her executed or sold to another man!

It is, to say the least, very interesting to find such stories circulating in a culture so far removed in time and place from our own. Whatever their historical veracity or their specific sexual content,

---

5. For this and other tales of the harem, see Eduğan, *Sexual Life in Ottoman Society*.

all of these stories serve as a reminder that the female residents of the harem still exercised a small degree of personal and sexual freedom. However, these small-scale experiments in personal freedom pale in comparison to those remarkable cases in which the women of the harem became the rulers of the empire.

THE POWER OF THE HAREM

Among the largest harems in history were those of the rulers of the Ottoman Empire. The Turkish Ottoman dynasty remained in power for over six centuries and held sway over large parts of Asia, Africa, and Europe until its collapse after World War I. From the late sixteenth century onward, women of the Ottoman royal family came to be major players in the political life of the empire. The rise to power of the imperial harem is one of the most dramatic developments in the history of the Ottoman Empire. During what is widely known as "the sultanate of women," the women of the harem, particularly the mother of the sultan and his closest concubines, played a leading role in both domestic politics and foreign affairs.

In order to understand how these women came to assume such an influential position in Ottoman life, we need to look first at changes introduced during the reign of Suleiman the Magnificent, who ruled the Ottoman Empire from 1520 to 1566. His period is generally viewed as the high point of Ottoman rule, while the years after his death are generally believed to have been characterized by decline and dissolution. Indeed, many authors argue that it was Suleiman's willingness to indulge his harem that opened the door to the rise of female power and led to the decline of Ottoman fortunes.

Prior to the reign of Suleiman, residents of the harem, including wives, concubines, sons, and daughters, lived in a separate palace from the sultan. Princesses were married off to provincial governors, while sons became governors themselves. Both were removed from the center of political power, the capital. When the reigning sultan died, all of his sons were considered eligible for the throne. The selection of a ruler was often decided through fratricidal wars.[6]

---

6. Among the Ottomans, every succession but one (Suleiman's own) for more than two centuries, from 1362 to 1574, was marked by executions or succession struggles that were resolved on the battlefield.

All this was changed by Suleiman and his immediate successors. Under his reforms the women of the harem (sisters, daughters, and granddaughters) were married to important court officials and thus remained in the capital. For their part, sons were no longer sent to serve as governors, but remained in the palace under the sultan's thumb. The imperial harem grew dramatically as it was expanded to hold the residences of mothers and sons. The division of power also underwent a decisive transformation, with women, particularly the sultan's mother and favorite concubines, acquiring new powers and the princes fading into the background.

In order to understand the ideas underlying this new division of political power we must delve into the deep symbolic relationship that existed between politics and sexuality among the Ottomans. This is presented with remarkable precision by Leslie Peirce, the author of a fascinating study of the Ottoman harem.

> Sexual maturity and political maturity were inextricable, and political control involved control of sexuality. . . . For males, political maturity coincided with the onset of fathering children, but for females maturity was marked by the cessation of childbearing, in other words, with a post-sexual status.

In other words, men usually began to exercise political power when they matured (sexually) and became heads of families, while women reached their political peak when they were no longer of childbearing age and believed to be no longer sexually active.

Given this association between sex and power, the biggest losers from these reforms were the Ottoman princes, who were rendered impotent in several senses. Rather than exercising power as husbands, fathers, and provincial governors, they were now kept in a status of perpetual immaturity. Hidden behind palace walls, excluded from public ritual, they were not even allowed to father children unless and until they achieved political power and became sultan.

If the princes were those who experienced the greatest decline in their power in the era of reform, it was the queen mother who emerged with the greatest status and most authority. Endowed with the title of *valide sultan*, she was responsible for the daily functioning of the harem and the royal household. She also received a higher stipend than any other court official, even the sultan himself. Usually, such a woman spent her early years as the *haseki* (favorite concubine) of a sultan, and rose to the office of *valide sultan* when he died and her son succeeded to the throne.[7]

In theory, at least, the role of the queen mother was essentially a domestic one based on her private relationship with her son. However, during the first half of the seventeenth century the ascension to the throne of a series of minor or incapacitated sultans transformed her position into a public role that influenced the entire empire.

Maypeyker Sultan, better known as Kösem Sultan, is remembered by the Turks as the most powerful woman of her time. She first assumed a position of influence as the *haseki* of Sultan Ahmed I (r. 1603–1617). She bore Ahmed many children and may have even become his only sexual partner. One European observer reported that she had "beauty and shrewdness, and furthermore . . . she sings excellently. . . . She continues to be well loved by the king . . . and is the favorite of the king, who wants her beside him continually."

However, the influence she enjoyed as *haseki* was nothing compared to the impact she had during her twenty-eight years as *valide sultan*. She served in this role not only during the sultanates of her sons Murad IV and Ibrahim II, but even during the first years of her grandson Mehmed IV's reign.

During the period from 1622 to 1623 the empire was ruled by Sultan Mustafa, a man who was known to have serious mental and physical problems.[8] In fact, power resided with his mother, the *valide sultan*. Not only was she the power behind the throne, she was directly responsible for some of the empire's most important decisions, including the appointment of high officials. Mustafa's incapacity was, however, too much for her to overcome for any length of time and in 1623 he was deposed and she sank into obscurity.

His replacement on the throne was Sultan Murad IV, but once again it was the queen mother, in this case Kösem Sultan, who held real power. Alongside the grand *vezir* (similar to a prime

---

7. It should be remembered that, far from coming from important families, such women were almost always slave concubines, who were not even legally married to the sultan.

8. He had, in fact, previously ruled for several months in 1617–1618 and had been deposed for just this reason.

minister) we see her dealing with problems like military provisions and salaries for the troops. Although she was usually careful to mention her son, the official ruler, in all of her correspondence, he was little more than a figurehead. Indeed, the governor of Egypt, who also happened to be her son-in-law, communicated directly with her rather than with either the sultan or the grand *vezir*.[9] The ongoing and very personal nature of her relationship with the grand *vezir* with whom she shared power is beautifully captured in a passage of remarkable candor, "You really give me a headache," she wrote. "But I give you an awful headache too. How many times have I asked myself, 'I wonder if he's getting sick of me?' But what else can we do?"

Ordinarily Murad IV's death in 1640 would have marked the end of his mother's reign. However, the appointment of his emotionally disturbed brother Ibrahim to succeed him not only kept her in office but increased her power. Things were not, however, smooth sailing. In contrast to her warm relations with some previous grand *vezirs*, she repeatedly clashed with Kara Mustafa Pasha, the current incumbent. The Venetian ambassador reported, "these two rulers [the grand *vezir* and the *valide sultan*] come up against each other and in doing so take offense at each other, so that one can say that in appearance they are in accord but secretly each is trying to bring about the downfall of the other." Eventually both were to fall. Ibrahim had the *vezir* executed in 1644, and exiled his mother when she interfered with his private life. Once again it appeared that Kösem Sultan's hold on the reins of power was, or at least seemed to be, at an end.

But circumstances conspired to return her, yet again, to the center of Ottoman power. During this period, curious stories circulated concerning her son, the Sultan Ibrahim. He is said to have been impotent until he was cured by aphrodisiacal plants and pastes. After

---

9. Although the marriages of princesses had always been used for political ends, no one seems to have pursued this route with the tenacity exhibited by Kösem. Her daughters Ayshe and Fatma were married six and seven times, respectively. (Some sources credit the latter with having had twelve husbands!) This was, at least in part, possible because betrothals began when the princesses were mere infants, so that they had been married several times before they reached puberty. Ayshe was widowed twice by the age of sixteen and is said to have only lost her virginity during her fourth marriage. Both women continued to take part in such political marriages well into their fifties.

this he became insatiable. He had his room decorated from floor to ceiling with mirrors so he could watch himself performing. He had a fresh virgin presented to him every Friday. On other occasions all the women of his harem assembled, stripped naked, and acted as mares to his stallion. His special favorite is said to have been an Armenian woman who weighed over 300 pounds.

None of this probably would have mattered, but he also began to prey on the wives and daughters of his officials and administrators. In one celebrated incident, he courted the daughter of the *mufti*, one of the most important religious leaders in his empire. When she refused to marry him, he had her abducted and brought to his harem. He forced himself upon her for a few days, but her obvious reluctance and unhappiness dimmed his pleasure. Eventually, he had her returned to her outraged father. Courtiers may have wanted a ruler who displayed sexual vigor and potency, but they didn't want to be subjected to a reign of sexual terror. In 1648, having failed to show he could govern adequately on his own, Ibrahim was deposed. The same *mufti* whose daughter he had abused issued a religious ruling declaring Ibrahim to be "a fool and a tyrant and unfit for government."[10] The terrified ruler fled to the sanctuary of his harem, but was forced to abdicate. Ten days later he was executed.

Although this should not have brought his mother, Kösem Sultan, back into the limelight, once again unusual circumstances were to her advantage. When her seven-year-old grandson, Mehmed IV, was elevated to the throne, his mother, who was only twenty-two or twenty-three at the time, was not senior enough to serve as regent. Important politicians asked Kösem Sultan to be the regent and *büyük* (senior) *valide sultan* for her seven-year-old grandson even as his mother, Turhan, assumed the role of (junior) *valide sultan*. She consented and would often sit at the sultan's side behind a curtain when he held court. Her strong support from the army put her in a position of unparalleled power.

Predictably perhaps, when Kösem finally fell from power, it was not because of any male rival, but the work of her daughter-in-law, the aforementioned Turhan. After three years of serving in the shadows while her mother-in-law exercised power, Turhan sought to assume real power, but Kösem resisted. In 1651 she was

---

10. For this story and other equally scandalous stories, see the chapter "Three Mad Sultans" in John Freely's *Inside the Seraglio.*

murdered by one of the court eunuchs! When news of her death became public, the people of Istanbul closed the city's mosques and markets for three days of mourning. Turhan herself turned out to be no less skilled than her predecessor and held similar influence during her reign as *valide sultan*.

CONCLUSIONS

The development of "the sultanate of women" is a fascinating chapter in Ottoman history, but it extends far further than that. Although it is easy to cite individual cases in which a woman's proximity to the centers of power allowed her to exercise influence, here we are dealing with a far deeper structural phenomenon.

First, it must be remembered that unlike many other women, including the Chinese concubine Yang Guifei discussed in chapter 1, Kösem Sultan and other women in the position of *valide sultan* did not exercise power because of their attractiveness as women. Although that may have been the reason they were chosen for the harem and became the sultans' favorites, they were able to assume authority only when they were widows and viewed as no longer sexually active. In contrast with men (most notably their husbands and sons), for whom sexual potency and political potency were directly linked, for these women the situation was exactly the opposite. Only when they were widowed and presumed to be no longer sexually active could they assume power.

One of the interesting questions about such women is where they came by the skills to exercise such power. After all, the training they received as concubines is not what we would usually think of as an equivalent to the Kennedy School of Government or a degree in area studies from Georgetown. However, I think there are at least two elements of life in the harem that probably served as excellent preparation for their later duties.

The women of the harem, and especially the one who became the favorite, had to be shrewd judges of character and very skilled at assessing a man's mood. They needed to know how to assuage anger, raise the spirits (and the libido) at times of despondence, and get what they wanted under difficult conditions. All of this was probably pretty good training for dealing with ministers and considering the demands of foreign representatives.

It must be remembered, moreover, that the harem was far more than a sexual institution. As the heart of the household of the rich and powerful, it must have been a place that reeked of politics and intrigue. Doubtless many a man unburdened himself by talking about his problems "at the office" before and after having sex with his concubines and wives. Any young girl with sufficient intelligence and curiosity was probably as well informed about the political life of her time as the sharpest of reporters are today. If she coupled this knowledge with a healthy bit of ambition, she might find herself not only hearing about great events, but also playing a part in them.

In the first two chapters I have focused my attention on societies in which men demonstrated their wealth, power, and potency by acquiring and providing for many wives and concubines. No ruler in China or the Muslim world found himself condemned for having lots of sexual partners or sleeping with a woman other than his wife. However, in many societies where monogamy was at least the officially expected code of behavior, a man was not free to openly boast about the number of sexual partners he had. One common alternative, popular to this day, was to marry an attractive woman many years his junior. It is to this "trophy wife" phenomenon that I now turn my attention.

SUGGESTIONS FOR FURTHER READING

Eduğan, Sema Nilgün. *Sexual Life in Ottoman Society*. Istanbul: Dönence, 1998.

Freely, John. *Inside the Seraglio: Private Lives of the Sultans in Istanbul*. London: Penguin, 1999.

Graham-Brown, Sarah. *Images of Women: The Portrayal of Women in Photography of the Middle East 1860–1950*. New York: Columbia University Press, 1988.

Lassner, Jacob. *Demonizing the Queen of Sheba: Boundaries of Gender and Culture in Postbiblical Judaism and Medieval Islam*. Chicago: University of Chicago Press, 1993.

Peirce, Leslie P. "Beyond Harem Walls: Ottoman Royal Women and the Exercise of Power." Pp. 40–55 in Dorothy O. Helly and Susan M. Reverby, eds., *Gendered Domains: Rethinking Public and Private in Women's History*. Ithaca, N.Y.: Cornell University Press, 1992.

———. *The Imperial Harem: Women and Sovereignty in the Ottoman Empire*. New York: Oxford University Press, 1993.

Seng, Yvonne J. "Invisible Women: Residents of Early Sixteenth-Century Istanbul." In Gavin R. G. Hambly, ed., *Women in the Medieval Islamic World: Power, Patronage, and Piety*. New York: St. Martin's, 1998.

Ari and Jackie: Trophy Wife Meets Trophy Hunter

If women didn't exist, all the money in the world would have no meaning.

—Aristotle Onassis

I'm not sure who first coined the term *trophy wife*, or if it even has a precise definition. However, it leapt into the headlines in August 1989 when the prestigious magazine *Fortune* published a nine-page cover story on the topic. This story reported a "growing trend among powerful chief executives who are discarding their long-standing spouses for 'trophy wives'—women typically younger . . . beautiful and very often accomplished."

Even if *Fortune* hadn't included the word "powerful" in its description of the phenomenon, I think I would have been justified in including a discussion of these marriages in this book. While I'm sure that many of these relationships are deep emotional bonds, it is worthy of note that you hardly ever see beautiful young women with *poor* or *unimportant* older men! On the face of it, at least, money and power seem to play a major role in this particular equation. Indeed, if the *Fortune* article is to be believed, "the money is less important . . . than the power conferred on a woman by her connection to a Very Important Man."

So common has this phenomenon become that the satirical comic strip *Doonesbury* was able to run a series of strips joking about a wealthy businessman who was such a stick-in-the-mud that he was still married to his first wife. And someone joked after a recent Academy Awards ceremony that one producer got so drunk at a studio party that he left with a woman his own age!

Most recently this phenomenon reached (one is tempted to say "descended") to its most farcical stage with the televising of the program *Who Wants to Marry a Millionaire?* The spectacle of a single anonymous male millionaire choosing from among a selection of fifty young attractive women could be said to have reduced the trophy wife phenomenon to its lowest common denominator: male wealth versus female beauty, with wealth making the choice. The rather dismal collapse of the show's eventual pairing into a series of unintended disclosures and mutual recriminations only served to deflect attention from its stereotypical premise. After all, the show wasn't about an anonymous beautiful woman choosing from a number of millionaires, or about a female millionaire choosing from attractive men! Consciously or unconsciously the producers had reproduced the trophy wife phenomenon as a form of (rather bizarre) theater.

Right off the bat, I think I should point out that there's nothing new about older men pairing off with younger women. Comparative studies carried out in many different cultures and historical periods have found this to be a widespread phenomenon. In polygamous societies, men continue to marry women of childbearing age, so as the men grow older the gap between the age of the husbands and each successive wife grows. In monogamous societies of the past, major gaps in the ages of husbands and wives were often the result of the man's remarriage after the death, often in childbirth, of his first wife. Modern singles ads, the lives of historical figures, and polygamous societies throughout the world all commonly present patterns of powerful men marrying younger, nubile women. Several of the cases we've discussed already (Emperor Ming Xuan) or will discuss in future chapters (Juan Peron) fit this pattern. Some scholars have even argued that there is a deep evolutionary disposition to such pairings.

What then are the specific factors that have led to the emergence of such a phenomenon in our own society in recent years?

There seems to be little question that the best starting point for an understanding of the "trophy wife" phenomenon is our rising divorce rate and the growing acceptance of divorce and remarriage as a "natural" part of an executive's life. Back in the days when divorce was a major obstacle to career advancement, comparatively few business leaders risked their careers through a marital breakup. A second marriage to a noticeably younger woman, which might be interpreted as a sign of instability or immaturity, was all but out of the question. True, some men married much younger women in a first marriage. But since a "normal" family life was often a prerequisite for advancement up the corporate ladder, most budding executives married early in their careers and these May–December romances were a rarity.

Today, there's been an almost complete turnaround. Divorce and remarriage are almost a standard part of an executive's career, and no one holds it against him. Indeed, as my teacher and colleague Helen Singer Kaplan noted, not only is there "no longer a prejudice against divorce and remarriage—almost the reverse. In some cases, the man with the old, nice, matronly, first wife is looked down on. He's seen as not keeping up appearances."[1]

One result of these men "trading in" their first wives for a newer, sleeker model is the emergence of significant age differences. While many modern executives initially married women close to their own age, divorce and remarriage made it possible for these large age gaps to appear.

However, the rising divorce rate is only part of the story. It provides the social framework that makes such marriages possible; it doesn't explain their prevalence. Several factors would appear to be relevant on this score. Certainly media images such as movies that portray actors such as Robert Redford or Sean Connery sexually involved with women half their age are part of the story. If such romances were portrayed as deviant or ridiculous (as they often are when a woman such as Cher or Joan Collins is the older partner), they might be less common. However, it can be argued that these movies reflect attitudes to such pairings as much as they shape them.

In the aforementioned *Fortune* article at least one psychologist with lots of experience counseling management types opined that

---

1. "The CEO's Second Wife," *Fortune*, August 28, 1989, 45. For her part, the first wife no longer has the protection of social norms. Suddenly she finds herself being judged by a new standard. If in the past she'd been expected to serve as mother, hostess, and wife, the new values condemn her for not being well read, socially connected, or glamorous enough. While her husband pursues his career and expands his horizons, she finds "her fate is sealed in four words: she didn't keep up."

the phenomenon is part of a growing culture of self-indulgence. "Indulgence is an issue for people who have worked very hard to get where they are. They feel they've earned it, they're entitled to it." Yet another factor cited is the rise of the businessman as celebrity. Second wives often add glamour and new social experiences to their husbands' lives.

Finally, there's at least one other factor. I must say that it came to me as somewhat of a surprise that the early discussions of this topic skipped over what to me, given my area of expertise, seemed an obvious part of the trophy wife equation. Perhaps they were being cautious or didn't want to offend the important people they were writing about. The older executive married to an attractive younger wife is not only sending the message that he could get her, but that he can hold her and keep up with her sexually. His potency, in all senses of the word, is confirmed for all to see.[2] It's as if he's saying, "If I can satisfy her in the bedroom, I can satisfy the stockholders in the boardroom."

ARISTOTLE ONASSIS: THE SHIPPING MAGNATE
WHO MARRIED AMERICAN ROYALTY

Although Jacqueline Kennedy's marriage to the Greek shipping tycoon Aristotle Onassis predated the *Fortune* article on trophy wives by many years, it had many of the trappings of such relationships, most notably the linking of an enormously wealthy business figure with a younger, beautiful, and socially accomplished woman.

Most Americans had never heard of Aristotle Onassis until he married Jacqueline Kennedy in October of 1968, but in the interlocking circles of international finance and entertainment, Onassis had been well known for over forty years. For a man who pursued women with the same combination of charm and ruthlessness that he brought to the business world, his list of lovers is striking not merely for its length (of which he was inordinately proud), but also for the number of famous women it

---

2. Of course, I should point out that anyone who assumes that an executive with a young wife is vigorous and dynamic is just as likely to be in error as the person who assumes that one happily married to the same woman for many years is dull and unimaginative.

3. In discussing Onassis in this chapter, I certainly don't mean to imply that most or even many business leaders are compulsive womanizers.

includes.[3] Although a big question mark should perhaps be put next to the name of Eva Peron,[4] his name has also been linked to the actresses Gloria Swanson, Veronica Lake, Greta Garbo, and Paulette Goddard as well as opera singers Claudia Muzio and, perhaps most famously before Kennedy, Maria Callas. In fact, in the peculiar way of the world, Onassis's path crossed not only with John Kennedy when he married his widow, but with his father Joseph Kennedy as well, who had had an affair with Swanson! There appears to have been much truth in Onassis's claim that he viewed every woman as a potential mistress.

~

Aristotle Socrates Onassis was a child of the twentieth century, born on January 20, 1900, near Smyrna (today Izmir), one of Turkey's most important seaports. His father was a tobacco merchant, and it was clear at an early age that his son was destined to follow his father's footsteps into the business world. Although clever with languages and precocious in math, Aristotle was an indifferent student who was once suspended for a week for goosing a female teacher.

According to his own testimony his earliest sexual partners included the family laundress and his French tutor. He was also a frequent and liberal patron of Smyrna's red-light district where the local prostitutes appreciated his charm, fine clothes, and generosity with his father's best tobacco. One of the girls was to teach him a lesson that he claimed to carry with him throughout his life: One way or another, money was the reason all women "did it." He was to have many opportunities to test this piece of wisdom during the next half century.

The list of women that Onassis slept with or claimed to have slept with is much too long for me to name every one of them. What is significant are the behavioral patterns that characterized these relationships. From the outset Onassis had a penchant for mixing business with pleasure, but even as a young man he had a clear set of priorities. Given the choice between working as an

---

4. After meeting Peron in Paris during one of her trips to Europe, Onassis had a mutual friend arrange a more private meeting. In exchange for a $10,000 donation to the Eva Peron Foundation, Onassis was able to have a private breakfast with the first lady of Argentina. The meeting was probably innocent, since Eva Peron showed no inclination to sleep with men simply for the experience (see chapter 4), but more scurrilous accounts were quickly in circulation.

electrician in the company of women telephone operators during the day and as an operator himself with men at night, he unhesitatingly chose the latter job, which paid more. In later years when a friend expressed wonder that Onassis would pursue an affair with the rather plain-looking wife of a business rival, he replied that he had no need to hear sweet nothings in bed, he much preferred sweet somethings, preferably something that could be used to make more money!

Forced to flee to Argentina as a refugee in the 1920s, Onassis tried to introduce the Eastern tobacco blends with which he was so familiar to a new audience. Moreover, in an audacious move he also sought to market cigarettes to women at a time when many were unwilling to smoke in public. In a move typical of Onassis's style and audacity he convinced his lover, the opera singer Claudia Muzio, to endorse his brand. Having gotten what he wanted, he then dropped her for a Russian ballerina, whom he persuaded to abandon her company and stay in Argentina. As Onassis biographer Peter Evans writes, sex "played a key role in his life; his business, his success, his fame all had their sources in a substratum of sex."

Onassis's first wife was a case in point. Athina (Tina) Livanos had it all. Greek by birth, British by education, and American by citizenship, she was a beautiful golden-haired blond, and most importantly her father was the legendary Greek ship owner Stavros Livanos. When the forty-six-year-old Onassis married the seventeen-year-old heiress it was, at least for him, a marriage and a merger made in heaven. Livanos had been one of Onassis's most bitter rivals, and thus marrying his daughter was a double triumph. Playing a modern Jacob to Livanos's Laban, Onassis cleverly avoided marrying Tina's older sister Eugénie in order to consummate the acquisition of a lifetime.[5]

If, as the saying goes, a gentleman never tells, Onassis was no gentleman. He would talk freely of the many women in his life at the drop of a hat, and often seemed to feel that his current lover should feel flattered to be included in such an illustrious (if not particularly exclusive) group. He once deposited a drunk Veronica Lake in the bed of another of his girlfriends, to show her that he could get a pretty girl whenever he wanted. He also graded his

---

5. Eugénie was to eventually marry yet another Greek shipping magnate and rival of Onassis, Stavros Niarchos. Eugénie committed suicide in 1970, and eighteen months later, Tina (since divorced from Onassis) married her late sister's husband!

dates in ten different categories including dress, love of parents, and seaworthiness!

In considering Onassis's womanizing one obvious but important point must be kept in mind: He was throughout his life a private individual. Rich as Croesus, widely written about in the popular press, friend and confidant of royalty, presidents, and prime ministers, but a private citizen nonetheless. He was answerable to neither public scrutiny nor senatorial review. His business colleagues were more interested in the bottom line he produced than in the bottoms he pursued. In the world he lived in, to quote his father-in-law, "The rules are that there are no rules."

Nowhere was Onassis more himself for good or for bad than aboard his yacht *Christina*. Named for his daughter and converted at a cost of four million dollars from a frigate, the 322-foot yacht was, to quote one guest, "The last word in opulence." Others thought it gave bad taste a bad name. The actor Richard Burton, no stranger to such matters, remarked that there was no "man or woman on earth who would not be seduced by the sheer shameless narcissism of this boat." To which Onassis replied, "I've found that to be so."[6]

When fully staffed it had a crew of sixty including waiters, valets, seamstresses, masseurs, and two chefs—so that guests could choose between French and Greek food. It had gold fixtures in the marble bathrooms and priceless works of both Western and Eastern art. At times the decor went far beyond good taste, such as the barstools covered with white whale foreskin. Onassis delighted in telling female visitors that they were sitting on the world's largest penis! He was perhaps insufficiently familiar with American literature or American slang (or both) to make the obvious reference to *Moby Dick*, but guests on the yacht may not have missed the Ahab-like obsessiveness of their captain.

JACKIE O

It was aboard the *Christina* that he first met Jacqueline Kennedy and her husband, the then Senator John Kennedy. According to Peter Evans, Onassis was captivated by her from the start, later telling friends, "There's something damned willful about her, there's something provocative about that lady. She's got a carnal soul."

---

6. Quoted by Evans, *The Life and Times of Aristotle Socrates Onassis*, 145.

Prior to his marriage to Jacqueline Kennedy, Onassis was best known for his passionate affair with the opera singer Maria Callas. The two first met in 1957, but it was only in 1959 that the "two most famous Greeks in the world" began their affair. Both were married at the time: Onassis to Tina and Callas to her agent and mentor, Giovanni Meneghini, but neither seemed to care much. They made only the most minimal attempts to hide their involvement from their spouses. Meneghini was patient in the hope that this would prove to be only one more in Onassis's long list of dalliances. Tina, however, had no such inclination to play second fiddle to the diva. Two highly publicized divorces followed.

The Callas–Onassis relationship was to continue for eight turbulent years. It was a meeting of two people accustomed to being the center of attention and having others sacrifice everything for his or her pleasure and career. Even their combined resources could not meet the needs of two such colossal egos. Onassis, moreover, was quickly up to his old tricks. Among the women whose company he cultivated was Lee Radziwill, the sister of American first lady Jacqueline Kennedy. It was through her sister that Jackie first came to know Onassis well,[7] and it was through Radziwill that he was invited to be a guest at the White House during the traumatic days immediately following John Kennedy's assassination in November of 1963.

It's hard to pinpoint precisely when Onassis set his sights on marrying Jacqueline Kennedy. He was a persistent visitor from 1963 on, but he certainly realized that he would have to be patient. The woman who led a nation's mourning could not easily transfer her affections to a controversial foreigner. While the Kennedys certainly realized that the thirty-seven-year-old widow was not destined to a life of celibacy, they hoped she would do nothing that did not serve the family's interests. By 1968, Bobby's presidential ambitions were yet another obstacle.

Still, for Onassis, Jackie was the ultimate prize. Almost thirty years his junior, beautiful, educated, famous, and politically connected, she brought with her as a dowry not wealth, but fame, dignity, and a place in history. Her sister Lee may have had aristocratic connections through her marriage to (defunct) Polish royalty, but Jacqueline Kennedy was the nearest thing the

---

7. It is interesting to note that in both his marriages Onassis dallied with sisters before deciding upon the one who was less expected! For her part, Jacqueline Kennedy twice married men who were compulsive womanizers.

Americans had to royalty. Not surprisingly, Onassis's children referred to her in private as "the Widow."

Once Jackie had given her consent and informed the Kennedys of her intentions, what remained was essentially a business negotiation. Onassis could not have felt more at home. His second wife, much like his first, was a beautiful acquisition. He had had months to think through the details of this particular negotiation and set them out with admirable precision. Jackie, for her part, made sure that the criticism she endured was worth the pain both financially and in terms of her personal needs.

Predictably, the Kennedy–Onassis nuptials produced a storm of protest in the American public. Admirers of the late president, still largely ignorant of his compulsive womanizing and other faults (see chapter 10), just couldn't understand how his widow could dishonor his memory with a foreigner whose only attraction appeared to be his enormous wealth. Critics of the Kennedy family remarked snidely that after years of other people doing it, the Kennedys now could kiss their *Own-asses.*

Jackie O's (as she was referred to) reasons for marrying Onassis may have been varied. He could when the mood struck him be immensely charming, nowhere more so than when trying to woo a woman. We must always recall that long before he joined the ranks of the world's wealthiest men, he had success with women. She may have also remembered fondly a cruise on Onassis's yacht in the summer of 1963 during which she recuperated from the death of her son Patrick, who died a few hours after his premature birth.[8]

His wealth, of course, should not be discounted as a factor. Although it was not commonly known at the time, Jacqueline Bouvier was not particularly well off when she married Kennedy in 1953. Although John Kennedy was one of the wealthiest men ever to serve as president, even he had trouble keeping up with her tastes in clothing. His death left her with a government pension and $150,000 a year from the Kennedy family trust. Hardly a pauper's life, but not a princely sum either.

Marriage to Onassis suddenly catapulted her into a totally new financial range. If the Kennedys had an oceanfront compound, Onassis owned an island; if the Kennedys always traveled first

---

8. Jackie's presence on Onassis's yacht was the subject of criticism in the House of Representatives. It is unclear whether this was a premonition or simply politics as usual. In any event, her husband asked her to return home.

class, Onassis owned an airline; if $5,000 a month on clothes seemed extravagant when she was married to the president, five times that much was the norm during her years with Onassis.

In Kennedy's unique circumstances, Onassis's enormous wealth may have had another attraction beyond the many obvious material benefits it offered. Following the assassination of her brother-in-law Robert Kennedy in June of 1968, Jackie may have genuinely been concerned for her safety and more importantly that of her children. Twice in a period of less than five years attempts to protect Kennedy men had proven dismally inadequate. "If they're killing Kennedys, then my children are in danger," she remarked. The intervention of a protective man with almost unlimited resources may have appeared particularly opportune. Indeed, there is something almost primordial in the image of a young, attractive woman marrying an older wealthy man with the power to protect her and her offspring.

I don't know what advice about marrying Onassis I would have given Jackie if she'd turned to me during this period. On the sexual side, I probably would have told her to make the best of it, fantasize about other men or circumstances if it helps, *but just don't let him know you're doing it!*

Whatever Jackie's reasons, she was not naïve about her marriage to Onassis. After her experience with John Kennedy and the Kennedy family in general, she was well schooled in the advantages and disadvantages of marrying money and power. By most accounts, after the first year or two, neither side was particularly pleased with the marriage, and newspaper reports at the time of Onassis's death in 1975 claimed that he had been contemplating a divorce. While some claimed it was extravagance that soured their relationship, however much Onassis may have resented her expensive tastes, he could afford them. Ironically, it may have been the very characteristics that attracted him to her that made Jackie such a poor trophy wife. Her beauty, intelligence, worldly experience, and independence may have been what made her so attractive, but the latter three also made her less than ideally suited to be displayed as proof of someone else's success.

TROPHY WIVES OR TROPHY HUNTERS?

The example of Jacqueline Kennedy also serves as an important corrective to the popular image of the trophy wife. Although trophy wives are often portrayed as uneducated "bimbos" intended to serve as mere ornaments, in many cases they are much more than that. While not everyone can be a Jackie Kennedy, second wives are typically not only younger than their predecessors, but also better educated, more worldly, and more socially skilled.

Given this profile, it would be rather naïve of us to underestimate the active role played by these women in the formation of such unions. Although the popular image has the male aggressively pursuing his female "trophy," this is not necessarily the case. While second wives agreed that it was important to let their potential mate *believe* that he had done the choosing, they did not sit back and wait for him to arrive at their doorstep. Introductions were arranged through friends, parties organized, and functions attended all for the purpose of cultivating a relationship. Indeed, serious questions must be raised as to who is the trophy and who is the hunter under these circumstances. As Kendrick, Trost, and Sheets conclude in their scholarly analysis of trophy wives, the younger attractive "females in question should probably get equal credit as trophy hunters; they are simply hunting a different type of game. . . . When females seek trophies . . . they seek social status, position . . . and resources rather than youth and physical attractiveness."

These second marriages, therefore, fit neatly into the context of the changing patterns of the American workplace. Current debates about such topics as trophy wives and sexual harassment at work often overlook the fact that the office is a very different place than it once was. No longer are women confined to the secretarial staff or other low-status and low-paying jobs. No longer do they have only jobs; increasingly they have careers. While there may still be a "glass ceiling," the typical office is full of bright, ambitious, successful young women working not only *for* men, but also *with* them. Many a senior executive finds himself spending much of his day in the company of such women. Why should he choose to spend his nights with someone any less interesting?

Such women, it must be remembered, are not mere trophies, but trophy *wives*. Although they may be resented by their stepchildren, detested by their predecessors, and given the cold shoulder by older women, they should not be reduced to one-dimensional characters from another era.

SUGGESTIONS FOR FURTHER READING

Connelly, Julie. "The CEO's Second Wife." *Fortune*, August 28, 1989, 52–66.

Evans, Peter. *The Life and Times of Aristotle Socrates Onassis*. New York: Summit Books, 1986.

Kendrick, Douglas T., Melanie R. Trost, and Virgil Sheets. "Power, Harassment, and Trophy Mates: The Feminist Advantage of an Evolutionary Perspective." Pp. 29–53 in David M. Buss and Neil M. Malamuth, eds., *Sex, Power, Conflict: Evolutionary and Feminist Perspectives*. New York: Oxford University Press, 1996.

Stassinopoulos, Ariana. *Maria: Beyond the Callas Legend*. London: Weidenfeld and Nicolson, 1980.

http://www.greece.org/poseidon/work/modern-times/onassis.html
http://foia.fbi.gov/aonassis.htm

Eva Perón: sleeping her way to the top

It is a time-honored female tradition to use sexual power as a way to try to improve one's position in the world, immortalized in literature in characters like Becky Sharpe in "Vanity Fair" and Lily Bart in "House of Mirth."

—Katie Roiphe[1]

If powerful men used their power to get sex (with both women and other men), women have often used sex (another kind of power) to gain access to power. As the previous chapter's discussion of trophy wives indicated, even if the differences in strategy are pretty clear, it's not always clear who's the hunter and who's the trophy in many of these relationships.

It's no accident that men have tended to use one strategy and women another. Given the way financial and political power has been divided up throughout most of history, there's been little alternative. I think it's important to emphasize this point, for a number of reasons. First, I need to stress that what we're looking at here is not a case in which men are inclined to one form of behavior and

---

1. *New York Times*, September 15, 1998.

women to another. The issue that lies at the heart of this difference is who has had power.[2]

One of the earliest examples we have of this phenomenon is found in the biblical Book of Ruth.

Ruth, a widow from the land of Moab, lives with Naomi, the mother of her deceased husband. They are so poor that they survive by gleaning the grains left in the fields by the harvesters. At Naomi's insistence, Ruth (literally) throws herself at the feet of Boaz, Naomi's wealthy relative.

> Bathe, anoint yourself, dress up, and go down to the threshing floor. But do not disclose yourself to the man until he has finished eating and drinking. When he lies down, note the place where he lies down, and go over and uncover his feet and lie down. He will tell you what you are to do. (Ruth 3:3–4)

He spreads his cloak over her, and in the early morning before it is light enough for anyone to see, he gives her an abundance of grain. The next day, he arranges to marry her. Ruth goes from poverty-stricken young woman to respected married woman. (Her grandson, David, became king of Israel.)

What a curious story, and in the Bible no less! And what a powerful caution against rushing to judgment and being too hasty to moralize. Ruth is a Moabite, descendent of a people who according to biblical tradition resulted from an incestuous relationship. The Israelites are forbidden to marry them or even accept their conversions to Judaism. She initiates a nonmarital sexual relationship that results not only in her redemption, but eventually in the birth of one of the most important figures in biblical history, King David.[3] What is the Bible trying to tell us?

I don't think its message is that the end justifies the means. I do, however, believe that it is trying to teach us that every relationship, whatever its external appearances, contains the potential for fulfillment and fruition. Ruth benefits from Naomi's open-mindedness and clever advice; Boaz and his descendants

---

2. In chapters 11 through 14, I discuss some interesting cases of women in power, and not surprisingly, we'll see that the roles are often reversed in these situations.

3. It is interesting to note that some modern interpretations of the story of David and Bathsheba suggest that she purposely bathed in a place where the king would see her, in order to find her way into his bed and win his favor!

benefit from Ruth's "immoral" behavior, as she shared his blanket in the middle of the night. I also think that this story reminds us what a deeply human book the Bible is. For all its "thou shalt nots," it also appreciates human nature and weaknesses.

DON'T CRY FOR ME ARGENTINA

Although many figures found in this book can be described as larger than life, nowhere is this truer than in the case of Eva (Evita) Perón. Her rise from obscurity and poverty to fame and power is certainly the stuff of fairy tales, but it's not totally clear if she should be cast as Cinderella or one of the wicked stepdaughters. Tim Rice and Andrew Lloyd Webber have produced perhaps the most popular and best known image of Perón in the hit musical and film *Evita*. Eva Perón as depicted by them is a shrewd social climber who uses both her wits and sexuality to climb to the heights of political power. The casting, after years of false starts, of the flamboyant singer-actress Madonna in the title role of the movie only further strengthened the impression of Perón as one of the twentieth century's great sexual entrepreneurs. Yet, to many of her followers Eva Maria Duarte de Perón was a devoted wife, selfless public servant, and saintly mother of her nation, whose only association with the name Madonna was her obvious resemblance to the Virgin Mary.

In the words of J. M. Taylor, "At the time of her death Eva Perón was arguably the most powerful woman in the world. But Argentineans giving vent to their hatred or expressing their love of Eva Perón remember her special power as emotional and intuitive, violent, mystical, uninstitutionalized." Or to quote another biographer, John Barnes, she was "one of the most loved and hated, powerful and capricious women in Argentina and the world."

Who was Evita Perón, and what role did sex play in her rise to and use of power? As they used to say in the old detective stories, let's look at the facts!

On May 7, 1919, a baby girl was born to an unwed mother in the small town of Los Toldos in the province of Buenos Aires, Argentina. Although she would for many years call herself Eva Maria *Duarte*, her father, Juan Duarte, never publicly recognized her or any of her four older siblings in his lifetime. In fact, when they tried to attend his funeral in 1926, his "legitimate" family protested their presence and a violent confrontation broke out.

In the end, only after the intervention of one of the deceased's brothers were they able to follow the coffin to the local cemetery.

We can only speculate how a childhood lived under these circumstances affected the thin, dark girl. Certainly at an early age, she learned firsthand both the advantages and disadvantages of a sexual relationship with a married man, who served both as lover and provider. Her home situation was neither a secret nor particularly unusual. In early twentieth-century Argentina, as in many other places, the roles open to women were wives, daughters, and mistresses. Men protected their wives and daughters, and if they had the means they also pursued and enjoyed their mistresses. Wives accepted their husbands' right to have mistresses and expected them to keep their relationships with them discreet.

This life lesson was repeated when Eva was twelve. Her family moved from Los Toldos to Junin, a city of about 30,000, where her mother's latest protector, a local politician, set her up in a small boardinghouse. This site was eventually to become part of Evita's legend, with its true purpose the matter of much dispute and debate.

According to Jorge Luis Borges, one of Argentina's most creative writers, the young Eva

> was a common prostitute. She [her mother] had a brothel near Junin. . . . I mean, if a girl is a whore in a large city that doesn't mean too much, but in a small town in the pampas everybody knows everybody else. And being one of the whores is like being the barber or the surgeon. And that must have greatly embittered her. To be known and to be despised by everybody and to be used.

Borges's testimony must be taken with a grain of salt. Although her mother's "boardinghouse" may have served other purposes as well, its primary function was probably to provide lodging. It also provided husbands for the Duarte girls. All three of Eva's sisters eventually married bachelors (an army officer, a lawyer, and a lift operator) who had stayed at the house. Thus none of the women in Eva's family were strangers to the notion that a sexual connection with the right man could markedly improve one's standing in life. Young Eva, however, appears to have set her sights higher than either her mother or her siblings, and getting out of Junin was her first goal.

Shortly after Eva's fifteenth birthday opportunity knocked in the form of a handsome young tango singer named Agustin Magaldi, who came to Junin for a series of performances. When he returned to Buenos Aires a few days later, Eva made the journey with him. Although he may have seen himself as the older patron of an innocent young girl, who seduced whom is certainly open to debate. From an early age Eva appears to have been willing to lie to or lie with anyone who could help her achieve her goals.

In the capital, Eva, like so many other young girls from the provinces, sought to pursue a career as an actress. Like many of them she may have also found other less respectable ways to supplement her income. One of her contemporaries remembers that Eva earned much more from her "moonlighting" than her acting. However, even if Eva never actually worked in the sex trade, the stigma of such employment was something she carried with her throughout her life even at the peak of her success. According to one well-known story, on a foreign trip First Lady Evita asked her Italian escort why the people kept calling her a "whore." "Think nothing of it, Señora," he is said to have replied, "I haven't been to sea for fifteen years, and everyone still calls me 'admiral.'"[4]

At first, the young girl with the strong provincial accent had little success. Not only did she lack classic beauty (eventually she dyed her hair blonde and only financial problems seem to have prevented her from having her breasts enlarged) and charm, she also had neither experience nor references. At times, she seems to have survived on willpower alone, but that she possessed in abundance.

One of her first parts was in a comedy called *La Señora de Perez*. The play was less memorable for the acting experience that it provided than for the fact that it marked her break with the singer Magaldi, who was replaced by an actor, Pascual Pelliciota. In the words of Perón biographer John Barnes, "It was the first of a long series of lowly paid bit parts and short-lived love affairs."

Another play in which she toured, in June 1936, was called *The Mortal Kiss* and is noteworthy for the irony of its theme. Financed by the Argentine Prophylactic League, it preached against the evils of sexual promiscuity in an attempt to cut down the rate of illegitimate births in rural Argentina.

Although Eva may not have accepted the message of sexual abstinence preached by the play, she appears to have understood that an unwanted pregnancy or illegitimate child would have dealt a fatal blow to her plans. She also appears to have had the ability to move from bed to bed with all the skill of a chess grandmaster. An

---

4. This story appears in almost every biography of Evita (cf. Barnes, *Evita First Lady*, 88).

affair with Emilio Kartulovic, editor of a popular film and theater magazine, opened doors and led to her first film role. (She is also rumored to have slept with the film's star as well.)

Aided by her influential patrons, Eva Duarte had begun by age twenty to achieve some success with radio parts and the promise of a film career. Her skills in the bedroom seem to have always surpassed her abilities as a thespian. In particular her relationship with a wealthy soap manufacturer, who was also a major radio advertiser, paved her way to national recognition. In 1943 she was cast, rather prophetically, in a radio series called *My Kingdom of Love*, in which she portrayed various famous women. In the course of these broadcasts she portrayed a variety of figures, including Elizabeth I and Catherine the Great (both discussed in this book), as well as Alexandra of Russia, the Empress Josephine, and the actress Sarah Bernhardt. During the coming decade she was to achieve fame that rivaled that of any of the heroines she depicted.

Up to 1943, Eva Duarte's ambition appears to have been limited to her acting career and her relationships confined to the bedrooms of those who could assist her in that goal. An important crossover role seems to have been played by Colonel Anibal Imbert, the Argentinean minister of communications under a military government formed in 1943. Whether Eva's affair with him was sparked by the fact that he controlled all the country's radio stations or already motivated by higher ambitions we may never know. It did bring her in touch with the military elite of the country and in particular with the man with whom her name was to be forever linked, Juan Domingo Perón.

It is not clear exactly when and under what circumstances Eva first met Juan Perón, but tradition records it as an earth-shattering event, literally. When a devastating earthquake struck Argentina in January 1944, Eva was at the forefront of a group of performers and politicians who organized a benefit concert. She attended as the escort of her lover, Colonel Imbert, but spent much of the evening seated at the side of another colonel, Juan Perón.

As usual, Eva was ruthless in getting what or whom she wanted. Within a few days of meeting Perón she had convinced him to dismiss his current mistress, a sixteen-year-old girl whom she sometimes introduced as his daughter. The young girl was no match for the more experienced Duarte, but it's doubtful if an older woman would have fared any better.

Given the norms of public and political life in the Argentina of her day, there was nothing remarkable about either the frequency or the ruthlessness with which Eva changed partners. It was, to be true, rather unusual for a woman to be openly aggressive and ready to grab the initiative. To the best of our knowledge, Eva always moved on well before her lovers had tired of her. What is especially striking, however, is the infallibility of her social–political instincts. Her climb to the top, often over the recumbent bodies of her lovers, appears to be steady and unfailing. Never does she appear to have seriously misjudged a man or bet (or bedded) the wrong horse. Perón was only the latest and the last in a series of shrewd choices.

There was, it should also be pointed out, nothing unusual in a high-ranking official like Perón openly having a mistress. Indeed, it would have seemed suspicious to many had this not been the case. When some conservative officers criticized him for being too public in his relationship with Eva, he remarked, "My adversaries charge that I associate with women, and I do of course. Do they expect me to go out with men?"

At the time when she first met him, Juan Domingo Perón was exactly twice Eva's age, forty-eight. Handsome, tall, and athletic-looking with jet-black hair, he had the type of personality that tended to dominate a room. One observer once remarked that when Perón entered a room it seemed as if everyone else had faded into black-and-white, while he alone appeared in bold colors. A career soldier, he was at the time he met Eva one of the most powerful if not most prominent of the group of army officers that ruled the country.

Initially, Eva's relationship with Perón served primarily to strengthen her professional position. By 1944 she was by far the highest paid performer in the country. Her position was also more or less invulnerable. One evening as she was about to begin her broadcast, an announcer was heard saying over a microphone inadvertently left open, "The tart is on." The government canceled all the station's commercials for two days.

If Perón gave Eva ready access to power, she gave him the benefit of her instinctive understanding of the workers and the poor. On her advice, he pursued a clear populist policy, which endeared him to the masses. She also gave him, in sharp contrast to her previous relationships, total commitment. Having thrown in her lot with Perón, she was prepared to stick by him no matter what the price. Their enemies were to pay a heavy price for failing to grasp this point. In October 1945, Perón was forced to resign his positions as vice president, minister of war, and minister of labor and welfare and was then arrested. In a fatal error of judgment, however, Eva was left at liberty. No sooner had the arresting officers left the room than Eva was on the phone calling union leaders, the minister of post and telegraphs (her mother's lover who owed her his position), and high-ranking police officers. The demonstrations she helped organize quickly brought Perón's opponents to their knees. Thousands of workers, coatless and some even shirtless in the hot sun, marched against Perón's arrest. He was released and triumphantly returned to power. Five days later he and Eva were married.

The length and focus of this chapter do not permit me to discuss the dramatic history of the Peróns from their marriage in October 1945 until her death less than seven years later in July 1952. As I noted in the introduction, this book does not attempt to offer complete histories of any of its characters. Suffice it to say that joined together, the Peróns were one of the most powerful and controversial couples in world history. Even today, almost a century after her death, the arguments about Eva, and the Peróns in general, have continued to rage. While the Argentinean union of food workers wrote to the pope suggesting that she be considered for canonization, anti-Perónists tried, with only limited success, to discredit her posthumously. I will not try to pass a verdict here on a figure whose biography has mystified far greater historians than myself. What I will try to do, however, is look at some lessons her life can teach us about the relationship between sex and power.

SEXUAL HARASSMENT

One of the biggest dilemmas I faced in preparing this book was how and in what context to discuss the issue of sexual harassment. On the one hand it's hard to think of a clearer example of the way in which power and sex are tied to each other. In a classic case of sexual harassment a male employer or teacher uses his power to demand sexual favors from a female subordinate or student, sometimes in return for an offer of a job, promotion, or grade. Such cases, whether they take place in the office, classroom, or barracks, are clearly not to be tolerated and need to be prosecuted to the letter of the law. Indeed, in recent years there has been a growing awareness of just how prevalent sexual harassment has been. Women have been educated as to their rights at the workplace, and men have become more aware of what behavior is acceptable and what isn't.

Be this as it may, it's difficult to discuss sexual harassment as a historical phenomenon. By this, I don't mean to claim that incidents of what we today call "sexual harassment" haven't been going on from time immemorial. Consider for example, one of the earliest recorded examples of sexual harassment.

The "handsome and well-favored" Joseph serves as a slave in the house of his master, Potiphar. Joseph is repeatedly approached by Potiphar's wife, but despite her entreaties, Joseph refuses to have sex with her. Finally, catching him alone in her house, she approaches him one last time. When he flees, she seizes his garment, and carrying it in her hand as evidence, accuses him of assault. The unfortunate Joseph ends up in prison. So long before Michael Crichton wrote and Demi Moore and Michael Douglas starred in *Disclosure*, a story of sexual harassment by a female, the Bible considered the theme.

The biblical story, however, is, as they say, the exception that proves the rule. It appears that the main reason that the biblical author is concerned with the story is not the basic injustice he perceives in the situation, but the sympathy he has for the victim, Joseph. In biblical times when polygamy and concubinage were as common as in either China or the Ottoman Empire, cases of what we would today call sexual harassment were probably too numerous to count.

Throughout most of human history, powerful people (usually men) have exploited their positions to have sex with people dependent on them for employment, positions, or other favors. We can certainly label these cases as "sexual harassment." The question is, does this rather anachronistic description tell us very much? The concept is relatively new, and in using it to describe incidents in the past we may be guilty of imposing our understandings on other people's lives.

There's yet another point that I'd like to consider. As the examples of both Ruth and Eva Perón teach us, shrewd women also used their sexuality as a means of improving their social, economic, or political position. One of the things that troubles me about much of today's rhetoric about sexual harassment is that it tends to assume that women are always powerless victims. In some cases in an effort to "protect" such women, rules are applied at the workplace or school that make even consensual sexual relations between employer and employee or professor and student punishable. In my mind, this is throwing out the baby with the bathwater. It's as if we've gone back in time to a period when women, whatever their age, were perceived as childlike innocents who had to be protected from men.

The normal life of the workplace with its sexual tension, flirting, dating, and yes, misunderstandings, seems to be replaced by a set of peculiar assumptions. Almost by definition, sexual relations between a man and a female subordinate are understood not only to have been initiated by the man, but to have been imposed on the woman. The possibility that the woman may have initiated the relationship, may have been attracted by the idea of seducing a powerful man, or may have been manipulating the situation to her advantage seems to have been eliminated. Eva Perón's admittedly unusual life story demonstrates just how inaccurate such assumptions can be. Whatever version of Evita's life one chooses to accept, it's difficult to view her as a victim. However difficult the early conditions of her life may have been, by the time she reached her early twenties she had certainly gained a great deal of control over her destiny.

In fact, her story is at some level so paradigmatic that perhaps it can help us coin a new term. In September 1998 the author Katie Roiphe wrote in the *New York Times*, "There should be a term connoting the opposite of sexual harassment: when a person of less power uses her [or his] sexual attractiveness or personal relationship with a person of greater power to get ahead." Maybe we should call it *Evitism!*

SUGGESTIONS FOR FURTHER READING

Baldwin, Louis. *The Loves of Their Lives: Enduring Romantic Relationships from Antony and Cleopatra to Today.* New York: Birch Lane, 1993.

Barnes, John. *Evita First Lady: The Biography of Eva Perón.* New York: Grove Press, 1978.

Rice, Tim, and Andrew Lloyd Webber. "Evita: The Legend of Eva Perón, 1919–1952." New York: Avon Books, 1978.

Roiphe, Katie. "Monica Lewinsky, Career Woman." *New York Times*, September 15, 1998.

Taylor, J. M. *Evita Perón: The Myths of a Woman.* Oxford: Basil Blackwell, 1979.

http://www.evitaperón.org

Dangerous Liaisons: Biblical Women and Fallen Men

If you allow yourself to take pleasure in base desire, it will make you the laughingstock of your enemies.

—The Wisdom of Sirach 18:31

At the beginning of the previous chapter, I considered the story of Ruth and the manner in which she charmed her way into Boaz's bed and improved her social status. Ruth is just one of a number of biblical women who used sex to get what they want. However, not all of them had as benevolent intentions as she did. In this chapter, I want to consider a number of other women from the biblical period. There's one very important difference between them and Ruth. The women I'm going to discuss below used sex not only or even primarily to gain power or improve their lot, but rather to bring about the destruction of a personal and national enemy. Although all these stories appear in the Bible,[1] none of them focus on classic religious themes. (God is not even explicitly mentioned in the Book of Esther!) Moreover, even their historicity is

---

1. The story of Judith is considered an extrabiblical apocryphal work by Jews and Protestants.

rather doubtful. However, if the biblical authors saw fit to compose, preserve, and in certain ways repeat these stories, they must have had a reason. As we shall see below, these stories are rich in symbolism and raise issues about the connections between sex and power that go far beyond any one narrative. They are, moreover, interconnected in a variety of ways, which at least hints at the possibility that the organizers of the biblical canon wanted to be completely sure that we got the message.

ESTHER: THE HEROINE IN HIDING

The Book of Esther provides a marvelous transition from the previous chapter to this one, because it contains themes from both. The book, which is a sort of historical romance, tells the story of how Esther got access to power (was chosen to be queen) because of her beauty and then used that power to bring about the downfall of her people's enemy, her husband's chief minister Haman. However, she is remembered not for her personal triumph, but for using her influence to save her people and bring about the destruction of the enemy. Scholars are divided as to whether the events related in this book really took place, and if so when. I'm not going to solve that mystery. What I would like to do is consider the lessons it teaches us about sex and power.

The Book of Esther opens with the story of a great feast at the court of Ahasuerus, the king of 127 provinces from India to Ethiopia. After seven days of feasting and drinking, the king commands that Vashti, his queen, be brought before his guests so that they can see her beauty. Apparently not wanting to appear before a group of drunken men, she refuses.[2] The king is enraged. His officials' response, is, however, even more revealing. Thrown into a panic, they advise him, "This deed of the queen will be made known to all women, causing them to look with contempt on their husbands. . . . The noble ladies of Persia and Medea who have heard of the queen's behavior will rebel against the king's officials, and there will be no end of contempt and wrath!" (Esther 1:18).

---

2. I've always thought that Vashti made the right decision. Once his courtiers departed, Ahasuerus probably would have wanted to have sex with her. Given his drunken condition, he probably wouldn't have been able to achieve an erection. Vashti would have been blamed for his impotence, and her fate might have been worse than mere banishment.

Fearing that the queen's show of independence will shatter the fragile fabric of patriarchy throughout the court, and even the empire, the king has her banished, so that "all women will give honor to their husbands, high and low alike" (Esther 1:20).

Vashti, like so many women under special scrutiny because of their husbands' position, pays a heavy price for her independence. As the "model wife" whose behavior is supposed to provide an example for all others, she is judged by an extraordinarily high standard. As biblical scholar Renita Weems notes,

> The story of Vashti's reign stands as a valuable lesson about the enormous pressures, demands, and responsibilities upon women who live public lives. It is a memorial to the price often extracted of public women when they step outside of their prescribed roles. Nancy Reagan, Rosalynn Carter, Eleanor Roosevelt—wives of modern American presidents—come to mind.

Having deposed his queen, Ahasuerus begins his search for another and arranges a vast beauty pageant so that he can choose from all the maidens of his kingdom. In the end, his choice falls upon a Jewess by the name of Esther. She hides her identity[3] and begins to serve him as his queen. At the same time, the king's chief minister, Haman, unaware of the queen's identity, plans to kill all the Jews in the kingdom. Guided by her uncle Mordecai, Esther works to save her people and depose Haman.

Taking her life in her hands, she invites the king and Haman to a banquet. There, after wining and dining them, she begs the king to save her and her people. The king is, of course, appalled at the idea that anyone would threaten his queen. When Esther reveals that it is Haman who (inadvertently) plotted against the queen, the king's anger cannot be contained. Haman and his sons are hanged.[4] The Jews, given the right to defend themselves, are spared.

Judged by biblical standards, Esther is a curious figure. On several levels she can be said to violate the word, or at least the spirit, of the Law. She marries a non-Jew, hides her identity, and presumably lives as a Persian in every way. Yet, eventually her behavior is revealed to serve a greater purpose: the salvation of her people.

---

3. In Hebrew, the name Esther hints at the idea of hiding (*l'hastir*).

4. As many commentators have noted, the Book of Esther begins with the downfall of a queen at the hands of officials in the midst of a royal banquet and ends with the downfall of an official at the hand of the queen in the midst of a royal banquet!

In a similar manner, Esther the woman appears neither as independent as her predecessor, Vashti, nor as dangerous as Delilah, whom I will discuss in a moment. Her path to power is typical of that of so many women working with men and through the system. In the words of Sidnie Anne White,

> Her conduct throughout the story has been a masterpiece of feminine skill. From beginning to end, she does not make a misstep. While in the harem, she earns the favor of Hegai, and follows his advice and the advice of Mordecai, both experienced in the ways of the court. She wins the king's heart, becomes queen and then, when danger threatens, skillfully negotiates her tricky course.

When compared to the stories of Delilah and Judith, which we shall consider below, what is striking about Esther is the indirectness of so much of her action. Esther does not hold power in her own right; it is her connection to men that makes it possible for her to act effectively. Even the destruction of her enemy, Haman, can only be carried out through the action and decrees of the king. Moreover, Haman's defeat is brought about not because he offends her personally, nor does he fall victim to her seductive charms. Rather, he is the victim of his hatred for her people as particularly personified by her uncle, and his downfall is sealed not by his own enchantment with Esther, but by her husband's.

In the stories of Judith and Delilah the role of women is far more direct. Neither appears to have used sex to improve her social or political standing. Both are depicted as dangerous women who bring about the downfall of powerful men. These men, however, as we shall discuss, are neither saintly nor blameless, and go a long way toward contributing to their own defeat.

SAMSON AND DELILAH:
THE BIGGER THEY ARE, THE HARDER THEY FALL

Probably the most famous biblical femme fatale is the temptress Delilah. The story of her relationship and eventual destruction of the Israelite hero Samson is one of the most curious stories found anywhere in the Bible. For anyone used to thinking of the Bible as a religious text, few stories are more perplexing than that of Samson and Delilah. While Samson is certainly remembered as one of the biblical judges, he can hardly be considered a heroic figure. Indeed, he is more antihero than hero.

Some scholars were so puzzled by the story that they suggested it was neither a historical account nor a folktale, but a myth. SaMSon's name is associated with the Hebrew word for sun: *SheMeSh*, while DeLiLah's recalls the Hebrew word for night, *LiLah!* Samson the sun burns his enemies' fields, but when his hair (the rays of the sun?) is cut, he is blinded—plunged into darkness. Eventually, like the sun reemerging at the end of the night, his hair grows back and his strength returns. What is this story but a personalized mythical account of the daily cycle in which the burning sun sinks into darkness every night?

Although I'm a constant reader of the Bible, I'm no scholar, and I'm not going to pretend to provide a definitive interpretation. In the context of this book, however, I'd like to focus on Samson and the part that his arrogance, pride, and downright stupidity play in his downfall.

Most popular interpretations of the story have tended to focus on Delilah, the archetypal temptress who uses her sexual wiles to attract and betray a man. Virtually all accounts agree that she was beautiful, although the Bible is silent on this point. She may have been motivated by her sympathy for the Philistines, but here, too, the Book of Judges offers no evidence (that she was a Philistine). Her motivation may simply have been money, although the text seems to make it clear that she was not a prostitute.

However, her postbiblical image notwithstanding, it's hard to be too critical of Delilah. Unlike Esther, she appears as an independent woman, identified by a connection with neither a father nor a husband. Whatever her motive might have been, she certainly couldn't have gotten very far without the help of her erstwhile victim. One of the most fascinating questions raised by the story is why Samson is such a willing dupe. Although Samson is remembered as a classic symbol of a powerful man, his compulsive self-destructiveness is even more remarkable than his physical strength. In fact, if Delilah's name has become synonymous with temptation, Samson's should probably be equated with compulsive sexual risk-taking. By the time he met Delilah, Samson already had a long history of dangerous liaisons.

When Samson was born, his mother dedicated him as a Nazirite, a special status that required him to avoid certain foods and drinks, and not shave his head. It did not, apparently, require abstinence from sex. The first woman whom Samson is associated with is a Philistine woman whom he planned to marry against his parents' wishes. Although she did not endanger his life like Delilah, her betrayal was, in many ways, similar. Samson had challenged the Philistine men to solve a riddle that he posed. When they could not do this, they threatened his bride and her family. She, foreshadowing his relationship with Delilah, berated Samson claiming, "You hate me, you do not really love me. . . . She wept before him . . . and because she nagged him, on the seventh day he told her"[5] the solution to the riddle. No sooner did she have the solution than she had told it to her countrymen. To add insult to injury, she also married his best man!

Samson's next partner was a prostitute from Gaza. Although there is no evidence that she betrayed him, once again his behavior put him in mortal danger. While he spent his time with her, the men of Gaza planned to kill him in the morning, but (knowing their plan?) he rose at midnight and departed, carrying their city gates with him!

Although both his happiness and his life were threatened, Samson seems to have learned nothing from either of these experiences. Indeed, they may have convinced him that he was in some way invincible. Like the politician who believes that he's too smart or too powerful to be caught in a scandal, he set forth on yet another sexual adventure. This one would eventually lead to his downfall.

Throwing caution to the wind, he fell in love with a woman named Delilah, who lived not far from Jerusalem. No sooner had he fallen for her than his enemies the Philistines approached her and offered her thousands of pieces of gold if she would betray him. Delilah seems to have readily agreed and set out to discover the secret of Samson's great strength. Three times Delilah asks him how she can *master* him, and he deceives her. First he tells her to bind him with bowstrings; next he tells her to bind him with ropes. The third time, he gets a little closer to the truth and tells her to weave his hair into seven locks. Each time, when he falls asleep, she wakes him by telling him that the Philistines (who are actually waiting in the wings) are upon him, and she discovers that his strength is intact.

While each of these could perhaps be interpreted as some sort of erotic game involving bondage or changed sexual roles, and each episode is a separate act of intercourse after which Samson falls asleep, the biblical narrative leaves little doubt that Samson was fully aware that Delilah's interest was not merely sexual. Yet, each

---

5. Judges 14:16–17.

time she awakens him by telling him that his enemies are attacking, he takes no precautions to protect himself. In fact, the lovesick Samson is unable to stop himself from following her down the road to self-destruction. When Delilah discovers that she's been lied to, she berates the strong man, claiming he has been mocking her and that he doesn't really love her. (As if putting yourself in mortal danger is the only way to prove your love!) Samson, for all his physical strength, responds with complete passivity and offers neither a defense of his actions nor a reprimand of his lover for plotting his betrayal. Rather, in a final desperate attempt to prove he really loves her, he reveals the true secret of his incredible virility. (Just as in a vain attempt to prove he loved his Philistine wife, he revealed the secret of his riddle to her.)

Even as the Philistines lie in wait, he tells Delilah: "If my head were shaved, then my strength would leave me. I would become weak, and be like anyone else." Delilah, with keen insight, knows he has told "the whole secret" to her and when he falls asleep in her lap (after yet another bout of lovemaking?) calls a Philistine in to shave his head.

It is this scene, so vividly depicted by Rubens, that graces the cover of this book. The artist has added another woman, perhaps a servant. However, given her age it is hard to avoid the association with motherhood and more specifically Samson's mother, who bore him and first held the secret of his hair and his strength. Moreover, the picture is redolent with sexuality. Delilah, her breasts exposed, does not even bother to cover herself in front of the "barber." Her left hand rests almost affectionately on her betrayed lover's back. Samson, although not yet clean-shaven, lies helpless, defenseless, impotent. The hair, which not even his mother dared to cut, is about to be lost because of his love for Delilah.

Shorn of his locks, having violated his oath of office (as a Nazirite dedicated to God), Samson no longer has his supernatural strength. The Philistines capture him, blind him, and enchain him to grind at a mill. Eventually his hair grows back, and when he prays to God his strength returns. In a final act of self-destruction, he grasps the center pillars of the temple, where the Philistines have brought him to be mocked, and, literally bringing down the house, destroys himself as well as his enemies.

As I noted at the outset, the story of Samson and Delilah is by any measure not exactly the sort of story we'd expect to find in the Bible. The tale of a hypermasculine hero with a weakness for

women is hardly the standard stuff of religious texts. Later interpreters, troubled by this image, sought to understand Samson's pri-
mary sin as human pride. Forgetting that his strength came from
God, he followed the road to destruction.

However, on a more human level (and as the stories of David
and Ruth remind us, the Old Testament is remarkable for its portrayal of human behavior), Samson can be seen as the man who
believes his physical strength makes him a real man. His lack of
understanding of women is monumental. Yet, he believes that
his muscles will win the day and preserve him from all dangers.
Like the government official who thinks his political power
makes him invulnerable to criticism and behaves with reckless
abandon, Samson believes his strength makes him immune to
his enemies. Like so many others, he only recognizes the limits
of his power when it is too late.

JUDITH AND HOLOFERNES,
OR HOW THE GENERAL LOST HIS HEAD

One can't help but wonder what the story of Samson and Delilah
would look like written from the Philistines' perspective. Samson
was, as we have seen, no saint, and Delilah's action was probably
considered rather heroic by his enemies. We can get some idea of
how Delilah might have been depicted if we look to other literature of the time. She is not alone in using her skills to attract a
man and bring about his violent downfall. The Bible has several
other stories of this type. One of my favorites is a lesser-known
work, the Book of Judith. Set in the sixth century B.C.E., the book
is a kind of folktale, telling how a beautiful and pious Israelite
widow named Judith saved her people by killing the Assyrian general Holofernes. Seeing her people threatened by a powerful enemy, Judith, a widow from the town of Bethulia, prays to God and
then sets out, accompanied by her maid, to meet the general. Captured by an Assyrian patrol in whose eyes she was "marvelously
beautiful," she is escorted to the tent of the general. When she is
brought into his camp, the soldiers "marveled at her beauty" saying, "Who can despise these people, who have women like this
among them. . . . They will be able to beguile the whole world!"
(Judith 10:19). After four days of wining and dining, Holofernes is
ready to bed Judith, who he muses "is not only beautiful in appearance, but wise in speech. . . . For it would be a disgrace if we

let such a woman go without having intercourse with her. If we do not seduce her, she will laugh at us."[6] Judith enters his tent and Holofernes' heart "is ravished with her and his passion (was) aroused, for he had been waiting for an opportunity to seduce her from the day he first saw her" (Judith 12:16). Like so many men in this situation, Holofernes drinks until he is dead drunk and collapses in a stupor. Judith seizes his sword, grabs him by the hair, decapitates him, and carries away his head!

Although Judith's status as a heroine and Delilah's as a villain somewhat cloud the issue, I don't think there's any question that the stories are remarkably similar. In both stories, the men involved are not "mere" men, but inordinately powerful: one with superhuman strength and the other a general. Yet, confronted by beautiful women, they become besotted and lose all judgment. Their downfall is made all the more dramatic because they are depicted as extraordinarily strong.

Yet another similarity is the obvious symbolism attached to the cutting off of the man's hair/head. Freud was only the first of many observers to identify such acts as a form of symbolic castration. Judith takes Delilah's deeds even further: While Delilah only sets the stage for Samson's defeat, Judith does the deed herself. The all-powerful man is defeated by a mere woman. The man who has come for sex is rendered powerless. His hair/head and all that they symbolize are lost, because of his inability to resist the sexual lure.[7] In the case of Holofernes, moreover, the text emphasizes this interpretation by noting that Judith cuts off his head, using his sword, which is lying over the bed. Thus it is Holofernes' reckless masculinity (symbolized by his sword) that results in his castration (symbolized by his decapitation).

～

I must admit that I haven't been able to find any recent historical examples of this kind of story. While there certainly is no lack of men brought down by their weakness for beautiful women, it's hard to find cases in which the woman's only purpose was to bring

---

6. Judith 12:11–12.

7. The limits of this chapter do not permit me to consider yet another biblical story, in this case New Testament (Matthew 14, Mark 6). Salome, the daughter of Herodias, dances for her uncle, Herod. When he promises to grant her whatever she may wish for, she asks for the head of John the Baptist. This is brought to her on a platter. Once again, the decapitation of a male enemy by a seductive woman is rich with symbolism.

about their ruin. It may be that such "castrating" women exist only in ancient stories that touch upon men's deeply rooted fears. But whatever their origin and historicity, they represent a remarkable, if unusual, meeting of both sex and power.

SUGGESTIONS FOR FURTHER READING

Bach, Alice. *Women, Seduction and Betrayal in Biblical Narrative.* New York: Cambridge University Press, 1997.

Bal, Mieke. *Lethal Love: Feminist Literary Readings of Biblical Love Stories.* Bloomington: Indiana University Press, 1987.

Ogden Bellis, Alice. *Helpmates, Harlots and Heroes: Women's Stories in the Hebrew Bible.* Louisville, Ky.: Westminster/John Knox Press, 1994.

Weems, Renita J. *Just a Sister Away: A Womanist Vision of Women's Relationships in the Bible.* San Diego, Calif.: LuraMedia, 1989.

Westheimer, Ruth K., and Jonathan Mark. *Heavenly Sex: Sexuality in the Jewish Tradition.* New York: New York University Press, 1995.

White, Sidnie Ann. "Esther: A Feminine Model for Jewish Diaspora." Pp. 124–29 in Peggy L. Day, ed., *Gender and Difference in Ancient Israel.* Minneapolis: Fortress Press, 1989.

european unions: political marriages and other mismatches

*Where there is marriage without love,
there will be love without marriage.*

—Benjamin Franklin

MATCHMAKER, MATCHMAKER

One of the themes that runs through this book is that of arranged marriages, specifically arranged marriages that are not particularly successful. Catherine the Great (chapter 13) had such a marriage, but it was mercifully brief. Elizabeth I (chapter 12) had to struggle to avoid a match, but may have had her heart broken in the process. Louis XV (chapter 7) seems to have been very happy with the Polish princess chosen for him, but eventually found comfort with a series of mistresses, most notably Madame de Pompadour.

Although all arranged marriages reflect a perception of marriage radically different from our own, not all are primarily about political power in the normal sense of that term. Many traditional societies view marriages not principally as the union of two individuals, but rather as arrangements designed to link two families socially and financially. Contrary to the words of the song, love and marriage [do not always] go together like a horse and carriage. As the historian John Boswell has astutely noted, in premodern marriages the connection usually began with property, continued with children, and hopefully developed into love or at least affection. In many modern marriages the process is just the opposite. It begins with love, continues with children, and ends with property in the form of a divorce settlement.

Heads of families, usually elder men, forged links with other households by arranging for younger members to wed each other. The exchange of members as well as the payment of either dowries (payments made to the groom's family) or bridewealth (payments to the bride's family) creates ties that are based far more on family interests than the desires or sentiments of young people. In traditional societies, much of the power of elder men rested in their ability to control the circumstances and timing of the marriages of other members. Younger men were dependent on the goodwill of their father or another senior male to secure them a bride. The situation of young women was even more precarious, since upon marriage they often left their immediate families to join their husband's household. A young woman betrothed to a cruel or abusive husband often found herself without any allies in her new home. A good match was therefore not only desirable, but often a matter of life and death.

Two of the best known examples of matchmaking in traditional societies are the Jewish *shadkhan* (immortalized as Yente in the musical *Fiddler on the Roof*) and the Japanese *nakado*.

I have some firsthand knowledge of the former, although not, of course, from my own marriages or that of my children. I remember a conversation with an ultra-Orthodox Jewish man in his apartment in Jerusalem on this very topic. Of course, he said, he and his wife would choose a husband for their daughter. "We certainly know her very well, maybe even better than she knows herself," he assured me. "And what does she know about being married?" he queried. Obviously, it makes more sense for her parents in consultation with other experienced adults to choose her life partner than for a young, inexperienced girl to make such a crucial decision. And he concluded triumphantly, "Our divorce rate is far lower than it is in the secular world."

I'm not sure I find his arguments really convincing, but they do serve as a stark reminder that marriage is not necessarily seen as a personal decision of the couple involved. In the ultra-Orthodox community, matches are made on the basis of a combination of family status (wealth, learning, history) and personal suitability (education, occupation, personality). To this day, many couples marry having barely met (and certainly never in private) prior to the wedding.

The Japanese case appears to have several elements in common with the Jewish example. In both societies, there are few opportunities for young people of the opposite sex to meet each other and get to know each other on their own. Matchmaking either by parents or by others on their behalf is thus one of the only ways for couples to get together. In both cases, moreover, there is a strong emphasis placed on filial piety, obedience to and dependence upon one's parents. One author even writes of "Jewish mothering in Japan." For obvious reasons, children who depend heavily upon their parents for emotional support well into their teens and young adulthood are inclined to accept their judgment on the choice of a marital partner.

In prewar Japan, when a family member reached marriageable age, it was the extended family or household that made decisions regarding the choice of a spouse.

A love marriage [was considered] as something improper, indecent, "egotistic," or something similar to an extra-marital affair in Western Christian moral codes. To be "proper" a marriage needed to be arranged by parents and other elder members of the families concerned.

Although family members occasionally handled all the arrangements themselves, it was far more common for a go-between known as a *nakado* to be involved at some stage in the process. In cases in which the two families were not acquainted, the go-between might be the first person to point out that family A had a son who could be an appropriate match for the daughter of family B. Even if the families knew each other or were related, the *nakado* might have been called in to handle the often lengthy negotiations required before a marriage could be agreed upon. Handling such sensitive matters through an intermediary was an excellent way of avoiding direct confrontations and disagreements between the two families. This stage could often be time-consuming and arduous, with many trips back and forth between the two families. No wonder the popular saying claimed that "The *nakado* needs a thousand pairs of sandals."

However, the role of the go-between did not end with the families' agreement to approve the match. He or she also played an important ceremonial role at the wedding and even continued to be part of the couple's life after they married. Like a workman held responsible for his product, the *nakado* was expected to mediate disputes between the couple and, should the need arise, even see to the divorce and return of gifts. For their part, a couple would usually maintain contact with their go-between, visiting on holidays and involving him or her in celebrations up to and beyond the birth of their first child.

Although the role of the *nakado* faded in the second half of the twentieth century as Japanese young people increasingly insist on choosing their own partners for "love" marriages, it remains one of the most interesting examples of how societies and families have sought to control the personal lives of their members.

POLITICAL MARRIAGES

Political marriages were even more complicated than your run-of-the-mill arranged marriage. In such cases the personal concerns of the two partners were clearly subordinated to larger considerations that went far beyond those of mere families. Such marriages preserved and expanded the wealth and political power of noble families. Parents chose spouses for their children with an eye to forging political and economic links with other families of a similar rank. Kösem Sultan, whom I discussed in chapter 2, repeatedly married her daughters to important court officials to secure their loyalty.

Nor is this only a matter of historical interest. Consider the following couple described in a British newspaper. "He is of noble wealth and birth. So is she. Between them they own or have a stake in a sizeable chunk of Scotland and London. Now they have announced their engagement—and one day their fortunes will come together in a multimillion golden cascade." Although this announcement was published in 1976, it probably could have appeared during almost any period in English history.

Royal Alliances

In the case of royal families, alliances between nations were forged and strengthened through the marriages of princes and princesses. Such marriages were often little more than political arrangements with two main purposes: (1) to forge an alliance between ruling families and their countries and (2) to produce a male heir to the throne. In many cases, sexual relations were treated as a purely functional part of the relationship. Once an heir had been produced, there was no further *need* for physical contact.

Consider, for example, the situation of Mary Tudor, Henry VIII's sister and Elizabeth I's aunt. When she was nineteen her brother, the king, arranged for her to marry an invalid thirty-three years her senior, King Louis XII of France. Although Henry was reportedly very fond of his sister, this did not deter him from using her as a pawn in his political maneuvering. (As in chess, pawns who move down the board successfully can become queens!) Mary was the prize that clinched a treaty between England and France. Six days after the two countries signed their treaty of peace and friendship, Mary and Louis were married (by proxy!).[1] Despite his ill health, Louis apparently harbored the hope that his marriage with Mary might produce an heir.[2] Foreign relations indeed!

Although this arrangement may seem peculiar to us, it was far from extraordinary in its day. Henry himself had married Catherine of Aragon, his brother's widow, to preserve the political alliance between England and Spain. His predecessor Henry VII had arranged for his daughter Margaret to marry James IV of Scotland in an attempt to strengthen his ties with *that* country.

Although both men and women were subject to such marriages, women clearly bore more of the burden. The son of a noble family could eventually gain a degree of independence from his father, but women usually went from being dependent on their fathers to being dependent on their husbands. Although King Louis appears to have been genuinely captivated by his young bride, one of the first things he did after Mary's arrival in France was order that all of her English ladies-in-waiting and servants be sent home. In one fell swoop, Mary found herself, like so many other women in such marriages, alone in a strange country, where even her servants were not of her choosing.

In spite of the fact that noble men and women were raised with the expectation that they would agree to a marriage that would advance their family's or nation's interests, this does not mean that

---

1. A second wedding with both present took place around two months later, on October 9.
2. In fact, he died less than three months after he first met her.

they were devoid of personal feelings or preferences. Although intermarriage between nobles and commoners was comparatively rare, within the ruling classes genuine attractions and affections often developed. Mary Tudor appears to have had her heart set on one of her brother's close friends, Charles Brandon, Duke of Suffolk. In fact, Henry appears to have promised her that should Louis XII die (as expected), she would be free to marry her beloved. Although he balked at fulfilling his part of the bargain, the couple took matters into their own hands (and, given Henry's track record, their lives) and married without his consent only six weeks after Louis died.

Mary Tudor was comparatively fortunate in her circumstances. The early demise of her husband and her brother's genuine affection for both her and the Duke of Suffolk meant she eventually ended up with the man of her choice. Many others were not so lucky. They spent years in foreign lands, married to men who viewed them as little more than heir-producing vessels. Social norms offered women few options even in the case of neglectful or abusive husbands. Since marriages were arranged to promote familial and national interests, divorce or annulment had consequences far beyond the individuals. Parents and other family members were hardly inclined to take back an unhappy bride, if it would result in an international crisis or even war. Moreover, while society usually turned a blind eye when dissatisfied husbands found solace with their mistresses and concubines, few noblewomen could expect to benefit from similar tolerance.

～

The tragic stories of Louise and Stephanie, two of the daughters of King Leopold II of Belgium, illustrate just how badly things could turn out for women in such political marriages. First, Leopold arranged for his seventeen-year-old daughter, Louise, to wed an Austro-Hungarian prince many years her senior. No one appears to have prepared her for her wedding night, and the traumatized bride ended up fleeing the house in her nightgown. Over the course of time, she seems to have accustomed herself to sex, but not to her husband. The marriage went from bad to worse. Several years after her marriage, Louise conducted an adulterous affair with a cavalry officer, who, following a duel with her husband, ended up in prison. Given the choice between returning to her husband and entering an insane asylum, she chose the asylum!

Leopold's middle daughter, Stephanie, did not fare much better. Her prospective husband, Prince Rudolph of Austria-Hungary, brought his mistress with him when he traveled to Brussels to meet her. He was, moreover, an alcoholic and a morphine addict. None of this probably mattered to Leopold, who was, after all, only interested in his daughter becoming empress. However, even this was not to be realized after Rudolph and his mistress died in an apparent double suicide. Stephanie eventually married a Hungarian count, whose lowly status so disappointed her father that he stopped speaking to her. Always one to harbor a grudge, it is said that toward the end of his life, King Leopold had but two dreams: to die a billionaire and to disinherit his daughters!

A Match Made in Hell

Such arranged political marriages were so common in bygone days that there is no shortage of cases to focus on. One that particularly caught my attention, however, is the story of the disastrous marriage of Princess Caroline of Brunswick to Prince George (the future King George IV) of England. Ever since I read a review of Flora Fraser's masterful biography of the queen, who lived in the late eighteenth and early nineteenth centuries, I've been fascinated by the subject. When I read the book, I was absolutely captivated, and I knew that we would have to discuss this episode in this book. It had a little bit of everything: adultery and accusations, bigamy and betrayal, scandalmongering press coverage, official hearings exposing private matters to the public eye. In an era before television and DNA testing, it had all the trappings of a modern-day media circus.

Princess Caroline Amelia Elizabeth was born in northern Germany on May 17, 1768. Her father, Charles, was both heir to a dukedom and a war hero. Her mother, Augusta, was the sister of King George III, Caroline's future father-in-law.[3] From the moment she first became aware of her status, Caroline must have been aware that she was intended to be the bride of one or another scion of a European royal family. Her mother, moreover, made no effort to hide the fact that a marriage between her children and her brother's was her ultimate goal.

---

3. Given the expectation that princes and princesses would marry those of a similar rank, such marriages of relatives, including first cousins, were common and in many ways inevitable. Taken as a whole, the royal families of eighteenth- and nineteenth-century Europe often appear as one large dysfunctional family. Caroline's daughter was, for example, married until her death to Leopold I of Belgium, the father of Leopold II, discussed above.

Princess Caroline could, for her part, have had no illusions concerning the risks inherent in such an arranged political marriage. Her own father had stated that "Royalty must make marriages of convenience, which seldom result in happiness" and spent most of his life estranged from his wife and living with his mistress. The rest of her family history was littered with the corpses of such failed arrangements. Her father's sister, Elizabeth, Princess of Prussia, referred to her husband, Frederick the Great, as "that stinking man." Her mother's sister, Queen Caroline of Denmark, was sent into exile and her marriage to the king of Denmark dissolved after she had a public affair with a minister at court. Princess Caroline's older sister Augusta had been abandoned by her husband, Prince Frederick of Württemberg, amid mutual accusations of promiscuity and licentiousness, and later died under mysterious circumstances.

Since Caroline's intended was also her first cousin, she shared with him many of the same family scandals. Prince George was the son of King George III, whose descent into insanity was recently chronicled so vividly in the movie *The Madness of King George*.[4] And his personal history left little cause for optimism. This was, after all, the same George IV who when he died was memorialized by the *Times* as follows: "There never was an individual less regretted by his fellow creatures than this deceased king. What eye has wept for him? What heart has heaved one throb of unmercenary sorrow?"[5] While this damning eulogy still belonged to the future, at the time of his engagement to Caroline, George IV was already a man with a checkered past, which included a long list of debts, a mistress, and, in the eyes of some, a wife.

In 1785, at the age of twenty-three, Prince George had fallen head over heels in love with a Catholic widow, Maria Fitzherbert, six years his senior. In a fit of passion, he even gave her a ring and had a marriage contract drawn up. Had it been recognized under British law, this marriage to a Catholic would have cost the Anglican prince his throne. However, under the Royal Marriage Act (passed after the disastrous marriage of George's uncle, Henry), he could only marry with the consent of his father. This was, of course, not forthcoming. Nevertheless, in the eyes of the Catholic Church (the absence of clergy notwithstanding), this was certainly

---

4. In fact, most authorities today believe that George was afflicted with a rare metabolic condition known as porphyria.

5. Quoted in Hobsbawm and Ranger, *The Invention of Tradition*, 109.

a valid marriage. They were to conduct themselves as husband and wife for the next eight years.

Several years after this suspect marriage and while still living with Mrs. Fitzherbert, George began a relationship with Frances, Lady Jersey. This was only the latest in a series of such escapades for the lady, who in the words of historian Amanda Foreman had, for the better part of two decades, "regarded all married men—except her husband . . . as an irresistible challenge." As early as 1777, her exploits had been the subject of a ribald newspaper article, which seemed to have been news to no one except her husband.

Not surprisingly, Lady Jersey quickly moved to remove George's "wife" from the scene. Her strategy was both remarkable and deeply cynical: reduce Mrs. Fitzherbert to the status of mistress by providing George with a legitimate heir-producing wife. Thus it was George's mistress, Frances, Lady Jersey, who chose Caroline, a woman of "indelicate manners, indifferent character, and not very inviting appearance," to be the future king's wife.[6]

George's own motives were no less self-seeking. Marriage, he believed, would provide him with an easy solution to his desperate economic situation. When he married, Parliament would pay off his debts and increase his income from £60,000 a year to £100,000. His impatience to wed was, therefore, not the typical eagerness of many grooms, but the calculated greed of an embattled debtor.

Even though Caroline arrived with few illusions (she had received several anonymous letters detailing the relationship between George and Lady Jersey), she must have been disappointed that her husband-to-be was not willing to make even the most minimal of efforts to develop a relationship. Upon meeting her for the first time, he moved to the opposite end of the room and asked for a brandy.

Be this as it may, the couple was duly wed and nine months later, almost to the day, a daughter, Charlotte, was born.[7] While in some cases the birth of a child may have saved such marriages, this pairing

---

6. Fraser, *The Unruly Queen*, 43. Lady Jersey always got special pleasure out of tormenting the wives of her lovers. In Caroline's case, she had herself appointed one of the princess's Ladies of the Bedchamber. In short, she was a woman "who could not be happy without a rival to trouble and torment."

7. On the day of his marriage, George sent a message pledging his love to Mrs. Fitzherbert, and on the day of the birth of his daughter, he sent her an impassioned love letter!

was clearly beyond salvation. Not only had George failed to get his eagerly expected increase in income, but his new bride was as popular with the public as the prince himself was unpopular. Her public appearances were frequently greeted with applause and cheers, while his continuing relationships with Lady Jersey, Mrs. Fitzherbert, and several other women drew widespread condemnation.[8]

From Failed Marriage to Public Scandal

In its early years, George and Caroline's marriage was, on the surface, no different from numerous other failed arrangements among families of a similar rank of their period. Over the course of time, however, what had begun as a fairly discreet failed marriage became an almost unprecedented public scandal. Caroline lost much of her innocence, while George decided that the best defense was a good offense. If he was congenitally incapable of reforming his own behavior and salvaging his reputation, he could at least besmirch hers.

Not that this was all that difficult. By all accounts, Caroline had a normal sexual appetite[9] and, while mindful of her public position, did have lovers. Although she made some efforts to be discreet, it was almost impossible for a person in her position to have real privacy. While press coverage of private matters was not what it is today, it must be remembered that she was constantly surrounded by attendants and servants. While it was naturally expected that they would look after the interests of their employers, the princess could never be sure whether her servants' loyalty was to her or to her estranged husband. George for his part repeatedly planted spies in her household in the hope of obtaining conclusive evidence that would allow him to divorce her.

In 1806 she was accused—although ultimately found innocent—of having borne a bastard child.[10] One of the chief sources

---

8. Lady Jersey's house was stoned, and on one notable occasion, the people of Brighton paraded two figures dressed as George and Lady Jersey through the town on donkeys.

9. A footman is said to have told one of Prince George's spies, perhaps on the basis of personal knowledge, that "The Princess is very fond of fucking."

10. This accusation was not as outlandish as it might seem. Georgiana, Duchess of Devonshire, an earlier victim of Lady Jersey's machinations, had borne an illegitimate child by the politician Charles Grey in 1891. Caroline did adopt a boy named Willy Austin, but it was never proven that he was her biological son.

for the accusation appears to have been one of George's informants. However, most of her servants rallied to her defense, and some may even have committed perjury on her behalf. Eventually the issue was dropped not only because the charge was probably spurious, but also because King George III had little interest in a full-scale airing of all the princess's grievances.

Eight years later, Caroline agreed to leave England and accepted £35,000 a year, as long as she stayed outside the country. She left, leaving behind both her husband and, more surprisingly, her daughter, Charlotte. Not only was she not present at Charlotte's wedding in 1816, but when Charlotte died in 1817, Caroline was neither properly informed of her death nor allowed to return to attend the funeral.

We may never know all the details of her period in Europe, which included an extended stay in Italy and pilgrimage to the Holy Land. However, this much appears certain: Shortly after her arrival in Europe, Caroline met a handsome Italian, sixteen years her junior, named Bartolomeo Pergami (or Bergami). He quickly assumed responsibility for her household and became her lover.[11]

None of this probably would have mattered had Caroline decided to remain abroad. However, in 1820 when George IV prepared to assume the throne, Caroline decided to return to England to press her claim to be queen. George, who had already tried, unsuccessfully, to divorce her, had no intention of accepting such a situation. Indeed, in her absence, much of his concern focused not on her physical presence, but rather on the question of whether her name would be included alongside the king's in the Church of England's liturgy. Meanwhile, negotiations continued to prevent her return.

On June 5, 1820, after a six-year absence, Princess Caroline returned to England as Queen Caroline. The crowds that awaited her return couldn't have been more enthusiastic. "God bless Queen Caroline!" they shouted as they mobbed. So rapturous was her reception that she was forced to take refuge in one of the hotels until an open carriage could be arranged to transport her through the cheering crowds. It was a portent of things to come. Everywhere she went cheering crowds mobbed her, and the king's anger grew.

---

11. In December 1814, Lord Sligo, who frequently informed on Caroline's activities, wrote, "I think it is likely that he [Pergami] does the job for her." Somewhat later he noted the damning evidence that Pergami's "room is next to hers. . . . He never goes to the bawdy house." Fraser, *The Unruly Queen*, 266.

Forced to delay his coronation until Caroline could be legally excluded, George sought every means possible to convince her to voluntarily relinquish the crown. She was offered a £50,000 allowance (at the taxpayers' expense). Attempts were made to pass a "Bill of Pains and Penalties" that, despite its ominous name, would essentially have provided a no-fault divorce. Finally, when all else failed, Caroline was put on trial before the House of Lords.

A Media Circus

Although it may not be difficult for modern readers—veteran viewers of Court TV—to imagine these proceedings, nothing quite like this had ever taken place in England or anywhere else in Europe. While several witnesses produced damning evidence of kisses, embraces, and shared beds, the defense was adept at discrediting most of them. Moreover, the king's use of spies and other paid informants and the general distaste at *his* behavior combined to win the queen sympathy. How could one not feel for a woman whose husband could not even find it within him to officially inform her of their daughter's death? Not surprisingly, the votes of the peers had as much to do with their political leanings as it did with the evidence.

Although it is common to cite the advent of television and even more recently the Internet as causes of much of today's obsession with the private lives of the rich and powerful, Caroline's trial was, for its time, as heavily covered as any event could be. Between 1750 and 1800, the number of newspapers and periodicals published in England rose by more than 150 percent, from a little over 100 to more than 260. Almost all of them covered the trial, and readers devoured the news avidly. Both the *News* and the *Times* increased their circulation by 27 percent during their period of in-depth coverage of the trial.[12] However, this was only one manner of publicizing the issue. A pro-Caroline pamphlet (one of several hundred) exposing the corruption of the Lords sold more than 100,000 copies. Over 500 cartoons on the case were published. Small wonder that a conservative bishop railed against "the seditious abusers of the liberty of the press [who used it] to poison and irritate."

As captivating as the trial may have been in and of itself, many credited it with levels of meaning far beyond the facts of the case itself. Some saw it as a symbol of the corrupt and fundamentally il-

---

12. According to Fraser, "Ladies stopped their maids from seeing the papers; soon peers would stop their ladies' own supply of papers."

legitimate political system and took their passions to the streets. The king's supporters were the most common victims. A mob stopped the Duke of Buckingham's carriage and threw three sheep heads at it. The Earl of Bridgewater was pelted with sheep entrails. Nor was the Church spared. A thirty-foot effigy of one bishop was hanged, and another clergyman had his windows broken. While Caroline welcomed such support, she also took pains to argue that her supporters were neither a mob nor uneducated. It would, however, be a grave mistake to believe that she was either a revolutionary or a democrat in spirit. Like so many others in her position, she welcomed support from any corner.

The continual involvement of thousands of women in so public an issue was also a major departure from earlier politics. Petitions ranging from a few hundred to, in one case, over seventeen thousand signatures were submitted by women. Lacemakers made her a special dress, while plait weavers prepared a bonnet for her. The rugweavers gave her a carpet. Much of the sympathy Caroline garnered was due to her loss of access to her daughter. It must be remembered that under English law of the time, and in sharp contrast to our own norms, mothers did not have legal authority over their children. Deprived of access to her daughter in both life and death, Caroline became "every woman." When she was "acquitted," women had their own celebrations. Cotton handkerchiefs printed with depictions of the trial; some even included a bust of the queen's lover, covered in decorations.

Caroline was to have little time to savor her victory. Not only was she still denied the formal recognition she craved, but in the ensuing months her health deteriorated dramatically. In August 1821, less than a year after her trial, she died. Even in death, she was not spared a final indignity. A plaque reading "Caroline of Brunswick, Injured Queen of England" was stripped from her coffin prior to its departure from England.

There are a variety of reasons why George's treatment of Caroline brought him so much criticism. He was not, as we have already noted, a particularly popular monarch, and even by the reigning double standard of the times, his hypocrisy screamed out. I'd like to emphasize yet another feature, on a much deeper social level, that I think was a major underlying cause of the condemnation that George's behavior produced: the rise of a different model of marriage.

As historian Lawrence Stone has documented in considerable detail in his classic work *The Family, Sex, and Marriage in England*

1500–1800, the seventeenth and particularly the eighteenth century saw the emergence of a model of marriage increasingly based on affection and friendship. Known as the "companionate marriage," this new model meant that more and more couples "in the eighteenth century began to put the prospects of emotional satisfaction before the ambition for increased income or status."

It is difficult to overestimate the consequences of such a change. Most importantly, it led to a significant transformation of relations between husbands and wives. Although it would be a tremendous exaggeration to speak of "equality," there was no doubt a major decline in what had been the near-absolute authority of the husband. This was reflected not only in an improved legal and economic situation for wives, but even in such daily customs as modes of address. In 1700 the topic of whether or not wives should address their husbands by their first names was the subject of stormy debate. Opponents of the practice believed it signified a lack of proper deference and respect, while supporters viewed the change as "the effect of tenderness and freedom."

One of the most interesting institutional revolutions connected to this change in the perception of marriage is the development of the "honeymoon." Hitherto, the term merely referred, as the name indicates, to the month after marriage, which was presumably characterized by goodwill and affection. Far from being accorded a measure of privacy, couples were under close scrutiny and their first night together, with its focus on the bride's virginity, was almost a public event. Friends and relatives not only celebrated with the happy (and nervous) couple long into the night, but often even accompanied them up into their bedroom.

In the eighteenth century, the honeymoon came to be associated, as it is to this day, with the idea that the couple would go away together and be left totally alone by their friends and families. During this period, they had the chance to get to know each other both physically and emotionally in a way that had never been possible in earlier times. Of course, these changes did not take place overnight and were not evenly distributed among all groups in society. Aristocrats and particularly royalty were still largely bound by the demands of status.

Despite the obstinacy with which they pursued such arrangements, the royal families of Europe were well aware of the price they exacted on both children and parents. Caroline's own father wrote, "These marriages not only embitter the lives of the parties to them, but all too frequently have a disastrous effect upon the children, who often are unhealthy in mind or body."[13] One need look no further than his daughter's life for confirmation of this statement.

SUGGESTIONS FOR FURTHER READING

Foreman, Amanda. *Georgiana: Duchess of Devonshire*. London: Harper-Collins, 1998.

Fraser, Flora. *The Unruly Queen: The Life of Queen Caroline*. New York: Knopf, 1998.

Harris, Barbara J. "Power, Profit and Passion: Mary Tudor, Charles Brandon, and the Arranged Marriage in Early Tudor England." *Feminist Studies* 15, no. 1 (1989): 59–88.

Hendry, Joy. *Marriage in Changing Japan*. New York: St. Martin's, 1981.

Hobsbawm, Eric, and Terence Ranger, eds. *The Invention of Tradition*. Cambridge, U.K.: Cambridge University Press, 1983.

Hochschild, Adam. *King Leopold's Ghost*. Boston, Mass.: Houghton Mifflin, 1998.

Laquer, Thomas W. "The Queen Caroline Affair: Politics as Art in the Reign of George IV." *Journal of Modern History* 54 (1982): 417–66.

Mullan, Bob. *The Mating Trade*. London: Routledge, 1984.

Stone, Lawrence. *The Family, Sex, and Marriage in England 1500–1800*. London: Weidenfeld and Nicolson, 1977.

---

13. Fraser, *The Unruly Queen*, 15.

Madame de pompadour: The mistress of the House

mistress n. *1. A woman who has authority or control; the female head of a household or some other establishment. 2. A woman employing or in authority over servants or attendants. 3. A female owner, as of a slave, horse, dog, etc. 4. A woman who has the power of controlling or disposing of something at pleasure. . . . 7. A woman who illicitly occupies the place of a wife. 8.* Archaic or Poetic. *sweetheart.*

I decided to begin this chapter by quoting some of the dictionary definitions of the term *mistress*, because this seemed to me to be the best way to point out just how complex the concept is. In modern American English, the use of the term has tended to be reduced to a variant of definition 7: *a woman involved in an illicit relationship with a married man.* However, both linguistically and historically the meanings of this term are far more varied and complex.

I think it is especially interesting that several of the meanings of the term concern not the fact of an illicit relationship, but that of a woman with power and control. In fact, according to the *Oxford English Dictionary*, even the common connection with an illicit relationship originated in the concept of "A woman who has *command* over a man's heart." Given the topic of this book, it's only natural that I should take this opportunity to explore the connection between power and this kind of relationship.

In this chapter, I've chosen to use the term *mistress* in a very specific way. First, I've excluded cases of short-term or casual relationships, which had few consequences for the parties involved. Somehow grouping these figures with those who held the semiofficial title of "mistress" does not really do justice to such arrangements. Second, I have also decided to distinguish between concubines in a harem or other polygamous arrangement and women whose relationships took place in societies that at least theoretically believed in monogamy. Not only have I dealt with concubines and members of the harems already in chapters 1 and 2, but I also believe that these arrangements were very different from those of the couples discussed here. Harems, as we've already seen, were accepted, even religiously sanctioned, features of the Muslim societies in which they existed. In this chapter, I'm concerned with people who, however public their relationships were, violated the official norms of their cultures.

Finally, I want to stress that the couples discussed here were not living in today's world of individual freedom and comparatively easy divorces. Often as not, they were bound in wedlock through the kind of political marriage I discussed in the previous chapter. If bad choices were made, they were not usually made by the couple, but by their parents or other guardians. The existence of mistresses was almost an inevitable side effect of such arranged marriages. It served, often as a safety valve, to relieve the pressure on those trapped in loveless and often sexless partnerships.

Indeed, at times the burdens placed on the heirs to Europe's thrones appear to have driven them beyond the borders of sanity. Prince Pedro of Portugal, the son of Affonso IV, fell deeply and endlessly in love with Inês de Castro, his wife's lady-in-waiting. As his mistress, she bore him two sons, before she was murdered by his father. When he became king, Pedro had her body exhumed, married her (they must have omitted the traditional "til death do us part"), and forced the entire court to pay homage to her corpse!

One way to ease the burden of unhappy political marriages was to permit the men, and to a lesser extent the women, to find love or at least sexual pleasure elsewhere. And this is exactly what many of them did. In fact, given the hundreds of women who spent all or part of their lives as the mistresses of important men, it was not an easy task choosing whom to discuss in this book.

REINETTE

Jeanne-Antoinette Poisson, better known as Madame de Pom-padour, was born to a comfortable Parisian merchant family in 1721. Her mother was a popular local beauty, who clearly knew the value of her assets. When a financial scandal plunged the family into bankruptcy and forced M. Poisson to flee to Germany, Madame Poisson rescued them all by winning the affection of a wealthy businessman, M. Le Normant de Tournehem. He took charge of her family, educated her children, and even made it possible for M. Poisson to return home. Thereafter, Tournehem and M. and Madame Poisson lived together in a rather unusual ménage à trois. Thus the young Jeanne-Antoinette received an early lesson in the ways of the world.

According to an oft-quoted family tradition, when Jeanne-Antoinette was nine a fortune-teller told her that she would win the heart of a king. Thereafter, her family called her "Reinette"—"Queeny." It is a testimony to the vast cultural gap that separates our own time from that of "Reinette" if we consider the family's reaction to this prediction. Imagine, for a moment, how most families would react today if they were told that their daughter was destined to be the mistress of an important man. It would not be an exaggeration to claim that the Poissons, while understandably skeptical, were also cautiously thrilled. While the position of queen was open to only a single woman of royal blood who held the position until her death, the position of the king's mistress, while much more tenuous, was open to many other candidates. If in the fairy tale *Cinderella* the women of the kingdom attended the ball in the hope of dancing with the prince and becoming his wife, women of eighteenth-century France had slightly more modest ambitions.

It's important to point out that although such "illicit" relationships are usually kept secret these days, this has been, by no means, the case throughout history. In the past, the position of the "king's mistress" was quite public. Such was the prestige of a monarch in those days that there was very little stigma attached to the position of his mistress. Moreover, the material advantages to her family were enormous.[1]

---

1. Although most of her family appears to have been thrilled when Jeanne-Antoinette became the king's mistress, her husband, M. d'Etoiles, who loved her deeply, was devastated. To his credit he never sought any special advantage from his wife's position. Indeed, while he remained a close friend of his brother-in-law M. Abel Poisson, he didn't speak to his wife for more than twenty years.

LOUIS XV

Prince Louis, the future King Louis XV, was born in 1710. He assumed the throne at age five following the death of his great-grandfather Louis XIV, also known as the Sun King or Louis the Great. Having reigned for seventy-two of his seventy-seven years, the Sun King had outlived his son, his grandson, and one of his great-grandsons. Indeed, by the time he died and another of his great-grandsons assumed the throne as Louis XV, the family had been almost destroyed by disease and incompetent medical care. Young Louis may have been ruler of France, but he was also a shy, lonely boy with no father, mother, brothers, or sisters.

Over the course of time, Louis matured into a bright, clever, brave, and handsome young man. His shyness, however, never left him, and even as a mature king, he was uneasy with strangers, especially beautiful women. Although plans were made to marry him off to a princess ten years his junior, it was eventually decided not to wait too long, and he was eventually wed to an exiled Polish princess, who thus became Queen Marie Leszcinska.

At one time, Louis appears to have been deeply in love with his wife and to have claimed, the opinions of others notwithstanding, that she was the most beautiful woman at Versailles. He certainly seems to have found her sexually attractive. She was to bear him no less than ten children. After this, she seems, perhaps not surprisingly, to have found every possible excuse to keep him out of her bed. In the words of biographer Nancy Mitford, "As she was extremely pious, he was never allowed there [in her bedroom] on the days of the major saints. By degrees the saints for whom he was excluded became more numerous and less important." Having more than fulfilled her duties as a wife and consort, she settled into an existence that did nothing to hold her energetic husband. Even her father, King Stanislas, is said to have remarked that the two dullest queens in Europe were his wife and his daughter! So when Louis's attention began to stray, he looked not only for beauty, but for wit, style, and grace.

Initially Louis's companions were three sisters, who one after the other (with occasional overlapping) became his mistresses. Madame de Mailly was succeeded in 1740 by her sister the Marquise de Vintimille, who died giving birth to the king's child a year later. Shortly after her death, Louis began his affair with a third sister, the Duchesse de Châteauroux. Her death from pneumonia in 1744 left the position of mistress to the thirty-four-year-old monarch open again. According to Nancy Mitford, the biographer of both Madame de Pompadour and Louis XV, "every pretty woman in the Île de France nurtured a secret conviction that she would carry off the prize" of becoming the king's mistress. Although yet another sister was available, Louis eventually looked elsewhere, and thus he found Madame de Poisson.

$\sim$

How did Jeanne-Antoinette attract the king and hold his attention until her death twenty years later? Not surprisingly, she seems to have been uncommonly beautiful. Even her rivals generally conceded that she "absolutely extinguished all the other women at the Court, although some were very beautiful." A close friend of the queen wrote that Jeanne-Antoinette was "One of the prettiest women I ever saw."

However, it was doubtful if she could have captured the king, much less held his affection until her death, had she not had other assets. In an era before radio, television, movies, and packaged music, the ability to entertain was not only appreciated, but also greatly prized in elite circles. Owing to the generosity of her mother's lover, young Jeanne-Antoinette received an excellent education in every possible subject. She could recite entire plays by heart, played the clavichord well, and was an enthusiastic gardener and botanist. She painted, drew, and engraved precious stone. She is said to have had an excellent sense of humor. Even before she became the royal mistress, she was a popular hostess, regularly entertaining and being entertained by such luminaries as Voltaire and Montesquieu.

Given our preconceptions surrounding the term *mistress*, it is perhaps surprising to note that the sexual side of the relationship was not one of its strong points. Madame de Pompadour was by her own testimony "cold of nature" and, in her early years, lived in constant fear that her lack of passion might disappoint the king. She tried every possible remedy, including a "diet to heat the blood," elixirs, and various other solutions. In the end, her doctor recommended quite sensibly that she simply look after her general health and get a bit more exercise.

Perhaps more than anything else, she held the king's attention by her uncompromising devotion to him. Although she was never particularly strong, whatever energies she had went into pleasing her king. Late-night dinner parties were followed by early morning masses. As an important, however unofficial, court personage, her social responsibilities were unending: letters to write, visitors to receive, house parties, work plans, etc. Even when she suffered a miscarriage, as happened several times during the early years of her relationship with the king, she remained in bed for only a day or two before resuming her normal schedule.

KEEPING THE JOB

Even had the physical side of the relationship not been so demanding, it was no easy task being the king's mistress. One of the most remarkable aspects of Madame de Pompadour's career is that she emerged not only unscathed from attempts to replace her, but usually with her status enhanced.

In 1752 a number of her enemies at the court, including one of her cousins, sought to replace her by introducing a pretty young girl, Madame de Choiseul, into the king's social circle. The king was clearly enamored of the young woman, but neither she nor her allies had the savvy to match wits with de Pompadour and her allies. In the end, Choiseul's careless handling of a letter from the king led to her and her husband being banished from the court. The king compensated de Pompadour for her anguish by bestowing the rank of duchess upon her.

A few years later, in 1756, reports circulated that Louis intended to replace Madame de Pompadour with a new mistress, one Madame de Coslin. Unfortunately for her supporters and allies, de Coslin spoiled the scheme by asking for too many presents and submitting too eagerly to the king's advances.[2] (De Pompadour certainly helped her cause by circulating a forged letter hinting at her rival's exaggerated financial expectations.) Once again de Pompadour was rewarded for her patience. She was appointed a member of the queen's inner circle.

Indeed, her relationship with the woman who could have been her greatest rival, the queen, offers an important clue to understanding her longevity. While several of her predecessors, most notably the Duchesse of Châteauroux, had deeply offended the queen, de Pompadour took great pains to cultivate her relationship with Marie. From the outset, she encouraged Louis to be considerate of his wife. On one notable occasion she encouraged him to give a beautiful gold and diamond snuffbox intended for her mother to the queen instead.

---

2. In the words of Nancy Mitford, "She gave herself like a whore and like a whore, she was abandoned."

As opposed to her rivals, she seems to have completely understood the limits of her position and how to order her priorities. Just as she was cautious not to offend the queen, it never seems to have bothered her that Louis had dalliances with other women. She even made discreet arrangements for him with local prostitutes. She valued her position at his side, far more than her place in his bed. "It's his heart I want," she said repeatedly. Indeed, if her testimony and that of others are to be believed, she stopped having sex with him during the second half of their relationship.

FRIENDS AND ALLIES

Of course, however devoted de Pompadour may have been to the king, her devotion was not completely selfless. From the start she used her relationship to accumulate power for herself and those close to her. As a woman, she could not be given any official position, but her male relatives could and were. Her mother's lover, "Uncle" de Tournehem, was made the superintendent of buildings, which put him in charge of palaces, public buildings, and the royal art collections. (Whatever her motives may have been, he was an excellent choice: putting the finances in order, organizing the inventories, and eliminating corruption.) When he died, her brother succeeded to the post and was made a marquis. Her father was also ennobled and given an estate.

De Pompadour also intervened regularly in the politics of the court. The Comte de Maurepos, one of the king's most experienced ministers, was also one of her most implacable enemies at court. Having known the king as a child and outlasted several of the king's mistresses, he apparently thought himself invulnerable. But his thirty-one years of service were brought to an end by de Pompadour, who had him exiled from the court.

As this case amply indicates, her political preferences were usually dictated by personality rather than ideology. Her allies and friends often prospered at the expense of more skilled and suitable candidates. Nowhere was this clearer than her long-running quarrel with the Comte d'Argenson. He blamed her, as did others, for his brother's dismissal from the court; she never forgave him for attempting to oust her from her position as mistress. Thus, despite his loyalty to the king and his acknowledged skill as a diplomat, d'Argenson found himself watching from the sidelines as less skilled hands, including de Pompadour herself, led Louis and France into an unpopular alliance with Austria and eventually the Seven Years' War.

THE VILLAIN OF THE PIECE

Given the influence de Pompadour exercised, it is easy to forget that the power she had was always wielded secondhand. Formally, it was Louis and not his mistress who rewarded her friends and family and dismissed her enemies. We are not the only ones to be misled by the circumstances. Contemporaries were all too ready to credit Louis with all of his successes and blame his mistress for all of his failures and shortcomings.

In the fairy tale existence of the royal court, the king's mistress was more often than not cast in the role of the wicked step-mother. Even when she served a popular monarch, she was a convenient scapegoat for any of *his* failings. When his popularity waned, her life could become almost unbearable. Replacing a king required a revolution; the downfall of his mistress meant merely finding a replacement.

In the case of Louis XV,

> to political disappointment was added contempt for a tyrannical and immoral king: His love affairs were never to be respected as those of his predecessor, Louis XIV, had been. On the contrary, they were excoriated because the king was inept enough to dis-dain Paris, to "rid himself" of popular princes, to indulge in se-crecy . . . at a time when his people were already becoming conscious of their rights and some of their desires. Louis XV's amorous activities, [were] seen through eyes filled with a new critical spirit which daily became more confident.[3]

From 1748 onward, Madame de Pompadour was one of the pri-mary targets of this new critical spirit. An unpopular peace treaty, high taxes, and a shortage of corn all turned Louis XV and, by as-sociation, his mistress into figures of ridicule. Although few sources, particularly in the court, were either brave enough or fool-hardy enough to attack the king himself, his mistress was not nearly so lucky. While direct attacks were rare, anonymous posters, pamphlets, and leaflets appeared on almost a daily basis. One par-ticularly popular form of attack was derisive poetry, most of which was slightly obscene and played upon her maiden name, Poisson (Fish). The poems, in which she was known as "Poissonades," were a more bitter and cruel form of the monologue jokes told at the ex-pense of public figures on today's late-night TV talk shows.

---

3. Farge, *Subversive Words,* 159.

In many ways, Madame de Pompadour found herself in a no-win situation. If she entertained lavishly, she was accused of wasting taxpayers' money. If she did not, it was claimed that she was preventing the king from meeting other women. Inevitably her building projects were criticized for being too lavish by some and too modest by others. At times the charges against her bordered on the bizarre. Following the disappearance of a young boy, a mob placed the blame on her doorstep and, chanting her name, stormed the house of her close ally, the chief of police. As the chorus of criticisms against her grew, her enemies and rivals at the court licked their chops in anticipation of her downfall and began to speculate as to who her successor might be.

It must always be remembered that the position of royal mistress was not decided by either an election or a popularity contest. Her tenure in office, like that of the king's ministers, was dependent upon the vote of only one person, the king, and despite her constant concerns, Madame de Pompadour appears to have had little to fear on this score. If the goal of her critics was to drive a wedge between her and the king, their barrage of criticisms had precisely the opposite effect. The king, who was notoriously shy by nature, simply withdrew further and depended upon her even more.

In the end, only death could separate them. Although she was only in her early forties, de Pompadour's health had been deteriorating for several years. By 1763 she was in the last stages of tuberculosis. Despite other concerns, Louis rarely left her bedside as the end of "a debt of almost twenty years and a sure friendship" drew near. Indeed, he withdrew only when it became clear that she could not confess and receive the last rites in the presence of a man who had for so long been her lover in direct contradiction to the Church's teaching. Even so, he watched her funeral procession from his balcony, standing coatless and hatless in a freezing storm, tears running down his face, "The only tribute . . . [he was] allowed to offer to a friendship of twenty years."[4] She was as greatly mourned in death as she had been despised in life.

CONCLUSIONS

Before we leave Louis and his mistress completely, it is useful to offer a few closing thoughts concerning their situation. In these days,

---

4. Princess Michael of Kent, *Cupid and the King*, 226.

when having a mistress is about as close as one can get to political suicide, it's useful to give some attention to how Louis's circumstances differed from our own. First, it must be remembered that he was not an elected politician, but a king in an era when kings, even the most unpopular, had a special status unlike that of any man. Not only was Louis expected to have a mistress or several mistresses, but as we have seen, the position of royal mistress was greatly coveted. Thus, whatever criticisms Louis may have faced during the period of his affair with Madame de Pompadour, none of it seems to have been focused on the simple fact of him having a mistress. People may have resented her influence, her extravagances, and her meddling in both domestic and international politics, but no one (or at least no one outside the Church) challenged the king's right to have a mistress. Her rivals sought to depose her or replace her, but not to discredit the institution she represented.

Second (and here we return to issues discussed in the previous chapter), even if Louis had not been the king, he and many of his contemporaries were trapped in arranged marriages that made marital fidelity extremely difficult, if not impossible. Not only was he not free to choose his wife, but he also lacked the option of an easy divorce. In a case like Louis's, where a combination of piety and pregnancy had led his wife to all but exclude him from her bed, extramarital liaisons were if not admirable, at least inevitable.

Finally, Louis lived in a time when even religious authorities had a far more forgiving view of human nature. The Catholic Church was remarkably discreet in its opposition to such arrangements. While Louis and others engaged in such relationships were denied access to the sacraments, they always had the option of a deathbed confession to restore them to a state of grace. Louis, to his great embarrassment, had made just such a confession at an early age. (He recovered both his health and his libido.) Madame de Pompadour was granted absolution just prior to her death, even though her legal husband refused to forgive her. Indeed, it may not be a coincidence that the phenomenon of mistresses seems to have been and still is particularly tolerated in Catholic countries, given their tradition of sin and forgiveness.

SUGGESTIONS FOR FURTHER READING

Elbl, Ivan. "'Men without Wives': Sexual Arrangements in the Early Portuguese Expansion in West Africa." Pp. 61–86 in Jacqueline Murray and Konrad Eisenbichler, eds., *Desire and Discipline: Sex and Sexuality in the Premodern West*. Toronto: University of Toronto Press, 1996.

Farge, Arlette. *Subversive Words: Public Opinion in Eighteenth-Century France*. University Park: Pennsylvania State University Press, 1995.

Princess Michael of Kent. *Cupid and the King*. London: HarperCollins, 1991.

Mitford, Nancy. *Madame de Pompadour*. London: Hamilton, 1968.

Woodbridge, John D. *Revolt in Prerevolutionary France: The Prince de Conti's Conspiracy against Louis XV 1755–1757*. Baltimore: Johns Hopkins University Press, 1995.

EiGHT

Tom and Sally: separate and unequal

"All men are created equal." So wrote Thomas Jefferson, and so agreed with him all the delegates from the American colonies. But we must not press them too closely nor insist on the literal interpretations of their words.

—John R. Commons[1]

NOT ONLY THE FRENCH

Although it is perhaps tempting to assume that there was something uniquely French about the type of relationship described in the previous chapter, that certainly does not appear to be the case. In England, for example, the decline of moral Puritanism from the mid-seventeenth century onward led to a decided change in the attitude toward both mistresses and illegitimacy. As Lawrence Stone has documented, already in the reign of Charles II (1660–1685) it appeared to some that "the whole court was engaged in an endless game of sexual musical chairs." The king himself was as sensual as he was popular and had at least fifteen mistresses during his career, several of whom bore

---

1. *Races and Immigrants in America*, new ed. (New York: Macmillan, 1920).

him children. Such behavior was so much the norm that one important official was urged to keep a mistress, lest he be "ill looked upon for want of doing so."

Throughout the eighteenth century, it was quite common for important Englishmen to have mistresses. Their wives appear to have accepted this with no more comment than Louis's Queen Marie. George II, a close contemporary of Louis XV, made no attempt to hide his mistresses from his wife, who said she "minded it no more than his going to the close stool."[2] The monthly publication *Town and Country Magazine* carried a regular feature on the sexual escapades of distinguished men.

More often than not, the female companions of such men were the daughters (or wives) of once well-off men who had lost their fortunes. (Here too the lives of many Englishwomen were similar to that of Jeanne-Antoinette Poisson and her mother.) Financial difficulties not only flooded the market with bankrupt businessmen, but also produced a ready supply of attractive, educated women who sought to maintain their previous standard of living through an arrangement with a wealthy and well-connected man. Relationships were thus arranged in which affluent men joined with women seeking to retain some measure of status and comfort in mutually beneficial arrangements.

COLONIAL VIRGINIA

On the other side of the Atlantic, in the southern states of colonial America, the phenomenon of wealthy men engaging in extramarital relationships assumed a particularly invidious form because of the widespread practice of slavery. While slavery was not unheard of and in fact had thrived during earlier periods in Europe, and continues into modern times in some parts of the world, in the eighteenth and nineteenth centuries it assumed a particularly developed form in the framework of the agricultural economies of the New World. Over a period of approximately 300 years, over twelve million people were exported from Africa to serve as slaves in the Western Hemisphere. While the majority of these were men, destined for agricultural work on plantations in Brazil, Jamaica, and the southern regions of North America, many were young women who engaged in both field

---

2. Stone, *The Family, Sex and Marriage*, 329.

and domestic work. For many such women, sexual exploitation was a common aspect of their lives.

The question of the relationship between slavery and racism in America has produced one of the stormiest debates in American history, much of it focusing on colonial Virginia. On the one hand are those who believe that prior to the introduction of slavery in North America, racism was only a negligible phenomenon. Racism, it is argued, emerged in full form as a justification for slavery and the immorality it represented. On the other hand, there are those who claim that the first American settlers were already deeply imbued with racist ideas, and their mistreatment of people of African origin was merely an inevitable outcome of this ideology.

An examination of the legal codes of the period in colonial Virginia offers valuable insight into the norms of the period relating to sex and power. In 1662 the colony's assembly decided that nonmarital sexual relations between members of different races should carry twice the penalty as the same "crime" committed by members of the same race. At the same time, it was decreed that the child of a black woman and a white man would inherit the status of his mother, and not, as was the common English norm of the time, that of his father.[3] Thus, they ensured that in almost all cases such "mixed" children would be slaves.

In 1691 the same assembly decided to ban interracial *marriages*. While the legislation applied equally to men and women, its stated purpose—to prevent "negroes, mulattos and Indians intermarrying English and other white women"—made it clear that the "protection" of white women was the primary purpose of the legislation. Indeed, while the existing ban on interracial fornication between white women and nonwhite men was retained, the penalties against white men who consorted with nonwhite women were dropped! Thus, while both white men and women were prohibited from marrying outside their race, it was no crime for a white man to have nonmarital sex with a black woman! While white women were placed on a pedestal and enshrined as the symbol of white superiority and racial purity, female slaves were rendered virtually powerless to resist sexual abuse and degradation.

---

3. Over the course of time, these laws evolved to the point where anyone with black ancestry would be classified as black. Thus, as one scholar has noted, a white woman could give birth to a black child, but a black woman could not give birth to a white child!

As striking as this contrast between women of different races may have been, it appears even more remarkable when we remember that it took place at a time of growing rhetoric about equality and freedom. No one individual personified this tension between word and deed more clearly than Thomas Jefferson, who preached equality, but owned slaves; who condemned miscegenation and led a household full of "mixed race" members.

THE FACTS OF THE CASE

In the fall of 1998, newspaper readers in the United States and around the world were startled to discover that DNA evidence provided a strong indication that a popular American president had had an illicit affair with a young female member of his staff. Almost immediately, the battle lines were drawn. Defenders of the president claimed that the evidence was not all that clear, and in any event, the "charges," even if proven, were irrelevant given the president's successes and popularity. In contrast, critics of the president said that the scientific evidence confirmed what they had long suspected and was conclusive evidence of his dishonesty and hypocrisy. I am referring, of course, to Thomas Jefferson and the accusations that he had a sexual relationship with and fathered several children by his slave Sally Hemings.

Although most Americans still remember that Jefferson authored the Declaration of Independence and served as the country's third president, in recent years the controversy regarding his personal behavior and morality has tended to overshadow his other achievements both personal and political. He served the state of Virginia as its governor and the United States as an ambassador, secretary of state, vice president, and, of course, president. He was, moreover, one of the outstanding thinkers and intellectuals of his time. His 10,000-volume library eventually served as the basis for the Library of Congress. He was not only the founder but also the architect of the University of Virginia. He knew several languages, and although his reputation as an inventor has been somewhat exaggerated, he was a clever designer of gadgets.

The balance of power in a relationship is often clearly reflected in the division of the historical evidence. Nowhere is this clearer than in the Hemings–Jefferson controversy. Given the vast quantities of information we possess about Jefferson and his life, it is humbling to realize how little we actually know about Sally

Hemings. Indeed, in keeping with her slave status, almost all of it reflects in one way or another her relationship with Thomas Jefferson and his family.

Sarah (Sally) Hemings was the daughter of Elizabeth (Betty) Hemings, a "mixed-race" slave, and John Wayles, an English-born Virginian who later became Thomas Jefferson's father-in-law. Born in 1773, three years before Jefferson penned the Declaration of Independence, she was the youngest of six children whom Betty bore to John following the death of his third wife in 1761. She became Jefferson's property through inheritance in 1774 and came to his home at Monticello with her mother in 1776. She was, of course, not only his slave, but also his wife Martha's half sister![4] Although we do not have pictures of her, all accounts seem to agree that she was unusually beautiful.

Martha Jefferson died in 1782 at age thirty-three, shortly after the birth of her sixth child. Her grief-stricken husband was devastated and retreated to his room for three weeks. Later he destroyed all of their correspondence. According to a well-established historical tradition, he had promised his dying wife that he would never marry again; no small undertaking for a vigorous man who was at the time only thirty-nine years old.

Throughout most of her early childhood, Sally assisted in the care of Jefferson's daughter Mary, and in 1787, she traveled with her to France to join Thomas, who was at the time serving as ambassador to France. (This period was movingly, if not always accurately, evoked in the Merchant Ivory film *Jefferson in Paris*.) When they returned to the United States in 1789, Sally was pregnant, and shortly after her arrival, she gave birth to a son. Rumors and his name, Thomas, notwithstanding, this child was almost certainly NOT Jefferson's.

To this point, there is almost no dispute about the facts. The same, however, cannot be said for almost all that follows. During the next several decades, Sally was to bear several more children, at least some of whom were descendants of Thomas Jefferson or one of his close relatives. Four of these survived infancy: a daughter named Harriet and three sons, Eston, Beverly, and Madison.

Both Eston, who lived his life as a white, and Madison, who lived his as an African American, are known to have believed that they were sons of Thomas Jefferson and to have passed

---

4. Tradition records that the two women resembled each other, which may explain, at least in part, why Jefferson found Sally so attractive.

these traditions down to their families. Indeed, Madison Hemings, in a document published in Ohio in 1873, wrote a short version of his memoirs in which he explicitly claimed Jefferson was his and his siblings' father.

It is doubtful if historians would ever have given any credence to Madison Hemings's claims, if it were not for the work of a Jefferson contemporary named James Callender. While Callender was not the originator of the gossip about President Jefferson and "Dark Sal," he was, more than any other single person, responsible for its public dissemination. At face value, this does not speak highly for the veracity of the tale. Callender was, by all accounts, a rogue and a scoundrel who frequently let his personal malice overshadow any interest he may have had in the truth. Indeed, it can truly be said that he brought to his work the worst features of modern tabloid journalism.

Ironically, Callender was, early in his political life, a strong supporter of Jefferson. Indeed, so ardent were his political views that he was indicted and convicted under the notorious Sedition Act of 1798 for defaming Jefferson's rival and predecessor, President John Adams.[5] When Jefferson became president in 1801, he pardoned all those convicted under the act and promised to restore the money they had been fined. Callender, who had already been released, was infuriated when the money he had been promised did not arrive on time. Indeed, Jefferson himself personally provided him with partial restitution and on several other occasions offered Callender financial assistance. Callender, however, had higher ambitions and when these were thwarted by Jefferson's refusal to appoint him as postmaster in Richmond, he turned against his onetime patron.

He began by recounting a well-known (and generally accepted) story concerning Jefferson's attempts to seduce the wife of one of his friends. This, however, was only a preliminary to his much harsher accusations concerning the president and "Dusky Sally." In the first of what was to become a series of diatribes he wrote:

> It is well known that the man, who it delighteth the people to honor keeps and for many years has kept, as his concubine, one of his slaves. Her name is SALLY. The name of her eldest son is Tom. His features are said to bear a striking though sable resemblance to those of the president himself. . . . By this wench Sally, our president has

---

5. The act under which Callender was tried and convicted was itself very controversial. It is, perhaps, significant to note that even prior to his attacks on Jefferson, Callender had a reputation for defaming his political enemies.

had several children. There is not an individual in the neighbour-
hood of Charlottesville who does not believe the story, and not a few
who know it.[6]

Other papers published by Jefferson's enemies were quick to
pick up the story, several resorting to rhyming verse to mock the
president. The following was set to the tune of Yankee Doodle:

> *Of all the damsels on the green*
> *On mountain or in valley*
> *A lass so luscious ne'er was seen*
> *As Monticellian Sally*

Whether their tone was bitter or humorous, the accusations leveled against Jefferson can only be properly understood in the context of the time. Although he may not have been technically guilty
of a crime, his offense was, in the eyes of many, much worse. Although slave masters rather routinely imposed themselves on their
female slaves, attitudes toward miscegenation were terribly complex. Jefferson was no stranger to the phenomenon, both through
his friends and family. However, he was also aware that many
viewed the interracial sex with a repugnance that most of us can
barely imagine.[7] It was for such individuals, including Callender, as
much a sin against nature as a crime against man. Jefferson was,
for example, only one of a number of individuals whom Callender
"outed," not because he objected to the exploitation of the women,
but rather to what he viewed as the perversity of the men.[8]

DNA OR DENIAL?

For almost two centuries, scholars of American history and Jefferson biographers either dismissed or ignored the Hemings–Jefferson

---

6. Gordon-Reed, *Thomas Jefferson and Sally Hemings*, 61.

7. Jefferson himself at times expressed his repugnance at the practice,
but this does not appear to have prevented him from having friendships
with men who had black slave mistresses, or (so it appears) having one
himself.

8. It should be noted in this context that only in the 1960s did the U.S.
Supreme Court rule that laws against miscegenation were unconstitu-
tional. Moreover, even in the later 1990s, one state still had such a law on
its books, although it was, of course, unenforceable.

relationship. Not only were such intimate revelations not part and parcel of conventional biographies of the time, but the accusations seemed absurd when leveled against a man who was one of the most respected figures in all of American history. While abolitionists and British critics of Jefferson and the American Revolution repeated the tale with glee, few serious scholars viewed Sally Hemings or her progeny as a significant part of Jefferson's story.

In 1974 historian Fawn Brodie became the first scholar to seriously evaluate the evidence for the Hemings–Jefferson connection. Although she at times exceeded the evidence at hand and her avowedly Freudian approach is certainly open to challenge, her book, *Thomas Jefferson: An Intimate History*, certainly succeeded in renewing public awareness of the story and sparking interest in the controversy. While several of the leading Jefferson scholars, including at least one who was a descendant of the Jefferson family, disagreed with her conclusions, the wider reading public was captivated by the story. Indeed, interest only increased with the publication of a historical novel, *Sally Hemings*,[9] and the treatment of the topic in several films about Jefferson's life.

This renewed interest in the topic culminated in 1998 with the decision to examine the DNA evidence on the issue. Using the same techniques that convinced some scholars of the validity of the tradition of priestly descent among certain Jews, samples were examined anonymously to determine if there was a connection between (known) members of the Jefferson line and African Americans who carried this as a family tradition. While the claims of descendants of Thomas C. Woodson, Hemings's first child, were not supported, the tests revealed, in the words of a report published on the official Monticello website (literally Jefferson's homepage), "a high probability that Thomas Jefferson fathered Eston Hemings" and, combined with other evidence, "that he most likely was the father of all six of Sally Hemings' children appearing in Jefferson's record."

~

Ultimately, even with the DNA evidence, we will never know for certain whether Thomas Jefferson fathered any of Sally Hemings's children. While Thomas Woodson's connection to Jefferson can be safely dismissed, the situation with regard to Sally's other children is more complicated. Since Jefferson had no other known male children, the most we can say about Eston Hemings (Jefferson) and

---

9. Barbara Chase-Riboud, *Sally Hemings: A Novel* (New York: Ballantine, 1994).

his descendants is that they are connected to *some member(s) of the Jefferson family*. If this case were being tried in a court of law,[10] the results might well be inconclusive. As one defender of Jefferson has written, "It is the responsibility of the accuser to prove the charge, not of the accused to prove his innocence." However, as we have seen several times in this book, historical proof is rarely of the same quality as legal proof. Several facts would appear to support the presumption that the most famous Jefferson of all, Thomas, was in fact the father of Sally's children.

Perhaps the strongest argument supporting the claim that Jefferson was Sally's paramour is the timing of her children's births. Without exception, they can be shown to have been born approximately nine months after one of Jefferson's sojourns at Monticello. While we cannot, of course, rule out the possibility that one of his other relatives repeatedly took advantage of family visits at such times to consort with Sally, this explanation appears to be something of a stretch. Why, we must ask, would such relatives who lived close to Monticello have not visited Sally on other occasions?

Yet another point that argues in favor of a special relationship between Tom and Sally is the fact that he eventually freed all of her children. Beverly and Harriet were allowed to leave Monticello in 1822; Madison and Eston were emancipated four years later in 1826. This is the only case in which Jefferson is known to have given freedom to an entire nuclear family of slaves. Given his precarious financial situation and the cost of slaves, this decision to free Sally's children would seem to hint at some sort of special relationship. On the other hand, even in his will, he never freed Sally, which would seem to argue to the contrary.[11]

RUSH(MORE) TO JUDGMENT

All things considered, and keeping in mind that I'm not a professional historian, I tend to believe that Thomas Jefferson was

---

10. Such a mock court was, in fact, convened in 1994 by the Association of the Bar of the City of New York. Its purpose, however, was not to determine his guilt, but rather the extent to which his hypocrisy diminished his reputation. Of course, in a real paternity case the alleged father's DNA would be available and any proof much more conclusive.

11. Sally was, however, freed after his death. Jefferson may have chosen not to free Sally to avoid the appearance of confirming the rumors about their relationship.

the father of at least some of Sally Hemings' children. Assuming this to be the case, how does it affect our understanding and judgment of the great man?

Right off the bat, it must be stated that the Hemings–Jefferson connection seems to have little to do with Jefferson's political performance in any of his many official positions. Even his most bitter enemies do not seem to have believed his relationship with Sally posed a *political* problem in the sense of influencing his conduct in office. However, Jefferson, more perhaps than any other American president, is remembered as much for what he said and wrote as for what he did. Through the Declaration of Independence and his numerous other speeches and pronouncements, Jefferson came to be remembered as the voice of the American Revolution. Indeed, later generations were quick to forget some of his more conservative and less enlightened statements on race and slavery, in the attempt to highlight his liberal views. How does Jefferson, the man and the humanist, stand up under the light of these new revelations about his personal life?

At least in part, our answer to this question depends on how we reconstruct (some would say imagine), the Hemings–Jefferson connection. It is interesting to note that those who argue that there was no relationship base their argument at least in part on the claim that Jefferson, the rationalist and humanist, could not have engaged in the coercive, perhaps violent, exploitation of a woman. Such defenders of Jefferson have tended to assume the worst regarding the Hemings–Jefferson connection and argued that if the relationship did in fact take place, it would have been totally out of character for him. Indeed, their language, sprinkled with legal terminology, leaves little doubt that if the "charges" against the "accused" are accepted, he must automatically be expelled from the pantheon of America's great leaders. In contrast, those who believe in the connection tend to put a more human face upon it.

Personally, I find it impossible to accept the idea that for a period of several decades Jefferson had an ongoing sexual relationship with a woman who consistently rejected and resisted his advances. For this to be the case, Jefferson would have had to have been not only a hypocrite, but a monster. However, at the same time, I'm rather doubtful about recent attempts to romanticize the connection. Whatever their other differences, Sally and Tom led most of their lives in completely different worlds. Their connection may very well have had some rich emotional content, but it was also probably far more important to her than it was to him. Most of her life must have revolved around Monticello, Jefferson's presences and absences, and the children she bore him. For him, all of these had to be placed within the larger context of his public and other private responsibilities and concerns.

Actually, in many ways, his relationship with Sally Hemings puts a strange twist on the accusations that Jefferson was a hypocrite. In most cases, when the private lives of the rich and powerful have become public, they are revealed to have fallen far short of the ideals they espoused. In Jefferson's case, it was already well documented that his attitudes toward slavery and Africans were in sharp contrast to his pronouncements on equality and freedom. However, I think that the possibility that he had a slave mistress with whom he shared at least a part of his life for many years softens and humanizes his image. Unlike many others, the latest revelations, if accepted as fact, show him in a somewhat more positive light than previously. His reputation may not be untarnished, but neither does it suffer great harm from recent discoveries.

SUGGESTIONS FOR FURTHER READING

Bardalgio, Peter W. "'Shameful Matches': The Regulation of Interracial Sex and Marriage in the South before 1900." Pp. 112–38 in Martha Hodes, ed., *Sex, Love, Race: Crossing Boundaries in North American History*. New York: New York University Press, 1999.

Block, Sharon. "Lines of Color, Sex and Service: Comparative Sexual Coercion in Early America." Pp. 141–63 in Martha Hodes, ed., *Sex, Love, Race: Crossing Boundaries in North American History*. New York: New York University Press, 1999.

Brodie, Fawn M. *Thomas Jefferson: An Intimate History*. New York: Norton, 1974.

Dabney, Virginius. *The Jefferson Scandals: A Rebuttal*. Lanham, Md.: Madison Books, 1991.

Foster, Eugene A., M. A. Jobling, P. G. Taylor, P. Donnelly, P. de Knijff, Rene Mieremet, T. Zerjal, and C. Tyler-Smith. "Jefferson Fathered Slave's Last Child." *Nature* 396 (1998): 27–28.

Gordon-Reed, Annette. *Thomas Jefferson and Sally Hemings: An American Controversy*. Charlottesville: University Press of Virginia, 1997.

Jacobson, Matthew Frye. *Whiteness of a Different Color: European Immigrants and the Alchemy of Race*. Cambridge: Harvard University Press, 1998.

Onuf, Peter S., and Jan E. Lewis, eds. *Sally Hemings & Thomas Jefferson: History, Memory and Civic Culture.* Charlottesville: University Press of Virginia, 1999.

Vaughan, Alden T. "The Origins Debate: Slavery and Racism in Seventeenth-Century Virginia." Pp. 136–74 in *Roots of American Racism.* New York: Oxford University Press, 1995.

Wilson, Douglas L. "Thomas Jefferson and the Character Issue." *Atlantic Monthly* 270 (November 1992): 57–74.

http://www.monticello.org/plantation

parnell and the englishwoman: a love story

I would rather appear to be dishonourable than be dishonourable.

—Charles Stewart Parnell

I suppose that a chapter on politics, divorce, and adultery may seem like a funny place for a love story. Generally our assumption about adultery is that it is inevitably somewhat tawdry and distasteful. And late nineteenth-century Ireland is probably not the first place one would think to look for a politician who sacrificed everything for love. For some reason, the Irish don't have a reputation as the most passionate people in the world. But from the minute I heard the story of the nineteenth-century Irish politician Charles Stewart Parnell and the Englishwoman Katharine "Kitty" O'Shea, I knew I had to include it in this book. It raises so many fascinating questions.

- How could a man whose wife had born three children while living apart from him convince a court that he had "discovered" only recently that she was unfaithful?

- How could he, despite his own numerous affairs, successfully sue her for divorce?
- Why did Parnell, who knew that being named as an adulterer would probably ruin his political career, maintain his silence and not defend himself?
- And finally, given the fact that the Parnell–O'Shea relationship was common knowledge for close to a decade, why, when it became public, did politicians react so strongly?

Not only is the Parnell–O'Shea romance a story that deserves to be told and thus made better known than it is today, it also combines so many of the themes that interest me here because all three partners to the triangle—Parnell, Mrs. O'Shea, and her husband, Captain O'Shea—present slightly different perspectives on the connection between sex, power, and politics. Captain O'Shea was willing to ignore his wife's adultery as long as it served his personal and political interests; Parnell was willing to risk his own and in many ways his country's political future to pursue a dangerous liaison. And Katharine O'Shea (later Katharine Parnell) was willing to pursue an illicit relationship for years even though it put both her and the man she loved at the mercy of her unscrupulous husband. One of my major sources for this story is the book *Parnell Vindicated: The Lifting of the Veil*, written by Henry Harrison, Parnell's private secretary. The book captured my attention both because it is a rare insider's view of someone else's adulterous relationship and because Harrison waited until all the parties to the story were long gone before publishing his book. I don't know what kind of financial incentives there were for him to go to press earlier, but I was pleased to be confirmed in my decision not to discuss the living in my own book.

I was also particularly taken by Harrison's explanation of his mentor's refusal to publicly discuss his personal life. "Parnell's silence . . . was based in some measure, doubtless upon his contemptuous dislike for the invasion of the privacy of his private life—a dislike that may today require some interpretation to a generation prone to turn households inside out for public inspection." How refreshing to know that already in 1931, seventy years ago, some people looked back on an earlier, purer age when public leaders' private lives were really private!

~

Charles Stewart Parnell was born on June 27, 1846, to a distinguished Irish family. His father, John Henry Parnell, died when he was thirteen, and he remained close to his American-born mother, who may have been one source for his strong suspicion of the British. After a rather undistinguished academic career at Cambridge University, he traveled a bit and then returned to Ireland. In 1875 he was elected to Parliament as a representative of the Irish Home Rule Party. Although initially dismissed by many as a naïve and spoiled young man, by 1880 he was the leader of the fifty-nine MPs of the Irish "Home Rule" movement. In the words of Irish historian Joseph Lee, "The rise of Parnell from the stumbling political novice of 1875 to the master politician and charismatic leader five years later constitutes the most brilliant political performance in Irish history."

In July 1880, the same year he rose to a leadership position, Parnell also met for the first time Katharine O'Shea, the wife of one his party members, Captain William Henry O'Shea. At the time, Katharine and William O'Shea had not lived together for several years, and she and their children were largely, if not entirely, provided for by Katharine's elderly aunt.

It was, as the saying goes, love at first sight. Parnell was immediately smitten. In a moving passage, Katharine recalls their first meeting.

> In leaning forward to say good-bye a rose I was wearing in my bodice fell out of my skirt. He picked it up and touching it lightly to his lips placed it in his button-hole. This rose I found long years afterwards done up in an envelope, with my name and the date, among his most private papers, and when he died I laid it upon his heart.[1]

Only a few months after their first meeting, Parnell was addressing his letters to her "My dearest love."

In the course of time, Parnell and "Kitty" developed a remarkably conventional domestic relationship. Although they formally maintained separate residences—which was not unusual given his many political commitments—there is little question that Parnell felt most at home at Mrs. O'Shea's house in Eltham, which he gradually equipped with everything he needed for his work and entertainment, including a science lab and cricket field.

During the next five years, the couple had three children. The first was born while Parnell was serving a prison term for his political activities in Dublin's notorious Kilmainham jail. Only a brief parole

---

1. Mrs. O'Shea's story, as told to Henry Harrison, appears in *Parnell Vindicated*, 118–32.

made it possible for him to hold his infant daughter in his arms before she died. The other two, Clare and Katie, born in 1883 and 1884
respectively, served to only deepen the couple's sense of a normal
family life.

How much did Captain O'Shea know about his wife's relationship with Parnell? He had strong suspicions in January 1881 when
he found Parnell's clothing and luggage at his wife's home. Later
that year, he challenged Parnell to a duel and was placated, almost
certainly by promises of political rewards and money. The birth of
three children during a period when his wife was living more or
less openly with Parnell must certainly have made the situation obvious to anyone with a basic knowledge of human biology.[2]

Perhaps the question is best answered by Katharine herself. "Did
Captain O'Shea know? Of course he knew. I do not mean that I or
anybody else told him so in so many words, except once. . . . There
was no bargain; there was no discussions; people do not talk of
such things. But he knew and he encouraged me in it at times."

It's not completely clear, as some have claimed, that Captain
O'Shea initiated Katharine's relationship with Parnell. But once he
became aware of it, he was willing to take full advantage of the situation. As Katharine herself recalled, "When he wanted to get Mr.
Parnell's assent to something or other and he was urging me to get
this assent he said, 'Take him back [home] with you to Eltham and
make him all happy and comfortable for the night, and just get him
to agree.'"

In the most famous incident of its kind, Parnell secured the parliamentary constituency of Galway for Captain O'Shea over the objections of his advisers and other party leaders. Whether, as some
have suggested, he did so to buy O'Shea's continued silence or he
had some other motive for his action, the episode is a clear indication of how Parnell's judgment and behavior could be affected by
his unusual domestic relationship.

In fact, Parnell made frequent use of both Captain and Mrs.
O'Shea as mediators in his negotiations with British officials and
party leaders. This inside track on sensitive negotiations and access
to important figures may have been just the sort of advantage the

---

2. It should be noted, however, that Kitty did concede in her biography that O'Shea could genuinely have believed that the first child was his!
However, the fact that the first thing Parnell did when released from
prison was visit Kitty and the child must have indicated that there was at
least a strong possibility that the child was Parnell's.

captain was looking for when he tacitly agreed to his wife's relationship with Parnell. (The sexual and practical aspects of the arrangement never seem to have troubled him terribly, although the growing affection and devotion of the couple for each other did at times distress him.) He also had no qualms about frequently approaching her for money, which came either from her aunt or Parnell.

For Parnell, a deeply private man, especially for a politician, the arrangement provided all the warmth and deep affection of a family life. Katharine O'Shea provided a constant refuge from his political struggles. She was, moreover, a shrewd political adviser and did much to improve the quality of his speeches, many of which she crafted for him. The irony of the leading Irish nationalist politician of the time being deeply involved with an Englishwoman cannot have escaped either of them. He clearly wished to formalize their relationship, but she steadily demurred in deference to her aunt.

For Katharine, who had been all but deserted by her husband, Parnell was a great "catch." Living today, more than a century after Parnell and O'Shea, it is difficult for us to imagine the situation Mrs. O'Shea was in. In an age prior not only to women's liberation but even women's suffrage, she would, to quote Henry Harrison,

> have been exposed to inconveniences and to social slights of which ladies similarly situated today [writing in 1931!] do not dream. She went from being the discarded wife of a not particularly successful politician, a social non-person, to being the intimate companion of the leading political figure of the time. But we shouldn't underestimate, however, the strong bond of love and respect that developed between Parnell and "Kitty." To quote from only one of his letters, "MY DEAREST LOVE. . . . It is quite impossible for me to tell you just how very much you have changed my life, what a small interest I take in what is going on about me, and how I detest everything which has happened—I think of you always, and you must never believe there is to be any 'fading.'"

To quote once again from Harrison, "He called her wife, treated her as wife, not merely in externals but in a fullness of spiritual communion and in a sharing of interests such as none but the most fortunate of marriages confer."

THE TRIAL

This arrangement continued with only minor difficulties for almost a decade. However, on Christmas Eve 1889, Captain

O'Shea filed for divorce from his wife and cited Parnell as co-respondent. Although he and Parnell had had a political parting of the ways several years earlier, O'Shea had delayed taking any action in the belief that when Katharine's wealthy aunt died, he (as her legal husband) would share in the inheritance. When she died in May 1889, it became clear that the old woman had cleverly left her money to Katharine in a way that totally excluded O'Shea. With no further reason for silence, he filed for divorce. Even then it appears likely that Captain O'Shea would have retracted his suit in return for a payment of £20,000 but the money was not available.

To the modern reader, O'Shea's filing must seem nothing less than bizarre. How could he, after turning a blind eye for almost a decade, claim to be the injured party in a divorce? Certainly his silent acquiescence for so long must have been viewed as consent to the relationship. His own record of infidelity (no less than seventeen affairs were alleged), moreover, must have been expected to count strongly against him. How was he, despite these facts, able to mount a successful case?

The first and most basic answer is that Parnell and Kitty O'Shea offered no real defense. Their silence seems to have been motivated by several considerations. First and most important, they were concerned with the fate of their daughters. Captain O'Shea had more than hinted in correspondence with his wife that should she oppose him, he was willing to claim in court that he believed the girls to be his daughters. In an era prior to both blood typing and DNA testing, it would have been almost impossible for Parnell and Mrs. O'Shea to conclusively contest such a claim. The risk of losing their daughters must have been an enormous deterrent.

Second, under the divorce laws of the time, it is not at all certain that Mrs. O'Shea could herself have successfully sued for divorce. Although the Matrimonial Causes Act of 1857 is justifiably referred to as "one of the greatest social revolutions" of the nineteenth century because it made divorce much more easily available, it also enshrined in law a sexual double standard that was to remain intact for more than seventy years. While the act made it possible for a husband to petition for divorce on the basis of his wife's adultery, a wife was permitted to petition only on the basis of *aggravated* adultery (adultery plus unwarranted desertion for at least two years, cruelty, rape, sodomy, bigamy, etc.). This blatantly unequal treatment was defended on the ba-

sis of an interesting bit of popular psychology. In the words of
one high-placed official,

> Although the sin in both cases was the same, the effect of adultery
> on the part of the husband was very different from that of adultery
> on the part of the wife. It was possible for a wife to pardon a hus-
> band who had committed adultery; but it was hardly possible for a
> husband ever really to pardon the adultery of a wife.

Whether one agrees with this claim or not (the specifics of the Parnell case do not appear to support it), the law would have made it
extremely difficult for Mrs. O'Shea to petition her husband for a
divorce.

Yet another consequence of the act was that divorce became far
more public than in the past. Indeed, as Barbara Leckie has discussed in her recent book *Culture and Adultery*, during the second
half of the nineteenth century, divorce trials became an immensely
popular front-page feature of almost all daily newspapers. Not only
was attendance at such trials a popular pastime (the writer Henry
James attended the Parnell trial), but others avidly followed these
real-life dramas through the press and in increasingly popular nov-
elizations. Parnell and Mrs. O'Shea probably hoped to keep the inevitable media coverage to a minimum by offering as little drama
as possible.

Finally, and this was probably of special concern to Parnell, only
a divorce would have allowed him to finally marry Mrs. O'Shea. In
nineteenth-century Ireland, as in most places of the time, adultery
was one of the only grounds for divorce. Today's grounds, including irreconcilable differences or irreparable breakdown, were unheard of. Indeed, throughout the first half of the twentieth century,
it was common for couples seeking a divorce to arrange for a witness to "catch" one of the partners in a seemingly adulterous situation in order to have legal grounds for separation. If Parnell and
Mrs. O'Shea had successfully denied the adultery, the divorce
might be denied and hence they could not marry. Parnell was willing neither to perjure himself nor to further delay his chance to
marry the woman he had loved for a decade.

THE AFTERMATH

Parnell must have viewed the court's ruling (after only two days of
hearings) in Captain O'Shea's favor with mixed feelings. On the

one hand, Kitty was finally free to marry him. On the other, being publicly identified as an adulterer dealt his political career a mortal blow and significantly weakened the movement he championed. To quote no less an authority of English politics than Winston Churchill, "Her Majesty's Government recovered in the Divorce Court the credit they had lost in the Special Commission [which investigated Parnell]."

Parnell's political allies, both Irish and English, proved to be remarkably fickle. Within three weeks of the divorce decree, his party split. When one supporter argued that Parnell should continue to be "master of the party," one opponent quipped that he wondered who the "mistress" of the party would be. The Catholic Church in Ireland called for Irish Catholics to repudiate him as well. The National Vigilance Association for the Repression of Criminal Vice and Immorality (what a name!) protested against him. Although he received a hero's welcome when he returned to Dublin in early December of 1890, his political days were numbered. While those in the know could forgive his personal misjudgment, they were far less tolerant of his political weakness. When his candidates were defeated in successive elections, Parnell was finished as a political force in Ireland.

On June 25, 1891, Charles Parnell and Katharine O'Shea were married. What had been a de facto marriage for years had become a legal reality: They were man and wife. Tragically, they were to have precious little time together, as his political and personal struggles had taken a terrible toll on his already precarious health. In early September of 1891 one paper described him as "a relic . . . all but a dead man." On September 27, 1891, he gave his last public speech. Caught in a downpour, he came home and took to his bed. On October 6 he died. Kitty movingly described his last moments.

> Late in the evening he suddenly opened his eyes and said, "Kiss me, sweet Wifie, and I will try to sleep a little." I lay down by his side and kissed the burning lips he pressed to mine for the last time. The fire of them, fierce beyond any that I had ever felt, even in his most loving moods, startled me, and as I slipped my hand from under his head he gave a little sigh, and became unconscious. The doctor came at once, but no remedies prevailed against this sudden failure of the heart's action, and my husband died without regaining consciousness, before his last kiss was cold on my lips.

It's hard to believe that such a story has never become a Broadway musical, or even an opera. Perhaps it will in the future.

TOO HIGH A PRICE?

More than any other figure I've chosen to discuss in this book, Parnell seems to have paid a price totally out of proportion to any fault he committed. While he was technically and legally an adulterer, we would certainly see his as a victimless crime. Only if we believe Captain O'Shea's rather farcical protestations of ignorance is it possible to view him as a wronged party.

However, it is doubtful that his contemporaries viewed things that way. The second half of the nineteenth century was a golden age for divorce journalism. In the wake of the Matrimonial Causes Act of 1857, reports of divorce proceedings became one of the most popular and most controversial forms of news reporting. Never before had the private workings of families been subjected to such public scrutiny. Divorces routinely received coverage reserved today for only the highest-profile criminal proceedings. Given the celebrity of its protagonists, the O'Shea divorce trial could not help but attract attention.

Within the mini–morality play of the nineteenth-century divorce, there was no room for the victimless crime that we perceive in the Parnell–O'Shea episode. Given Parnell and Kitty's refusal to mount a defense, Captain O'Shea had no problem depicting himself as the innocent party: betrayed by both his wife and his friend. Parnell was thus cast as the rogue and destroyer of a family.[3] This was, in the eyes of its time, not a "no-fault" divorce, but a divorce in which the fault was all too easy to assign.

It was, nevertheless, perceived primarily as an issue of family and morality rather than politics. Although the involvement of an Irish politician with an Englishwoman would appear to be ripe for charges of conflict of interest, this does not seem to be the case. Whatever reproaches may have been directed at Parnell, no one seems to have believed that he allowed his involvement with Mrs. O'Shea to compromise his political integrity. Indeed, her hospitality and writing skills seem to have allowed him peace of mind and increased his political effectiveness.

It is, however, harder for us to be quite so sanguine about the other part of this unusual triangle. Parnell must have realized that

---

3. As late as the 1990s, as noted a historian as Gertrude Himmelfarb could write of "philandering politicians like Charles Parnell and Charles Dilke," thus associating Parnell with a man who had numerous affairs, often several concurrently. As we saw above, it is hard to think of a man less deserving of the label "philanderer."

his unusual domestic relationship put him and the cause he championed at the mercy of the unscrupulous Captain O'Shea. The fault was only compounded by his willingness to use O'Shea as an intermediary and promote him politically at the expense of better qualified and more reputable candidates. While no one can be blamed for falling in love, Parnell's relationship with *Captain* O'Shea clearly crossed the line between private and public. Whatever we may think about the *morality* of Parnell's behavior, it is harder to be charitable concerning his political judgment on this matter.

This being said, it is still hard to understand why Parnell fell so far and so quickly. Other leaders we have looked at survived greater misjudgments. However, it must be remembered that Parnell, in contrast to the other figures we have discussed, was an elected politician. His position depended not on his birth or the title he held, but on his personal popularity and effectiveness. No revolution was required to remove him, no change in the essentials of the political system required to replace him. While being publicly labeled as an adulterer may have hurt Parnell, it was his political weakness that led to his downfall.

Looking at things from a slightly different perspective, Parnell's case also serves to highlight yet another aspect of the importance of power. Put rather simply, powerful politicians are judged by a different standard than weak ones. The powerful may be forgiven for lapses in their sex lives; they are rarely forgiven for losing their power. The minute it became clear that Parnell's domestic troubles had made him politically vulnerable, his fate was sealed.

SUGGESTIONS FOR FURTHER READING

Bew, Paul. *Charles Stewart Parnell.* Dublin: Gil and Macmillan, 1991.

Harrison, Henry. *Parnell Vindicated: The Lifting of the Veil.* New York: R. R. Smith, 1931.

Himmelfarb, Gertrude. *The De-Moralization of Society: From Victorian Virtues to Modern Values.* New York: Knopf, 1994.

Hurst, Michael. *Parnell and Irish Nationalism.* London: Routledge & Kegan Paul, 1968.

Leckie, Barbara. *Culture and Adultery: The Novel, the Newspaper, and the Law 1857–1914.* Philadelphia: University of Pennsylvania Press, 1999.

Lee, Joseph. *The Modernization of Irish Society 1848–1918.* Dublin: Gil and Macmillan, 1973.

JfK: All the president's women

Kennedy, the politician, exuded that musk odor of power which acts as an aphrodisiac to many women.

—Theodore H. White

John F. Kennedy, the politician I've chosen to focus on in this chapter, couldn't be more different than Charles Parnell. Although both of them were Irish or at least of Irish descent, they had little in common in either their political lives or their adulterous relationships. Parnell's one affair, a long-term relationship that eventually culminated in marriage, cost him his political career. In contrast, Kennedy's compulsive womanizing was largely ignored by his contemporaries and never became a political issue. We've seen the circumstances behind Parnell's fall; now let's try to understand Kennedy's apparent immunity from scandal.

Of all the figures I've chosen to write about in this book, none caused as many second thoughts as John F. Kennedy. Although he and his wife fall within my self-imposed limitation of not writing about living people, they are in some strange way very much "alive" even today. More importantly, if the people I discuss in this book range from those who are not widely remembered outside their native lands (Christina of Sweden and Charles Parnell) to those whom recent films have once again made household names (Eva Perón and Elizabeth I), none of them, not even Thomas Jefferson, can compete with John Kennedy for familiarity or renown. Several hundred books have been written about the Kennedys and each new success or family tragedy produces magazine recaps, television specials, and rebroadcasts of old film clips. If the challenge of discussing Catherine the Great or Queen Caroline is how to introduce the average reader to such complex and interesting characters in a few thousand words, in the case of Kennedy, it's how to shed new light on a story that has been so brightly illuminated by so many for so long.

As we've already seen, it is not always easy to uncover the truth about famous people's intimate lives. In the case of John Kennedy, however, the record seems remarkably clear. Since the record is pretty well established, I'm not going to simply retell the story. Rather, I'll focus on a number of crucial questions:

- Why did he do it?
- How was he able to get away with it?
- How important is his compulsive sexual behavior in evaluating his presidency?

THE KENNEDY OBSESSION

Although there's a common tendency to blame today's alleged decline in sexual morals on relaxed standards of the press and other media, especially movies, I'm rather skeptical of such explanations. Already in this book, we've seen plenty of examples of behavior that would have raised eyebrows long before the existence of either the movies or television. Certainly, Kennedy, who lived in an age when network and movie standards were still fairly strict, didn't need their influence to encourage his behavior. He had plenty of examples far closer to home.

By all accounts, the young JFK was a rather quiet and vulnerable child. He was the only one of the Kennedy children who seems to have been a reader from an early age. He almost died from scarlet fever when he was two and a half and suffered from a variety of illnesses throughout his childhood, indeed throughout his entire life. Various authors have speculated as to the connection between his infirmities and his sexual behavior. Mark J. White, for example, in a fascinating study of Kennedy's private life, wrote, "JFK's poor health made him feel that he should enjoy himself as much as he could, while he could, as he would probably not live a long life. His health, in other words, or rather lack of it, fostered a live-for-the-moment mentality." In contrast, John Hellmann, emphasizing the tension between Kennedy's desire to be a "man's man" and his chronic health problems, suggested that "acutely concerned with his appearance and masculine image, Kennedy had compensated for his lack of athletic prowess with sexual conquests."[1]

This last comment also places attention on the family environment in which John Kennedy grew up. Much of his early life was spent in the shadow of his older brother, Joe Jr., who, until his death in World War II, was his father's favorite and carried with him the family's dreams of "making it." At least one friend viewed this as the key to Kennedy's behavior, telling Kennedy biographer Nigel Hamilton that "all that macho stuff was compensation—all that chasing after women—compensation for something he hadn't got, which his brother Joe had."

Joe Jr. was not the only influence on young John's perception of women. His father, Joe Sr., made it clear that there was sex and there was marriage and told all his sons "to get laid as often as possible." John once came home from school to find that his father had laid pornographic magazines out on his bed, open to the most revealing pictures of women. Joe Sr. had numerous affairs and made little attempt to hide them from either his wife or the rest of the family. Not only did he bring one of his mistresses to Hyannis Port to have dinner with his family, when he traveled to Europe with her, he invited his wife along for the trip! He also appears to have repeatedly attempted to seduce both his daughters' friends and his sons' girlfriends! Neither his father's behavior nor his mother's passive acceptance of the situation can have done much to cultivate JFK's respect for marriage or for women.

Whatever the causes may have been, throughout his adult life—both before and after he married Jacqueline in 1953, while in Congress, the Senate, and the White House—John Kennedy was remarkably promiscuous. Although it's possible to dispute an incident here and there, he appears to have compulsively pursued women

---

1. And from the same author, "The young Kennedy's intimate friends inferred that he knew that his skirt-chasing was 'displacement' a futile attempt to . . . prove the manhood his body failed to realize on the athletic field."

with little regard for the risks involved. Some were famous (Marilyn Monroe and Jayne Mansfield); others such as Judith Campbell (Exner) only became known when they told their stories. They included White House staff members (among them his wife's press secretary), campaign workers, prostitutes, and total strangers.

In recent years there has been a tremendous amount written about sexual addiction. According to this view, people who engage in compulsive sexual activity are similar to alcoholics, overeaters, and smokers. Was JFK such a sex addict? I have to say, I've never found such explanations very convincing either personally or professionally. This doesn't mean that I'm underestimating the seriousness of such behaviors and the pain they can cause. However, I think we need to be careful about blurring the line between physical addictions and psychological compulsions. Kennedy's personal behavior was certainly reckless and at times even compulsive. To be sure, he's said to have told one of his friends that if he didn't have sex for several days (and I don't think he meant with his wife), it gave him a headache. If, however, his was an addiction, one can only wonder how he lived with it during his period at sea during World War II, prior to the famous *PT 109* episode.

MEET THE PRESS

Put rather simply, John Kennedy had the sex life that he did while in office because he could. The press, as I'll discuss in more detail below, was not willing to investigate or publicize his behavior, and none of his political advisers or allies were willing or able to control him. Perhaps, most importantly, his wife permitted it. There can be little question that Jacqueline Kennedy was well aware of her husband's behavior. According to some stories, Joseph Kennedy promised her a million dollars when she, fed up with his betrayals, threatened to divorce John and ruin his political career.[2] In the end, she seems to have made her peace with her husband's behavior, although at times her bitterness crept out. On one occasion she is said to have identified two staffers as her husband's lovers to an Italian reporter!

---

2. As I indicated in chapter 3, her subsequent marriage to another womanizer, Aristotle Onassis, would seem to say something about her choice of men. Indeed, her father was also said to have behaved similarly toward her mother.

In general, however, and particularly after his death, there was no more assiduous cultivator of the Kennedy legend. It was she who first invoked the image of "one brief shining moment" and Camelot in describing his period in power.[3]

As for the press, it's hard to remember in our post-Vietnam, post-Watergate era of no-holds-barred press coverage that the press's treatment of Kennedy's affairs was, in those days, the norm rather than the exception. It was not that Kennedy was a Teflon president, but rather that the press followed a very different set of rules. One needs merely to watch the films of Kennedy-era press conferences to see how different things were from today's events. Moreover, since reporters are, after all, only human, there was little incentive for them to dig too deeply into stories that would almost certainly never be printed.

From a public relations point of view, a great politician doesn't necessarily have to have a great relationship with the press. He does, however, need to *understand* his relationship with the press. Kennedy, our first television president, and one who understood his relationship with the press as well as anyone, once said rather prophetically, "They can't touch me while I'm alive, and after I'm dead who cares?"

In order to understand how different these times were, one need not look at the coverage of JFK's sex life. As we noted above, Kennedy was troubled by health problems throughout his life. However, like Roosevelt and Eisenhower before him, he was able to ensure that only minimal information about his conditions reached the general public. Such "private" information was not considered of relevance to his public service, and although his back problems and his rocking chair were well documented, the seriousness of his situation was not known or at least not reported. In fact, the Kennedy image of athleticism, including sailing and touch football, was carefully crafted to overshadow his real health concerns. To this day the medical records of his death are more available to the public than those of his life.

It is not surprising that the first detailed discussions of Kennedy's indiscretions came about against the background of the Watergate scandal and the new standards being applied to presidential behavior. It was the Senate Select Committee of Intelligence, headed by Democrat Frank Church of Idaho, that first discussed in public the

---

3. Ironically perhaps, in the Arthurian legend it is the queen who betrays the king and not the other way around, as in the American Camelot.

relationship between Kennedy and Judith Campbell (Exner). Even then, it was decided to refer to her merely as a "friend." Then as today, Washington insiders generally protected each other and were careful not to throw the first stone.

While the *Washington Post*, which had been so instrumental in the downfall of Richard Nixon, sought to downplay the implications of the Kennedy scandal by placing it on page 6, Nixon loyalist William Safire asked a series of trenchant questions in his *New York Times* columns. Although Exner was discreet about her relationship with Kennedy in a December 1975 press conference, her 1977 no-holds-barred autobiography confirmed her affair with Kennedy and substantiated it with much undeniable detail.

Once the taboo against discussing the president's private affairs had been broken, the way was open for a floodgate of revelations. Marilyn Monroe, Frank Sinatra, Fidel Castro, and the Mafia all became the subject of intricate stories of sex, espionage, and intrigue. Even a former White House kennel keeper wrote a tell-it-all memoir of skinny-dipping and wild parties. So many stories were written about Kennedy's escapades that some defenders wondered, if all the stories were true, how he found the time to govern and fulfill his official duties!

If during the period from 1960 to 1975 the Kennedy years were idealized and media coverage suffered from an absence of rigor, the ensuing years have seen the press eager to compensate for past lapses. No president's, indeed no family's, behavior has been subject to as much analysis of normally private matters. One wonders how other politicians would have borne up under such scrutiny.

Few Americans, for example, seem aware of or concerned with the sex life of Kennedy's successor, Lyndon Johnson. Yet, Johnson is said to have bragged that he had "more women by accident than Kennedy had on purpose." For a variety of reasons his numerous affairs don't seem to have captured the imagination the way Kennedy's did and still do.

PUBLIC OR PRIVATE?

As we saw in chapter 7, in societies in which leaders and rulers were allowed or even expected to have extramarital liaisons and mistresses, adultery was not an important political issue. However, it must also be remembered that even in those situations in which adultery is frowned upon and viewed as a serious lapse in morality, it is not automatically viewed as a *public* matter. In plenty of countries around the world, the American (and to a lesser extent British) concern with politicians' private lives is seen as a rather bizarre aberration. Why should we care who our leaders sleep with, if they do a good job in office?

At least one of the reasons why Kennedy's infidelities have continued to fascinate the public is that no previous politician had ever sought to blur the line between public and private the way Kennedy did. His father, who had experience in the film industry and close connections in the world of publishing, crafted his son's rise to power with a skill that any Hollywood producer or scriptwriter would have admired. Although JFK was, at least at the beginning, much like an actor following a script, he soon began to genuinely enjoy his role. With a beautiful wife, and as the first president since Theodore Roosevelt with young children, Kennedy developed with the assistance of his close aides a carefully crafted image of youth, vigor, and a happy family life. Consider, for example, this rather idealized posthumous recollection offered by Theodore Sorenson, JFK's speechwriter and sometime alter ego: "His election, to her surprise, strengthened instead of strained their marriage. Those were the happiest years. Jacqueline and the children, contrary to her fears during the campaign, saw more of her husband than ever before, and he found with her a happiness and love he had never known before."[4]

If turnabout is fair play, why shouldn't the press, which for years was expected to cover the Kennedys' "ideal" family life, devote attention to all their faults and weaknesses? The question, therefore, is not whether Kennedy's indiscretions should be mentioned, but how prominent a place they should take in the discussion of his achievements.

In his defense, it should be noted that whatever Kennedy's failings may have been on a personal level, there is little indication that they were reflected in the way he formulated policy or conducted his administration. The recklessness and compulsiveness that characterized his sex life find no echo in his conducting of domestic matters or foreign affairs. Kennedy the risk-taking philanderer was also Kennedy the cautious statesman.

However, although it would certainly be a mistake to judge Kennedy's presidency solely on the basis of his sexual behavior, it would be equally naïve to argue (as some of his defenders have)

---

4. As quoted by White, *Kennedy: The New Frontier Revisited,* 257.

that his private conduct had no bearing on his public record. While Kennedy does not appear to have appointed his partners to important positions or allowed them to directly influence his decision making, his recklessness made him vulnerable on several counts. He was, for example, unable to replace J. Edgar Hoover at the FBI for fear that Hoover might retaliate by releasing embarrassing information. His long-running relationship with Campbell appears to have involved him with both organized crime figures and perhaps even some bizarre plots to assassinate Castro. Even more seriously, had Kennedy's indiscriminate womanizing come to the attention of hostile countries, they might have used the information against him or even attempted to entrap him into more damaging behavior.[5] Indeed, Kennedy was at times so concerned with pursuing his liaisons that on at least one occasion he abandoned the officer holding the bag containing the codes to America's nuclear arsenal!

All in all, therefore, I am not inclined to be as forgiving as some of Kennedy's admirers who see his sex life as totally irrelevant to our judgment of his presidency. The quote with which I began this chapter from Theodore White seems to both shift the blame to the women and take a certain "boys will be boys" attitude. Even Kennedy's own "And after I'm dead who cares?" point of view is more than a little problematic. First of all, WE CARE! We may not have a right to expect our leaders to be saints or angels, but we probably do have a right to expect them to lead *by example*. Kennedy, who sought to mobilize the American public with a vision of sacrifice and public service, clearly did a disservice to the idealism he espoused. True, he was neither a great moralist nor an ethical teacher, and thus he can be spared the charges of hypocrisy leveled at Jefferson. However, the image of leadership and family he presented was greatly at odds with his own practice.

Second, and perhaps even more important, Kennedy's behavior, although it was revealed only after his death, contributed—along with Vietnam, Watergate, Irangate, and the more recent problems of the Clintons—to an erosion of trust and the development of a

---

5. Although this may seem far-fetched and more the stuff of spy novels than fact, it should be remembered that the French ambassador to Moscow was entrapped in just this manner in 1958, and in 1963 British war minister John Profumo was forced to resign when it was revealed that he had had an affair with a model named Christine Keeler, who at the same time was also sleeping with an attaché at the Soviet embassy.

deep cynicism about politics and politicians. While Kennedy's private infidelities do not deserve to be judged with the severity that is applied to a politician's betrayal of his *public* duties, neither can they be dismissed as irrelevant to the creation of an atmosphere of alienation and disillusionment.

~

What does all of this add up to? Personally, I tend to agree with actress Shirley MacLaine's oft-quoted remark that she preferred a president who did it to women to one who did it to the country. This also seems to be the view of the American public, 80 percent of whom indicated that they would vote for a candidate even if they knew he had committed adultery. John Kennedy may not have been the great family man of his public image, but neither should his private behavior deflect our attention from a fair and reasonable evaluation of what he was able to accomplish in his all too brief period as president.

SUGGESTIONS FOR FURTHER READING

Brown, Thomas. *JFK: History of an Image.* Bloomington: Indiana University Press, 1988.

Hagood, Wesley O. *Presidential Sex: From the Founding Fathers to Bill Clinton.* Secaucus, N.J.: Carol Publishers, 1997.

Hamilton, Nigel. *JFK: Reckless Youth.* New York: Random House, 1992.

Hellmann, John. *The Kennedy Obsession: The American Myth of JFK.* New York: Columbia University Press, 1997.

Kessler, Ronald. *The Sins of the Father: Joseph P. Kennedy and the Dynasty He Founded.* New York: Warner Books, 1996.

Reeves, Thomas C. *A Question of Character: A Life of John F. Kennedy.* London: Maxwell Macmillan International, 1991.

White, Mark J. "Behind Closed Doors: The Private Life of a Public Man." In Mark J. White, ed., *Kennedy: The New Frontier Revisited.* New York: New York University Press, 1998.

cleopatra: Life and Death on the Nile

What is not often associated with Cleopatra was her brilliance and her devotion to country. . . . She fought for her country . . . was a born leader and an ambitious monarch who deserved better than suicide.

—The Ministry of Tourism, Egypt

No book on sex, power, and politics would be complete without devoting at least several chapters to the special circumstances of women leaders.[1] Although there have been some notable exceptions, throughout most of history women rulers and political leaders have been viewed as something of an anomaly or even a contradiction in terms. Leadership was by definition a male prerogative. Not surprisingly perhaps, authors in the past seeking to praise female rulers sometimes found little alternative but to describe their subjects as "kings." In fact, in some societies since the term "queen" was reserved for the spouses of kings, there was no

---

1. Although we have already commented on several women who had power and influence, including the Chinese concubine Yang Guifei, the *valide sultan* Kösem Sultan, Evita Peron, the biblical Queen Esther, and Madame de Pompadour, all of these were dependent to a significant degree on male leaders for their position. Delilah and Judith exercised power over their victims, but never held any official position.

alternative but to refer to a female ruler by the equivalent male term. Elizabeth I herself is said to have remarked, "I may have the body of a weak and feeble woman, but I have the heart and stomach of a king."

Even in the second half of the twentieth century, democratically elected prime ministers such as Golda Meir of Israel, Margaret Thatcher of Great Britain, and Indira Gandhi of India have been seen as exceptional figures. Like their predecessors from earlier centuries they have tended to be unusually strong leaders and have often been characterized in masculine terms. Thatcher, for example, was known as the "Iron Lady," and Israelis frequently joked that Golda Meir was the only real man in her cabinet. Of course in bygone days, women leaders were not elected (until the twentieth century women could not even participate in the election of male leaders in most countries), but usually inherited power in royal families because of the absence of a suitable male heir.

As we'll see in a moment, the unusual situation of a woman with an "abnormal" amount of power was often translated into the image of a woman of unusual or ambiguous sexuality. In the next four chapters I've chosen four female rulers, each of whom found a different solution to the "dilemma" of being both powerful and female: Cleopatra VII of Egypt used her sexuality as a key part of her political arsenal and won the favor of both Julius Caesar and Mark Antony; Elizabeth I chose (at least publicly) to deny much of her female side by not marrying and promoting her image as the "Virgin Queen"; Christina of Sweden went in the opposite direction and, having guaranteed the stability of her realm, abandoned power in order to lead her life freely as a woman; and Catherine the Great of Russia held on to both her throne and her sexuality and used her power to assure herself of access to a regular supply of partners.

CAESAR AND CLEOPATRA

Like the biblical Delilah or Shakespeare's Juliet, Queen Cleopatra of Egypt is one of those women whose fascinating story has transcended time and space and given her an almost mythological status. Although she was the seventh Egyptian queen to bear the name Cleopatra, her fame is so great that the others are generally known only to historians specializing in the period. Both Shakespeare and George Bernard Shaw felt called upon to dramatize her story, and every few years another film seeks to translate her mys-

tique to the silver screen. Whether your image of Cleopatra is Elizabeth Taylor, Claudette Colbert, or one of her more recent incar-
nations, once you've seen her or heard her story you're not likely
to forget it.

~

Although some people have suggested that Cleopatra's story is yet
another example of a woman sleeping her way to the top, I don't
think this is necessarily the best way to look at things. Unlike Evita
Perón, whom I discussed in chapter 4, Cleopatra started off pretty
close to the top. She was, after all, born into a royal family with
strong traditions of divine kingship, and by the time she was eighteen she was ruler or at least co-ruler of Egypt. Hers is much more
the story of a woman who used her seductive charms, intelligence,
and understanding of people to turn her country's enemies into her
lovers and allies.

Cleopatra was born in 69 B.C.E. in Alexandria, Egypt. One of the
many misconceptions about her is that she was an Egyptian. Indeed, in recent years as the controversy over the racial identity of
the ancient Egyptians has grown, there has been an increasing tendency to portray her as an African or at least of "mixed race."[2] Although her maternal line is not completely clear, she was, in fact,
a Ptolemy, one of the last in the line that stretched back to the political heirs of Alexander the Great of Macedonia. When Ptolemy
XII (Auletes) died in the spring of 51 B.C.E., he left his kingdom to
his eighteen-year-old daughter, Cleopatra, and her twelve-year-old
brother, Ptolemy XIII.

According to local practice, Cleopatra had to have a consort, either a brother or a son, and she was accordingly "married" to her
brother, as co-ruler. Such "incestuous" unions had been going on
for centuries in Egypt, and this one would certainly not have raised
any eyebrows. It is not that the Egyptians or the Ptolemies routinely accepted incest as a norm. Rather, much as in ancient
Hawaii, this violation of the norms usually applied to commoners
was a striking expression of the special, in fact divine, status of the
rulers. It preserved their pure blood and unique position. In the
case of Cleopatra, moreover, there was at least an implied limitation of her power to rule as well.

However, the young queen was far too ambitious and politically
ruthless to accept any attempts to curb her appetite for power. Almost immediately, she dropped her brother's name from official

---

2. See my comments on the problems in using this term in chapter 8.

documents and his portrait from coins. Styling herself "mistress of the two lands, the goddess Philopator," she sought not only sole control over the kingdom she had inherited, but to return Egypt to its ancient glory.

Her task was not an easy one. At home, powerful court officials, led by the eunuch Pothinius, opposed her drive for power and favored her brother Ptolemy. Internationally, her predecessors had for years been losing territory to the emerging Roman Empire. Cyprus, Syria, and Cyrenaica had already fallen, and the riches of Egypt were clearly too valuable a prize to be ignored. Moreover, internal disputes such as the one between Ptolemy and Cleopatra were just the sort of situation that the Romans routinely exploited to get a foothold in new territories.

When the Roman general and future emperor Julius Caesar appeared off the coast of Alexandria in 48 B.C.E., he was drawn to his destiny by neither Cleopatra's charms nor the conquest of Egypt. His archrival Pompey had sought sanctuary in the country only to be assassinated as he stepped ashore. Never one to pass up an opportunity, Caesar disembarked and almost immediately began to intervene in Egyptian affairs. Although Caesar had indicated his intention to mediate between the rival Egyptian claimants to the throne, Ptolemy's supporters believed that they could convince him to act in their favor. They had not counted on Cleopatra's skills and just how vulnerable to them Caesar would prove to be.

Although both Ptolemy and Cleopatra were invited to appear before Caesar in the morning, she preempted her rival by having herself smuggled through enemy lines the night before, hidden in a carpet. Thus, in the words of historian Günther Hölbl, "these two remarkable people, both of whom were characterized by their political genius, their determined ambition and a sense of adventure, met as man and woman." By nightfall they were lovers, and by the time Ptolemy arrived at the palace the next morning, his claim to the throne was critically weakened. Politically it may have been expedient for Caesar to have favored Ptolemy's faction, but his personal involvement with Cleopatra dictated his policies. Not only had she regained the throne, but Egypt was able to reclaim Cyprus as well.

How did she do it? And in only one night? There could have been no shortage of women willing to make themselves available to the heroic Roman. So what was so special about Cleopatra? While opinions appear to vary on the matter, the consensus would seem to be that Cleopatra was not an incredible beauty. Coins and

Aristotle & Jackie Onassis

Eva & Juan Perón

Ruth & Boaz

Esther Confounding Haman

Samson & Delilah

Judith & Holofernes

Louis XV

Madame de Pompadour

George, Prince of Wales (the future George IV)

Frances, Countess of Jersey

Maria Anne Fitzherbert

Caroline Amelia Elizabeth of Brunswick

Catherine the Great

Thomas Jefferson

Charles Stewart Parnell

John & Jackie Kennedy

Cleopatra & Caesar

Cleopatra & Antony

Elizabeth I

Robert Dudley

Christina of Sweden

Phillip d'Orleans

John Adams

Abigail Adams

Abraham Lincoln and His Family

Franklin & Eleanor Roosevelt

Lucy Mercer

Lorena Hickok

statues that have survived from her period indicate that at least by current standards she was shorter, heavier, and had a bigger nose than is considered attractive today. However, she certainly knew how to make the most of what she had.

Egyptians had a reputation in the ancient world for being skillful lovers, and none can be said to have personified this as much as Cleopatra. She is said to have owed her flawless skin to regular baths in ass's milk. Later generations were to remember her as having mastered not only the application of cosmetics, but also the use of perfumes. She is said to have known how to both use and make contraceptives and abortifacients, and even a cure for baldness, which included burnt mice, horse teeth, bear-grease, and deer marrow, is attributed to her![3]

Whatever skills Cleopatra may have had in the area of lovemaking and cosmetics were supplemented by her keen intelligence, education (she is said to have known seven or eight languages), and deep understanding of people. Caesar may have also been attracted by the fact that Cleopatra as an Egyptian woman was much less sheltered and isolated than her Roman counterparts. Her youth was doubtless also part of her attraction to the fifty-two-year-old general, although it clearly awakened more than mere paternal feelings within him. Indeed, we cannot ignore the possibility that because she was so much his junior, Caesar may have seriously underestimated Cleopatra and believed that the young queen would be his puppet.

In fact, his choice of Cleopatra plunged Caesar into the vicious politics of the Ptolemaic court with its fatal combination of incest and fratricide. Cleopatra's hold on the throne was only established after a civil war that left Ptolemy XIII dead and her married to her eleven-year-old brother, Ptolemy XIV.[4] No sooner had the blood been washed away than Caesar and Cleopatra set off on an extended tour of her kingdom, traveling by royal barge up the Nile. By the time they returned to Alexandria, Cleopatra was visibly pregnant.

Several weeks before the birth of his son, Caesarion (Ptolemy Caesar), Caesar departed for Syria. In July of 46, he returned to Rome in triumph where he was feted and granted a ten-year dictatorship. However, his popularity began to fade within a few

---

3. Some believe that Caesar, who was beginning to suffer from baldness, may have availed himself of this cure!

4. Ptolemy XIV and a sister were both later to meet their deaths through Cleopatra's hand.

months when he had Cleopatra brought to Rome to join him. Conservative Romans were offended by her luxurious lifestyle, her "Eastern" ways, and her claims to be the latest incarnation of the goddess Isis. One indication of the honors that Caesar bestowed upon her was a golden statue of her placed in the temple of Venus Genetrix, which symbolized her role as both lover and mother. By the time of his death on the Ides of March, 44 B.C.E., Caesar had not only recognized Caesarion as his son, but indicated his intention of flouting Roman tradition and marrying the unpopular foreigner.

ANTONY AND CLEOPATRA

Caesar did not mention either Cleopatra or Caesarion in his will. Fearing she and her son might suffer the same fate he had, Cleopatra traveled back to Alexandria. In her absence Ptolemy XIV had let the country slip into chaos. Never one to let sentiment stand in her way, she had her brother killed and named her four-year-old son as her co-regent. All of this, however, was by way of an intermission, as she waited to see whom Rome would send to her next: Mark Antony or Octavian (later Augustus).

It was the former, and in 41 B.C.E. Cleopatra was invited to Tarsus (in modern Turkey) by Mark Antony. However dramatic and eventful the encounter between Cleopatra and Julius Caesar may have been, it was this encounter and later affair with Mark Antony, with its majestic themes and tragic end, that secured the queen's place in history.

For the woman who had captured Julius Caesar in a day, Mark Antony must have seemed like comparatively easy prey. Not only did he lack the military genius of his predecessor, but he also showed a clear weakness for wine, women, and (for all we know) song. If Cleopatra had traveled to meet Caesar hidden in a rug, for Antony she took the opposite tack. Pulling out all stops, in a scene memorialized by countless authors and artists, she invested much of her failing country's wealth in making an impression. She arrived dressed as Aphrodite, the goddess of love, flanked by attendants and handmaidens who fanned her.

The couple spent the winter of 41–40 together, and later in the year Cleopatra gave birth to twins, whom she named Alexander and Cleopatra. By this time, however, their father, Antony, had returned to Rome, where, in an attempt to resolve his political prob-

lems, he had married Octavian's sister, Octavia.[5] She was a beautiful and intelligent woman, popular among the populace, and probably no less skilled politically than Cleopatra herself. Antony's political skills were, however, a totally different story. If he had just
stayed put, there's no telling what he might have achieved.

In the fall of 37, Antony returned to the East and had Cleopatra
brought to him. Although several years and his marriage to Octavia
had transpired since their last meeting, little appears to have
changed between them. Their twin children were recognized by
Antony, an act that cannot have pleased Octavia, who had only
produced a single daughter. Moreover, Antony restored Egyptian
control of not only Cyprus but several other territories as well, including the rich lumbering kingdom of Chalkis in Lebanon, Judea,
and parts of Crete and Cyrene. Although there were good political
and economic reasons for Antony to bestow these "gifts" on
Cleopatra, his Roman enemies, most notably Octavian, had a political field day condemning his generosity as the folly of a lovesick
fool paid for at the expense of the Roman citizenry. They may not
have been totally mistaken.

Whatever Antony's motives, his return to Cleopatra and division
of territories divided the Roman Empire both geographically and
personally between East and West. While he and Cleopatra attempted to rule the East as a royal, in some senses even divine,
couple (they were married in 34),[6] Octavian controlled the West
and organized against them. Their self-indulgent lifestyle and
Antony's legal divorce of Octavia in 32 did nothing to help
Antony's cause. When it was revealed that Antony had acknowledged Cleopatra's son Caeserion as Julius Caesar's son (and, in theory at least, heir) and requested in his will that he be buried alongside Cleopatra in Egypt, his fate was sealed. Amidst rumors that he
intended to move the capital of the empire to Egypt, in the year 32
the Roman senate revoked his authority and declared Cleopatra to
be an enemy of the state.[7]

---

5. As we saw in chapter 6, marriage was often a means of creating or
cementing political alliances.
6. The fact that Antony minted coins on which both he and Cleopatra
appeared is a testimony to the depth of their connection and the honor
with which she was viewed.
7. It is typical of the gender-biased judgments of this and other periods
that Cleopatra, the Egyptian queen acting in the best interests of her country, should have been much more harshly condemned than Antony, the
Roman, who was her consort.

For much of the next two years, Octavian's armies drove Antony and Cleopatra back to Egypt. On August 1, 30 B.C.E.,[8] Octavian entered Alexandria in triumph. Antony, believing that Cleopatra was already dead, attempted to commit suicide. She was, in fact, very much alive, and he died in her arms. Some have speculated that Cleopatra may have encouraged his suicide, in order to leave her free for a clear shot at Octavian, but other sources record her genuine grief at his passing.

Octavian permitted Cleopatra to bury Antony with royal honors and kept her alive as a living symbol of his triumph. This proud daughter of the Nile had, however, no interest in being a testimony to another's victory. At first she tried to starve herself to death, but relented when Octavian threatened to punish her children. Eventually, after a relaxing bath and a sumptuous meal, she committed suicide by snakebite. She was only thirty-nine years old and had outlived Antony by a mere ten days.

Cleopatra's death from a cobra's bite remains one of the most striking images of her story.[9] The cobra was a symbol of both Egypt and the goddess Isis, with whom the queen identified herself. Thus hers was a double suicide as she ended her human life through a creature that represented her divine being. The snake is/was also, of course, a symbol of immortality and thus was an appropriate choice for this deathless queen. Whether this was a staged act or merely a story spread by her supporters, her death represented the reaffirmation of her divine status and her sacred right to rule her country.

A WOMAN FOR ALL SEASONS

Despite her ignominious end, Cleopatra achieved an immortality that her pharaonic predecessors would have truly envied. During the comparatively short period while I wrote this chapter, I was able to read about a new Cleopatra exhibit at the British Museum, see a recent film about her on the Hallmark Channel,

---

8. Of course, since our month of August is named after Octavian (Augustus), this was not the name of the month at the time. It is interesting that the month named for this Roman emperor is not the month of his birth (September), but the month of his defeat of Antony and Cleopatra.

9. The term *aspis* (asp) refers to a snake capable of puffing up its neck into a shield or hood.

and view the Discovery Channel's fascinating documentary *In Search of Cleopatra*. Most publicists would be thrilled to get that sort of coverage for a living client, much less one who's been dead for over 2,000 years!

Of course the Cleopatra who has survived often bears little resemblance to the historical figure, either in her appearance or in the deeds attributed to her. All you have to do is look at a gallery of portraits of Cleopatra to realize the extent to which every generation has reimagined her, according to its own standards of beauty, femininity, and seductive behavior. Giambattista Tiepolo's eighteenth-century frescoes and Cecile B. de Mille's 1934 film spectacle are only two of the more memorable images passed down over the years. As Mary Hamer has shown in her fascinating study *Signs of Cleopatra*, the story of Cleopatra has achieved an almost mythic status in Western culture. For almost two millennia it has been rewritten and reinterpreted, usually to carry thinly veiled messages about the status and behavior of women.

Although some of her enemies would later refer to Cleopatra as a "whore," there is really no evidence that she was promiscuous. Indeed, while we can't be certain about the facts, the only documented relationships she had were with Caesar and Antony. Nor would it appear very fair to characterize her as an Egyptian Delilah, enticing her lovers to their doom. Neither Caesar nor Antony was a political novice when he met her, and any blame for the decisions they made under her influence must certainly be evenly divided.

At least in part, Cleopatra's story remains so fascinating because it involves some of the most important events and people of ancient history. Yet, while the events are very well known, she remains something of a mystery. Because her portrait is sketched so dimly, everyone seems to have felt the right to rewrite this fascinating woman's life. In thirty-nine years, she lived more than most people do in twice that time. And she left a legacy that was a hard act to follow, even for the female rulers I'm going to discuss in the next few chapters.

SUGGESTIONS FOR FURTHER READING

Hamer, Mary. *Signs of Cleopatra*. London: Routledge, 1993.
Hawley, Richard, and Barbara Levick, eds. *Women in Antiquity: New Assessments*. London: Routledge, 1995.

Hölbl, Günther. *A History of the Ptolemaic Empire*. London: Routledge, 2000.

Hughes-Hallett, Lucy. *Cleopatra: Histories, Dreams and Distortions*. London: Bloomsbury, 1989.

Rowlandson, Jane, ed. *Women and Society in Greek and Roman Egypt*. Cambridge: Cambridge University Press, 1998.

http://www.discovery.com/stories/history/cleopatra/todaysact.html

Elizabeth I: courtship, power, and the politics of virginity

> *The world has suffered more from the ravages of ill-advised marriages than from virginity.*
>
> —Ambrose Bierce

BORN NOT TO RULE

It is one of the curiosities of English history that three of the country's most durable monarchs were women: Elizabeth I (r. 1558–1603), Victoria (r. 1837–1901), and Elizabeth II (r. 1952–). Each of these was in her own way an unlikely ruler, but none more so than Elizabeth I. Elizabeth's birth was a bitter disappointment to her father, Henry VIII, and his second wife, Anne Boleyn. He had divorced his first wife, broken with the Catholic Church, and executed his friend Thomas More in an attempt to secure the succession through a male heir. When she was born on September 7, 1533, no one could have believed that Elizabeth would ascend to the throne only twenty-five years later. Three years after her birth, the execution of her mother for adultery, incest, treason, and witchcraft and a parliamentary act declaring Elizabeth herself to be illegitimate made her eventual succession seem even less likely.

However, as is well known, Henry's desperate actions and numerous marriages produced only one son, Edward. He succeeded his father in 1547, but died six years later. Edward was succeeded by his half sister Mary, who died in 1558, and thus, against all odds, Elizabeth assumed the throne.

Elizabeth's reign was a golden period of national success and the flowering of culture. Among the artists and scholars who worked in this period were Edmund Spenser, Christopher Marlowe, Francis Bacon, and, as was so brilliantly depicted in the Academy Award–winning movie *Shakespeare in Love*, William Shakespeare. The English victory over the Spanish Armada in 1588 inaugurated a period of international supremacy and world leadership.

AN UNMARRIED WOMAN

It is interesting to speculate how Elizabeth's childhood experiences may have influenced her attitude toward power, men, and marriage. Her mother and several of her kinswomen were executed in the course of political-marital intrigues. Catherine Parr, Henry's last wife, who was as much as anyone a mother figure for Elizabeth and largely responsible for the excellent education she received, died in childbirth. If this was not traumatic enough in and of itself, Elizabeth then found herself pursued by her stepmother's second husband, Thomas Seymour, who wanted to marry her!

It would obviously be a bit simplistic to conclude that Elizabeth refused to marry because of such experiences. True, it is reported that at age eight, following the execution of both her mother and her third stepmother, Catherine Howard, she told a confidant that she would never marry. However, from my experience this sort of attitude is not exactly rare among small girls. After all, as comedienne Lily Tomlin once noted, if everyone did what they planned to do at age eight, we'd live in a world of cowboys, fighter pilots, ballerinas, and nurses!

It must always be remembered that once she became queen, Elizabeth's decision not to marry was no longer the private decision of a private individual. For a people who viewed their monarch as God's representative on Earth, a female ruler was far more than a curiosity. In a patriarchal society in which every woman was subordinate to at least one man, she stood at the head of the nation, subservient to none. She was a cultural anomaly who did not fit the accepted social categories. And as anthropologist Mary Douglas has taught us, such anomalies are often viewed as powerful and dangerous.

One way to "solve" the problem of a female ruler was for her to marry a suitable man of noble or even royal blood who would govern in her name. In the early part of her reign, Elizabeth gave her subjects some reason to hope as she pursued numerous courtships with various degrees of seriousness. During the early part of her reign, her clear favorite was Lord Robert Dudley. Unlike so many others, Dudley's friendship dated to the period before she assumed the throne. Upon her accession, she appointed him to a major household post that required his constant presence at her side. In his favor, he was both English and a Protestant. He was, however, the son and grandson of executed traitors. Most importantly, he was married. And his wife's mysterious (and perhaps too convenient) death from a broken neck after apparently falling down the stairs may have technically freed him to marry, but left him with an even greater burden of scandal. Although Dudley's closeness to the queen secured him a place on her council, estates, and the title of Earl of Leicester, he was never able to carry off the ultimate prize.

At the same time that Elizabeth flirted with Dudley, she and her council also pursued other avenues. Many of these potential arrangements had all the characteristics of the political marriages I discussed in chapter 6. At the time of her accession, the king of Sweden had approached her on behalf of his brother, but Sweden was not sufficiently important politically to justify such a match. A union with Archduke Charles of Austria was intended to strengthen ties with the Hapsburgs, while marriages to Henry of Anjou or Francis of Alençon were designed to secure an alliance with France.

It is difficult to determine how serious Elizabeth ever was about any of these men. It is possible that if her councilors had been able to unite around a single candidate, they might have been able to force her hand. However, this was virtually impossible since she took their advice individually and not as a group. Her strategy of divide and rule generally achieved its purpose of giving her the upper hand, and as time progressed, it became increasingly clear that it was not her intention to consummate any of her courtships with marriage.

Not only did this leave her country in the irregular situation of being ruled by a woman, but it also threatened England with political chaos in the not-too-distant future. As we have already seen,

Elizabeth only came to power for want of a better alternative. She was, unless she married and bore an heir (either male or female), the last Tudor ruler. As has been noted by Elizabethan scholar Carole Levin, "Had Elizabeth died in the first decade of her reign there might well have been a disputed succession and bloody civil war." Small wonder her refusal to either bear or name an heir caused anxiety verging on terror. Although this somewhat dissipated during the middle of her reign, it grew again as she aged, and instability once again loomed.

THE VIRGIN QUEEN

One of the most remarkable official responses to Elizabeth's unusual situation was the promotion of the cult of the Virgin Queen. There is probably no better indication of the cultural gap that separates most of us from the England of Elizabeth's time than this particular aspect of royal pageantry. To be sure, in some traditional (particularly Catholic) societies, virginity under special circumstances still enjoys a high religious status. However, more commonly in today's world it is the subject of skepticism and derision, if not outright scorn. It is hard to imagine any modern politician mounting a campaign to strengthen his or her position based on the theme of virginity. Indeed, modern female politicians who have never married are often suspected of being either lesbians or simply sexually deprived.

In Elizabeth's case there were, of course, special circumstances. Henry VIII's controversial and violent break with the Catholic Church and its enormously popular cult of the Virgin Mary left a void for many believers. The fortuitous fact that Elizabeth herself was born on September 7, the eve of the feast of the nativity of the Blessed Virgin Mary, was viewed by many as no mere coincidence. Many of her subjects viewed her as a suitable substitute for the Virgin Mary, describing her visits as a blessing and claiming she had the ability to heal with her touch. In a particularly impressive ceremony on Maundy Thursday the queen, often dressed in blue (the color of the Virgin Mary), would wash the feet of both noble and common women (the number equaled her age) and make the sign of the cross on each foot.

Thus Elizabeth's virginity, or at least the public perception of it, sent a powerful political-religious message. Her special status as ruler was enhanced by an aura of sanctity and purity. The dangerous and potentially disruptive fact that she had neither married nor borne an heir suddenly became something to be admired and even venerated. While other medieval women had become the subject of admiration and even worship by living chaste and holy lives, Elizabeth was virtually unique in combining this with the political power of a monarch. Hers was not merely the spiritual influence of the pious woman, but the layering of saintly behavior upon the base of immediate and visible presence of the monarch.

Chastity and purity were, however, only two of the meanings that Elizabeth's virginity sent to her nation, for she presented herself, like Mary herself, as a virgin mother. One of the most striking aspects of Elizabeth's self-portrayal was her public display of part of her body, most notably her breasts and belly. During this period it was the practice for all unmarried women to leave their breasts uncovered (a piece of authenticity omitted in modern films seeking to depict the period). Thus this display was, on the one hand, an integral part of Elizabeth's maidenhood. However, as University of California Professor Louis Montrose has noted, in Elizabeth's case the bosom also carried with it the idea of a selfless and bountiful mother. "The image of the queen as wet nurse seems to have had some currency. . . . The queen was the source of her subjects' social sustenance, the fount of all preferments." Thus the Virgin Queen's display of her body sent a message that was both political and sexual, erotic and nurturing. No male ruler could rival her in this.

DISSIDENT VOICES

The cult promoted by Elizabeth and her supporters was not without its detractors. In fact, if even a portion of the stories told about Elizabeth during her reign were true, she could be said to have more in common with Catherine the Great (see chapter 13) than with the virgin she was so often compared to. Almost inevitably, Elizabeth's favorites were claimed to be her bedmates, and their status a reward for both political and sexual services. Among those alleged to have risen to power in this manner were the aforementioned Robert Dudley (later made the Earl of Leicester), Sir Christopher Hatton, and Sir Walter Raleigh. Quite frequently such men were said not only to have gained Elizabeth's favor but, reflecting gender assumptions of the time, to actually be holding the reins of power. A mere woman could not, of course, be ruling so effectively!

We shall return to this theme in the next chapter and our discussion of Catherine. However, it must already be noted that there were marked differences between the perception of such alleged lovers of the queen and the mistresses of kings like Louis XV and Charles II. First, while such mistresses were, as we have seen, a widely tolerated phenomenon, no such leeway was granted Elizabeth. None of our sources seem to treat the possibility that she had a sex life as either natural or desirable. The gender bias is obvious. Second, and here too a double standard operated, while many a mistress was accused of having too much influence on her lover, none were in a position to assume power in any official capacity. Most had little if any power independent of their royal connection. Even the granting of noble rank conferred more honor than authority. The queen's alleged lovers, in contrast, were usually men who held a certain amount of power in their own right and could, in theory, use her bedroom as a means of enhancing their already lofty status.

It must also be remembered that, according to the understanding of the time, the queen's body was never viewed as merely personal and private. Elizabeth's mother's alleged adultery was not only a betrayal of her husband the king, but an act of treason against the state. In a similar fashion, accusations that Elizabeth had been debauched or violated referred not only to her personal status, but also to the sanctity and inviolability of the kingdom itself. So far as the queen's body was concerned, the idea of personal privacy had no significant meaning. It would, in the terms of the time, have been virtually meaningless to argue that her sex life was no one's business but her own.

Elizabeth's detractors did not limit themselves to disputing her virginity. Charges of illegitimate children and even infanticide circulated throughout the queen's reign, usually peaking at moments of national crisis. In 1570 a man was condemned to lose both his ears or else pay a fine of a hundred pounds for claiming that Elizabeth had two illegitimate children by Robert Dudley. A decade later a laborer was reported to have said that the queen had two children by the Earl of Leicester. Although two seems to have been a particularly popular number in such rumors, charges that the queen had three or even as many as five bastards circulated. Clearly, such rumors reflected not only concern with Elizabeth's behavior, but also the intense anxiety (which only grew as the years progressed) over the problem of succession. As late as 1601, when Elizabeth was sixty-eight, rumors circulated that she had had a child by Robert Dudley's stepson, the second Earl of Essex, who was precisely half her age.

The same year was also an especially fruitful time for stories of royal infanticide. Elizabeth, according to these stories, had all or some of her children exiled or murdered (in most cases burned). In the words of Robert Shephard,

> In these rumours, the earlier fears that Elizabeth may have offspring conjoined with frustration and anger that the queen, now past child-bearing age, had left the succession question as unsettled as she had found it. A bastard might have been better than nothing. These tales reflect heightened animus against Elizabeth. In them, she stands accused of a double sin: first, having illegitimate children and then, committing infanticide. These stories suggest that she had been both sinful in the past and deficient in providing for her nation's future.

As much as I'd like to resolve the contradiction between the extreme views presented above, this is not within my power. Although I am very skeptical regarding the most outrageous stories that circulated about Elizabeth's behavior, I also wouldn't like to stake my reputation on her having been a virgin. While the traumatic events of her childhood and youth may have left her with a deep suspicion of men and even more so of political marriages, by all accounts she was an intelligent, vibrant woman well aware of her appearance and the impact she had upon men. As her numerous courtships indicate, she enjoyed "playing the game" and having male suitors. She does not, for example, appear to have followed the example of some female ascetics and deprived herself of nourishment or attempted to minimize her attractiveness. In the end, we shall never know.

What I think is particularly noteworthy, however, is not the question "Was she or wasn't she?" but the manner in which the political concerns of the time developed into a debate over the sexual behavior of the queen. Public anxiety over the need for an appropriate ruler and an heir came to focus upon the very private behavior of this particular woman. Moreover, as I indicated above, the greater the anxiety, the more outlandish the stories that circulated about her.

This set me to thinking. I doubt if this is the only case in history in which concern over political issues was expressed as concern over a leader's sexual behavior. It might be interesting to try to chart such a connection. In times of stability and prosperity do people pretty much ignore their rulers' sex lives, or at least treat them as irrelevant? After all, if everything is going well, what do we care what our leaders do in private? On the other hand, in times of crisis, it may be much easier to focus on the personal lives of our rulers than on the issues that really concern us! Several of the cases we've examined so far seem to support this analysis: the Emperor Xuan and Yang Guifei; Louis XV and Madame de Pompadour. I'll let the professional historians figure this one out!

SUGGESTIONS FOR FURTHER READING

Berry, Philippa. *Of Chastity and Power: Elizabethan Literature and the Unmarried Queen*. London: Routledge, 1989.

Doran, Susan. "Why Did Elizabeth Not Marry?" Pp. 30–59 in Julia M. Walker, ed., *Dissing Elisabeth: Negative Representations of Gloriana*. Durham, N.C.: Duke University Press, 1998.

Douglas, Mary. *Purity and Danger: An Analysis of Concepts of Pollution and Taboo*. New York: Praeger, 1966.

Levin, Caroline. *The Heart and Stomach of a King: Elizabeth I and the Politics of Sex and Power*. Philadelphia: University of Pennsylvania Press, 1994.

MacCaffrey, Wallace. *Elizabeth I*. London: E. Arnold, 1993.

Montrose, Louis Adrian. "*A Midsummer Night's Dream* and the Shaping of Fantasies of Elizabethan Culture: Gender, Power, Form." Pp. 65–87 in Margaret W. Ferguson, Maureen Quilligan, and Nancy J. Vickers, eds., *Rewriting the Renaissance: The Discourses of Sexual Difference in Early Modern Europe*. Chicago: University of Chicago Press, 1986.

Shephard, Robert. "Sexual Rumours in English Politics: The Cases of Elizabeth I and James I." Pp. 101–22 in Jaqueline Murray and Konrad Eisenbichler, eds., *Desire and Discipline: Sex and Sexuality in the Premodern West*. Toronto: University of Toronto Press, 1996.

Walker, Julia M., ed. *Dissing Elisabeth: Negative Representations of Gloriana*. Durham, N.C.: Duke University Press, 1998.

catherine the great: no horse's tale

Continue dear Madam, to defend virtue, and ridicule vice, while ignoring the grumbling of envious people, stupidity, and meanness.

—Catherine Dashkova, president of the Russian Academy of Art and the Academy of Science, to her patron Catherine the Great

If the sexual needs and desires of Queen Elizabeth I were the subject of contradictory speculation and rumor, those of Catherine the Great of Russia produced scandal and outlandish exaggeration. Throughout the second half of her life, the court and diplomatic circles were kept buzzing by stories of her string of young, virile male favorites. Her death was the topic of prurient interest for decades, and even today it is popularly believed that her demise was directly related to her sexual excesses.

Born on May 2, 1729, Sophie Fredericke Auguste von Anhalt-Zerbst was the daughter of a minor German prince. In 1745 she married (or since it was an arranged marriage, was married to) Grand Duke Peter of Holstein, heir to the Russian throne. Like many such political linkages, the match was not a particularly successful one, and the intelligent and ambitious Catherine soon developed an independent coterie of supporters in St. Petersburg. Although Peter succeeded to the throne in 1762, his erratic behavior and political ineptness quickly led to his overthrow on July 9 of that year. The imperial guard placed Catherine on the throne, and several days later (some say at her instigation), Peter was murdered. Thus a princess of foreign birth became the supreme ruler of all Russia.

In contrast to her late husband, Catherine was a shrewd politician and cultivated favor with both the local gentry and foreign intellectuals such as Voltaire and Diderot. Although she was initially an advocate of moderate reform and modernization, a peasant rebellion at home (1773–1775) and the French Revolution abroad turned Catherine into an archconservative. During her reign, the territory of the Russian Empire was greatly increased until it extended to the Black Sea and included large tracts of Polish territory.

Although assessments of her reign differ, by any standards she was an unusually powerful and passionate leader. Perhaps most surprisingly, since she is hardly remembered as a feminist hero, she did much to advance the education of women. At the empress's initiative, her friend and confidante Catherine Dashkova became the first woman to hold a government position when she was appointed director of the Academy of Sciences in 1783. Later that same year, she also became the president of the Russian Academy of the Arts. Empress Catherine is also credited with establishing the Smolny Institute for Girls in St. Petersburg.

THE THRONE AND THE BED

Her achievements in these and other areas are usually overshadowed by fascination with her personal life, in particular her penchant for younger male court favorites, who were also often her lovers. As we have seen above, Catherine was not unusual among rulers in combining a passion for both power and numerous sexual partners. Nor was there anything particularly noteworthy in the fact that in the later years of her life, these partners were inevitably younger, less experienced, and less powerful than she was. However, as is so often the case, because she was a woman her contemporaries reacted very differently than they might have had she been a male ruler. While a king might be celebrated for his virility and applauded for continually demonstrating it with an ever-increasing number of ever-younger partners, Catherine was the subject of gossip and condemnation. And while male rulers might reward their female sexual favorites with valuable gifts and even allow them certain political influence, only in exceptional circumstances could they be appointed to official positions. In contrast, Catherine sometimes placed several of her lovers in offices, and thus her dalliances quickly moved from the private into the public realm. Nevertheless, it should be noted that she never married any of her favorites and thus all of them were denied the title of emperor.

Catherine's amorous adventures began before her husband's death and her own elevation to the throne. Gregory Orlov, one of the participants in the coup that brought her to power, was also her lover at the time and had been for the best part of two years. Indeed, in April of 1762, three months before the coup, she had borne him a son! After she gained the throne they were virtually inseparable, appearing together at public ceremonies and sharing a bed in more private moments. Orlov was by all accounts neither very intelligent nor very ambitious. He inspired neither jealousy nor overt hostility. Although he and Catherine wished to marry, her political advisers vetoed the idea. So for the next ten years, he stayed by her side offering support, sometimes advice, and on some occasions even initiating policies. Gregory Orlov remained Catherine's favorite until 1772. Indeed, she showed tremendous patience as he grew increasingly restless and pursued numerous dalliances. However, when he decided to marry his thirteen-year-old cousin, she had no choice but to dismiss him and look elsewhere.

Orlov's place was taken by a man who is probably the best known and most significant of Catherine's partners, both emotionally and politically, Grigory Aleksandrovich Potemkin. Unlike many of Catherine's later favorites, Potemkin had a distinguished career in his own right both before and after he shared her bed. True, he was a "favorite" and his power rested on his relationship with Catherine, but he was also a gifted statesman. Potemkin first came to her attention for his part in the coup that placed her in power. He also distinguished himself in the Russian–Turkish War of 1768–1774, and it appears that only after this did their sexual relationship begin.

At first glance, Potemkin would seem to have been an unlikely choice of favorite. Catherine had known him for years and, as far as we can tell, had never given him a second glance. He was a hard-living, hard-fighting, and hard-playing military man who had lost his left eye in uncertain circumstances. At age thirty-four he was ten years younger than Catherine, but more a hardened veteran than a callow youth. He became the most important figure in her life, and together they not only made love, but also history. In his position as vice president of the College of War, he was the country's de facto minister of defense.

Fortunately for the historian, much of their correspondence has survived, and we are able to judge both the depth and the content of their relationship. Based on the queen's use of such terms of endearment as "my dear husband," "dear spouse," and "my darling husband" and her reference to "sacred bonds," the noted historian John T. Alexander has suggested that Catherine and Potemkin may have been secretly married. Her use of such expressions as "golden cock," "golden tiger," "lion in the jungle," "my dear soul," "my dear friend," and "my heart" suggest both "animal" passion and deep devotion.

We will probably never know why they stopped being lovers around 1776. Catherine's statement that their disagreements were "always [about] the question of power never that of love"[1] is intriguing. However, Potemkin was to remain a close confidant and valued aide until his death in 1791. Indeed, none of the men who followed him can truly be said to have taken his place politically or personally.

His position (at least as lover and court favorite) was taken by Colonel Peter Zavadovskii, a Ukrainian officer who, like Potemkin, was ten years Catherine's junior. Although well educated, he was far less experienced politically than his predecessor, and it may well be that Potemkin encouraged Catherine's involvement with a man who would not be a serious rival for political influence. Although "Petrushinka" quickly captured Catherine's affections (her letters to him repeat many of the pet names she had used for Potemkin), he never emerged as an independent political force in his own right. While Potemkin had been kept busy with diplomatic duties and other projects, Zavadovskii was much more at her beck and call. Indeed, when he chafed at not having enough to do or not getting enough of her attention, she gently reminded him that she did have an empire to run!

Zavadovskii remained in favor for only eighteen months, but even in "disgrace" continued to serve his queen loyally in a variety of positions, supervising public schools, banks, and medical education at her behest. For his part, he named his favorite estate Ekaterinindar (Catherine's Gift), and its furnishings included both a statue and a full-length portrait of his former lover.

---

1. Alexander, *Catherine the Great*, 206.

None of Potemkin and Zavadovskii's successors were either as capable or as affectionately remembered as they were. Semen Zorich was a compulsive gambler; Ivan Rimskii-Korsakov betrayed her with one of her close friends, the Countess Bruce; and A. Dimitriyev Mamonov fell in love with one of her maids of honor. Probably the greatest damage to her reputation was done by Platon Zubov, her favorite from 1789 on. Following the death of Potemkin in 1791, he inherited many of the senior man's posts, but possessed none of his merits. The influence he exercised on foreign affairs was out of all proportion to his abilities, and Catherine's reputation suffered accordingly.

A LEGEND IN HER TIME

As John T. Alexander, one of the most insightful biographers of Catherine, comments, over the course of time stories of "Catherine's sexual insatiability assumed virtually mythic proportions in Russia and abroad." According to one popular story, two women at Catherine's court served as "testers," assigned to screen potential male partners.

No story appears to have been too lurid to pass into popular lore. Thus when Alexander Lanskoi, a twenty-three-year-old officer of the horse guards, died of fever, informed sources claimed that he died "in action" as the result of an overindulgence in aphrodisiacs.[2] During her lifetime some observers speculated that her behavior would shorten her life and her reign, but she ruled for thirty-four years and died at the age of sixty-seven of natural causes.

Given Catherine's position and power, it is not surprising that within Russia, her sexual behavior was the subject of much talk, but rarely mentioned in public or in the press. Foreign observers were much freer to gossip, particularly after they had returned home.

While the stories that circulated about Catherine during her lifetime were often outrageous and scurrilous, none can compare to the rumors that surrounded her death. According to a popular tale often repeated, but only rarely written down, Catherine met her demise when a horse being lowered upon her for sexual purposes fell on her and crushed her to death. This tale has even been

---

2. His death in 1784 may have been of diphtheria. He left his fortune to Catherine, but she with typical generosity saw that it was divided among his mother, brother, and five sisters.

elaborated by some to include the story that hidden in the depths of the Kremlin vaults are the shoes of Catherine's favorite mount (pun intended), forged into the shape of hearts! The story of Catherine and the horse has shown incredible longevity and is often the only thing the average person knows about her. Only a few weeks ago, I heard it mentioned yet again on the popular television game show *Hollywood Squares!*

After her death and with the passage of time, even within Russia her behavior became the subject of open discussion. Inevitably her life became the subject of drama and film, with George Bernard Shaw presenting her as witty and worldly and Tallulah Bankhead, Jeanne Moreau, and Marlene Dietrich portraying her on screen. Perhaps the bit of casting that did the most to consolidate Catherine's reputation for profligacy was when the "Queen of Sex" Mae West wrote and starred in a revue called *Catherine Was Great!* Only in recent years, with a changing appreciation for the position of women, has Catherine's reputation been somewhat rehabilitated as, for example, in the 1995 English/German biographical film starring Catherine Zeta-Jones. Here, for perhaps the first time, Catherine appears as an attractive, intelligent, and ambitious princess, with a healthy but not excessive sexual appetite.

WAS CATHERINE A NYMPHOMANIAC?

Although it has been frequently speculated even by serious scholars that Catherine was a "nymphomaniac," this diagnosis fails to hold up to any serious scrutiny. The psychiatric community no longer recognizes nymphomania as a real condition. And it is difficult to think of a clearer case of the term being used to pass a value judgment. Catherine's behavior was no more abnormal than the position she found herself in, and whatever the root cause of her behavior, it was not so-called nymphomania.[3]

Despite the unrestrained speculation that surrounded her, during a period of forty-five years, Catherine can be firmly said to have slept with only a dozen men and not the three hundred sometimes claimed. This number is hardly remarkable by today's standards or

---

3. Some authors have sought to draw a connection between Catherine's behavior and the claim that even in her sixties she had not reached menopause. Even if this was true, there is no reason to connect her behavior to the fact that she continued to menstruate.

even in comparison to many male rulers of her time. In fact, several of the men discussed in this book were far more promiscuous. I find it significant that in the CD-ROM encyclopedia that I use, the article on Catherine mentions her lovers, but a longer article on John F. Kennedy makes no mention of his! Similarly, the biography of her compatriot, Peter I (also known as Peter the Great), makes no mention of the fact that he banished his wife to a convent and engaged in innumerable affairs with both men and women.

All in all, it's hard to say that Catherine deserves the reputation she has. In addition to her husband of seventeen years, several of her "affairs" were multiyear relationships and a number of others seem to have reflected genuine affection, at least on her part. She and Orlov were together for a dozen years, and while her affair with Potemkin lasted only three years, their friendship continued for five times that long. As unlikely as it might seem, the historical record appears to indicate that several of her lovers "dumped" her, or at least that their ardor cooled before hers. She was always generous and rarely vindictive even when betrayed. As a rule she only gave her favorites public political responsibilities when she deemed them qualified. And while her judgment on such matters may have lapsed in her later years, she was not alone in this. It is hard to claim that the functioning of the state was seriously compromised by her behavior, however embarrassing some may have found it.

Catherine was victim of the double standard not only with regard to her number of lovers, but also with respect to their ages. Orlov's seduction and marriage of his thirteen-year-old cousin have scarcely blemished his reputation, and Zavadovskii's marriage to a countess more than thirty years his junior apparently raised few eyebrows. But Catherine's dalliances with men of similar youth were considered scandalous. And while it might be argued that it was as much her lovers' station in life as their age that disturbed observers, it must also be remembered that, in her case, no man was of equal rank or power.

All in all I can't help but feel that Catherine has been badly served by history or at least by historians. It's almost as if there's been a campaign to blot out her real achievements by depicting her as some sort of sexual deviant. Somehow it seems as if a powerful, sexually active female ruler was just too much for people to handle. So she was turned into a figure of ridicule both in her own day and our own. The older she got, the greater the ridicule became. The "horse story" is really only the pièce de résistance in what is a fairly systematic campaign of defamation.

When we read Catherine's letters and the record of her life is reviewed, it's hard to escape the sense that she may have been trying to use sexual encounters to fulfill other emotional needs. Never has the saying "It's lonely at the top" been more true.

It is certainly unfortunate that her private life has tended to overshadow her very real achievements as a ruler. She governed Russia with almost absolute authority for over three decades, from 1762 to 1796. She was well read, intelligent, pragmatic, and hardworking. While her policies may not have been particularly enlightened by today's standards (or even those of her own time), for most of her reign she served her country loyally and well. She deserves a better epitaph than a dirty story and a smirk.

SUGGESTIONS FOR FURTHER READING

Alexander, John T. *Catherine the Great: Life and Legend.* New York: Oxford University Press, 1989.

de Madariaga, Isabel. *Catherine the Great: A Short History.* New Haven, Conn.: Yale University Press, 1990.

Mamonova, Tatyana. *Russian Women's Studies.* Oxford: Pergamon, 1989.

FOURTEEN

christina of sweden: nothing feminine but her sex

I think, therefore I am . . . single.

—Anonymous female philosopher

Of all the figures I have chosen to discuss in this book, none is less known or more mysterious than Queen Christina of Sweden. Although mention of her today generally produces little more than a blank stare, in the 1930s she was the subject of several biographies and a film starring her countrywoman Greta Garbo. Even today, serious scholars remain mystified by many aspects of her life. To quote an extensive catalog prepared by the National Museum of Sweden to honor her extraordinary life, "Her character is frequently bewildering. Recent research . . . has produced widely different conclusions regarding her life."

~

Christina Vasa was born on December 6, 1626, the only child of King Gustavus of Sweden. Her mother, Maria Eleonora, is said to have been deeply disappointed at having given birth to a girl and paid her little attention. When her father died in battle six years later, her mother was paralyzed with grief, and Christina herself became the nominal queen of her country. Even prior to his death, Gustavus had commanded that his daughter be raised as a boy and be prepared for life as a prince.[1] Whatever his motives may have been, following his untimely death the princess's guardians had no choice but to follow this policy to the letter. If a (by definition inferior) woman was to become ruler of their country, she must in every way possible be given the skills and abilities of a man. They could not have found a more apt pupil.

Christina herself professed little interest in clothes and handicrafts, but showed a keen natural inclination for athletics, horsemanship, and hunting. She mastered languages including Latin, French (a French diplomat remarked that she spoke the language as if born in the Louvre!), German, and Dutch effortlessly and was prodigious in philosophy, mathematics, theology, and astronomy. One of her tutors offered her what he perceived as the highest possible praise, "it rejoices me that she is not womanly, but of good heart and deep understanding."

During the twelve years of Christina's minority, the Privy Council that ruled the country in her name gradually sought to erode the power of the monarchy. Had they succeeded, Christina and, even more significantly, her heirs would have found themselves reduced to the role of mere figureheads. The council failed, however, to reckon with the willful young queen. In December 1644, at age eighteen, she came to power. By 1646 she was pursuing policies of her own, and by age twenty-two she was ready to restore the council to its "proper" place in the political system.

To those who were troubled by the issue of succession, which would have required her to marry and bear an heir, she stated, "I tell you here and now, that it is impossible for me to marry. So it must be, and I will not adduce reasons. Enough that I am not so inclined."[2] Using popular support to overcome council opposition, she solved the problem of succession and maintained her own independence. Through a series of shrewd political moves, she had her cousin Charles Gustavus designated hereditary prince and her successor in 1650.

---

1. This is in sharp contrast to Catherine the Great, who as a small girl was forced to do all sorts of "women's work," which bored her to tears.

2. Unlike Elizabeth I, Christina was completely consistent on this issue and left no room for doubt in either word or deed. She had no courtships that we know of.

While Christina doubtless had clear personal reasons for her decision, we should not ignore the larger religious-cultural background. Her studies had imbued her with a deep interest in Catholicism. ("She hath nothing feminine about her but the sex" wrote one of the Jesuits she came to know when she was contemplating a secret conversion to Catholicism.) Swedish law at the time decreed that anyone accepting Catholicism would forfeit all their rights and titles. Although the law never envisioned that the person in question would be the ruler of the country, Christina had no desire to create a political crisis by making her faith a public issue. Nor did she seek to impose her faith on others. Christina had no wish to emulate either Henry VIII in promoting religious turmoil or Elizabeth in creating a succession crisis. Temperamentally, she does not appear to have been inclined to emulate Elizabeth's virginity either. Abandoning the throne appears to have been her only option.

Christina first expressed her desire to abdicate the throne in August 1651.[3] However, there was so much opposition to the move that she was persuaded to wait for almost three years before carrying out her plan. On June 6, 1654, the twenty-seven-year-old queen abdicated the throne and set out for Rome. Only a few days after her departure she had her hair cut short, put on the coat and trousers of a man, and continued on horseback, calling herself Count Dohna.

Throughout her journey to Rome, Christina appears to have done everything in her power to draw as much attention as possible. Indeed, her abdication journey appears to resemble a triumphant tour as much as anything else. As she journeyed across Europe royalty and common folk alike flocked to see her because of her (male) dress, her learning, and the unusual company she kept. She arrived in Hamburg, for example, accompanied by two Jewish residents of the city and wearing a simple coat "such as the men wear and a woman's skirt . . . on top of the man's trousers. Her hair hung free, cut like a man's." Although she had abdicated, she was inevitably treated with all the honors due to visiting royalty. In November 1655 she publicly renounced Protestantism, was accepted into the Roman Catholic Church, and set out on the final stage of her journey to Rome.

Christina arrived in Rome on December 23 to an unprecedented welcome. Preparations for the arrival of this distinguished convert

---

3. At the same time, she took her first steps toward a conversion to Catholicism.

had taken months. Mounted pages, cavaliers, trumpeters, and drummers accompanied her procession, which eventually numbered thirty-six carriages. She was received by the pope and traveled in his coach. The occasion of her arrival was proclaimed a public holiday. She was established in a palace from which she hosted academic discussions and concerts. The magnificent art collection that she brought with her from Sweden was regularly supplemented with new acquisitions.[4]

For the next thirty years, with only brief sojourns elsewhere, Christina resided in Rome, hosting artists, scholars, authors, clergy, and politicians, often devoting herself behind the scenes to politics and even the election of popes. When she died in 1689, the pope ordered a memorial for her erected in St. Peter's, the most important shrine of Catholic Christianity.

SAINT OR SINNER?

Christina's life, as we have described it thus far, would appear to make her a possible, if rather unusual, candidate for canonization: a devoted daughter of the Church and patron of the arts, who sacrificed her kingdom for her faith. But there is another side to her legacy, which puts a very different slant on things.

If Catherine the Great left behind her a reputation for sexual profligacy, and Elizabeth the official image of a Virgin Queen, Christina's legacy, like Cleopatra's, is far more ambiguous. Every generation, including her own, seems to have interpreted her life slightly differently. Some of the accusations against her are just sort of silly, like the claim that she became a Catholic in order to be able to live in Italy far away from Sweden's harsh winters! Most are more malicious and concern her sexual behavior and identity.

French enemies of Christina appear to have been the first to attempt to impugn her reputation by attacking her sexuality. Pamphlets published in French while she was trying to mediate in a war between France and Spain accused her of being an aggressive "tribade" (a female homosexual who takes the male role), who "hit" on almost every woman she met. These texts, which were eventually

---

4. Her collection of medieval manuscripts of saints' lives was so impressive that the work of publishing such lives had to be suspended for a time to permit the incorporation of her material.

translated into Latin, German, and English and republished for decades, were to shape her image for years to come. Scurrilous as they were, they were not without a kernel of truth.

There is little question, for example, that Christina had, at various times in her life, strong feelings for the women around her. It's hard, for example, to read from her letters to Ebba Sparre, her lady-in-waiting, without gaining the impression that the two had an extremely intimate relationship. Three years after leaving Sweden Christina wrote to Ebba, "If you remember the power you have over me, you will also remember that I have been in possession of your love for twelve years; I belong to you utterly . . . and only when I die shall I cease loving you."[5]

How well Christina understood these feelings and when, if ever, she acted on them cannot be stated conclusively. Certainly, her contemporaries and many others believed her to be a lesbian, although this ignores some fairly well-documented relationships with men, including one of the cardinals of Rome! We may be a little closer to the truth if we accept that Christina was bisexual, that she had sexual relations with both sexes.

One of the questions about Christina that has fascinated her biographers was whether her sexual orientation was innate or the product of her environment. In a manner reminiscent of current debates of "nature versus nurture," they've argued over whether she was born (either psychologically or physiologically) with certain tendencies or whether she was the product of her unusual upbringing and situation in life.

On the one hand, we have those who felt that Christina was "ruined" by having been brought up as a boy. All that learning, all that preparation for leadership, all those male pursuits left her, they claim, a mixed-up young woman with a totally confused gender identity.

On the other hand, some of Christina's detractors have more biological explanations. A few even went so far as to suggest that her unusual behavior, as well as her refusal to marry, was the direct result of her being a hermaphrodite, that is, someone with the genitals and reproductive organs of both sexes. To my mind, this is a bit far-fetched. Hermaphroditism is an extremely rare condition. (Today it is usually dealt with by a combination of hormonal and sur-

---

5. Of course, the Garbo film could only hint at this aspect of her character by showing her as hurt and disappointed when she catches one of her female friends with a man.

gical treatments.) In the absence of any firm evidence, I would hesitate to jump to so far-reaching a conclusion.[6]

Whatever Christina's sexual preferences may have been and whatever roots they may have had in either her makeup or her upbringing, the diverse speculation about them was and is clearly rooted in what has been perceived as her "contradictory" role as an intelligent, independent, and powerful female ruler. (In this at least, she was not unlike Elizabeth I.) Whatever her physical condition, Christina was, in a sense, a *symbolic* hermaphrodite, a woman with the "equipment"—power, skills, wealth, intelligence—of a man. She immersed herself wholeheartedly in the politics of her country, the diplomatic conflicts of her neighbors, the intellectual life of her era, and the religious controversies of her century. If in her own day it could be stated that "She had nothing feminine about her but the sex," today she might be much more readily understood as a model woman in many respects.

WOMEN ON TOP

The women I have chosen to discuss in the last four chapters are, of course, only four among many women who held power over the ages. In selecting these four, with their fascinating life stories, it has not been my intention to suggest that all women rulers have had unusual sex lives. Many female rulers led personal lives that (at least as far as we know) were not markedly different from many of their subjects. Even in the case of these four, their exceptional behavior is as much a product of speculation and exaggeration as of fact. However, the women that I chose offer fascinating opportunities for comparison and speculation.

It is interesting to note some of the parallels that appear in the careers of these four women. All were by any measure successful rulers. Even Cleopatra, whose short reign ended in defeat and death, managed to preserve her country's independence for far longer than could have been expected. Christina, whose reign was by far the shortest, made a major contribution to political stability before she abdicated the throne. Both Elizabeth and Christina had to walk the tightrope of the Catholic–Protestant tensions of their

---

6. Some of Elizabeth's detractors also sought to explain her refusal to marry as the product of a physical abnormality that made it impossible for her to have sexual relations!

times, the former championing the Anglican cause, the latter converting to Catholicism. Detractors of both sought to "explain" their decisions not to marry, not as a free rational choice, but as the result of physical abnormality. Both were accused of being at the same time virtually asexual and (in this they were joined by Catherine) hypersexual. Both Elizabeth and Catherine were accused of promoting their sexual partners to high-ranking positions. One theme that appears to run through the lives or at least the histories of each of these women is that both their contemporaries and later authors appear to have treated them with rather obvious disdain. However successful they may have been, it seems pretty clear that the simple fact of a woman holding such power made many people uncomfortable. It's almost as if writers felt a need to degrade such women as a warning that such situations should not repeat themselves.

It would be nice to believe that the special dilemmas these women faced as female rulers are a thing of the past, but I fear they are not. As I noted at the beginning of the chapter on Cleopatra, the sexuality or at least the femininity of even twentieth-century female rulers was often impugned. Perhaps in the twenty-first century we'll reach the stage at which a woman can hold power and still be seen as being, in every respect, a normal woman.

SUGGESTIONS FOR FURTHER READING

Bjurström, Per. *Feast and Theatre in Queen Christian's Rome.* Stockholm: n.p., 1966.

Christina Queen of Sweden: A Personality of European Civilization. Stockholm: Nationalmuseum, 1966.

Faderman, Lillian. *Surpassing the Love of Men: Romantic Friendship and Love between Women from the Renaissance to the Present.* New York: William Morrow, 1981.

Porter, Roy, and Lesley Hall. *The Facts of Life: The Creation of Sexual Knowledge in Britain 1650–1950.* New Haven, Conn.: Yale University Press, 1995.

Roberts, Michael. *Essays in Swedish History.* Minneapolis: University of Minnesota Press, 1967.

Waters, Sarah. "'A Girton Girl on a Throne': Queen Christina and Versions of Lesbianism, 1906–1933." *Feminist Review* 46 (1994): 41–60.

Westheimer, Ruth, ed. *Dr. Ruth's Encyclopedia of Sex.* New York: Continuum, 1994.

gay Leaders: closets and cabinets

Jonathan made David swear again by his love for him; for he loved him as he loved his own life.

—1 Samuel 20:17

A PROBLEM OF DEFINITION

In the last chapter we saw just how hard it was to make any definite statements about Christina's sexual preferences and behavior. Not surprisingly, perhaps, her case is not the only one of this kind. Although many societies have been far more tolerant than our own toward homosexuality, same-sex relations have often been defined as a "sin," a "crime," a "disease," or any combination of these three. Obviously, this presents several problems for the historian.

Except in those cases in which people have been public about their homosexuality, we are often left with little more than speculation and/or accusation. While some historians have been tempted to suggest that any man and especially any woman (like Christina) who did not marry was homosexual, we really need to be much more cautious. Not only are there many historical examples of denied, repressed, or simply absent sexuality, but as we shall see below, the fact that someone had married and had children does not preclude their involvement in long-lasting relationships with members of the same sex.

Secondhand sources create yet another kind of problem. Although today's gay and lesbian activists are happy to *claim* hundreds of historical figures as part of their community, in the past it was much more common for people to *accuse* their enemies of such behavior. Clearly we need to exercise caution and try not to err in either direction.

However, probably the biggest problem with the labeling of a historical figure as "homosexual" is that it does a grave injustice to the historical material itself. The very idea of identifying a particular person primarily on the basis of his or her sexual orientation is of comparatively recent vintage. The terms *heterosexual* and *homosexual* seem to have first appeared in Germany in the middle of the nineteenth century and to have been used in the context of the debate over the criminalization of "unnatural fornication." In English, "heterosexual" was first used only in 1888, and "homosexual" followed four years later in 1892. Indeed, in this context it's interesting to note that for quite some time *both* "homosexual" and "heterosexual" referred to what were viewed as perversions! As Jonathan Ned Katz, one of the pioneers of gay and lesbian studies, notes, "In 1901, a Philadelphia medical dictionary was still defining 'heterosexuality' as 'Abnormal or perverted appetite toward the opposite sex.' . . . As late as 1923, I discovered, the authoritative Merriam-Webster dictionary was defining 'heterosexual' as a medical term meaning 'Morbid sexual passion for one of the opposite sex.'"

Of course the fact that the term *homosexual* didn't exist until comparatively recently doesn't mean that same-sex relations didn't exist before this time. The biology of sexual behavior probably hasn't changed all that much over time. But, the idea of someone *being* "a homosexual" or "a lesbian" is a fairly modern idea. People may have been having sexual relations with members of the same sex since time immemorial, but this defined something they did and not who they were. Throughout most of history, in the words of Robert Shephard, people "had no concept of homosexuality [or heterosexuality?] as a distinct sexual orientation . . . as a fundamental, permanent, and indeed defining part of one's overall personality." What this means is that we are probably missing the point when we devote too much time to trying to define (in our own terms) a historical figure's sexuality. Rather, we must attempt to understand their behavior within their own social and cultural context.

THEMES, NOT NAMES

Because of what I've just said, I'm not going to use this chapter to present a list of famous people who were homosexuals or try to determine what a particular person's sexual preference was. Several of the books I've consulted and listed below offer such lists and I encourage readers to look at them. Instead of summarizing what has already been done, I'd like to consider a couple of themes related to homosexuality and lesbianism in history, which are still of relevance to today's debates. Only after doing that will I look at a particular episode in which sex, power, and politics came together.

One of the hottest issues in today's debates over homosexuality is the question of same-sex marriage. Given these debates, I would really be remiss if I didn't say a few words on the subject. As I never tire of telling people, I'm basically rather conservative in my views on sex and relationships. At a time when so many heterosexual marriages end in divorce and so many heterosexuals seem disenchanted with marriage, I find it interesting and refreshing that homosexuals are ready to fight for their right to be part of this institution. I wonder how many of them (or their opponents) realize that same-sex marriages have a long and venerable history.

In 1994, shortly before his death, the Yale historian John Boswell published a fascinating study entitled *Same-Sex Unions in Premodern Europe*. In this truly impressive work, ranging widely over centuries and civilizations, Boswell demonstrated that not only were such unions, in various forms, widespread in the ancient world, but also that at one time both the Catholic and Eastern Orthodox churches both sanctioned and sanctified them in ceremonies strikingly similar to heterosexual marriage ceremonies!

Now anyone can draw whatever conclusions they want from these historical facts. However, at the very least they are striking reconfirmation of a theme that has followed us throughout this book: Sexual norms have varied tremendously over space and time.[1] They also serve to point out that recent calls for the recognition of same-sex unions are not as novel or unprecedented as many might believe.

---

1. Of course, one of the reasons why such unions were officially sanctioned is that the understanding of marriage at the time was very different from our own. We've already seen numerous examples of this in the discussion of political marriages, the attitude toward polygamy, and the toleration and even encouragement of concubines and mistresses.

Yet another topic that's been in the headlines a great deal in recent years is the question of gays in the military. The famous (or
some would say infamous) "Don't ask, don't tell" policy adopted of
late in the United States seems to have placated many without really satisfying anyone. It's interesting to note that many other
armies (that of Israel is one example) seem to function without ex-
cluding gays and lesbians.

Historically, many successful armies seem to have functioned best
by choosing their soldiers for their military skills and not for their
sexual practices. Eugene of Savoy's (1663–1736) sexual preferences
may have been ambiguous, but his ability to lead his men was never
in doubt. Even more interesting is the case of his contemporary and
friend, Phillip, Duc d'Orléans (1640–1701). Known as "Monsieur,"
he was public in both his transvestitism and his homosexuality. According to Vern L. Bullough, one of the foremost scholars of the history of sexuality, he "rode into battle wearing makeup, powder, rib-
bons, and jewelry, but no hat allegedly for fear of messing his hair."
His *second* wife wrote, "Except in time of war, he could never be prevailed upon to mount a horse. The soldiers said of him that he was
more afraid of the sun, or the black smoke of gunpowder [ruining
his appearance], than he was of musket bullets."

As we shall discuss in some detail below, homosexuals were
prominent among the German military leadership in the late nineteenth and early twentieth centuries. Even the "Iron Chancellor,"
Otto von Bismarck, conceded that he had known successful generals who were homosexual.

In societies in which sexual preference was a minor or even in-
significant issue, gay soldiers and politicians led an existence not
remarkably different from their heterosexual counterparts. Many
others, however, living in less sympathetic circumstances, had to
lead their lives in fear of being blackmailed, "outed," dismissed,
and prosecuted. Although individuals often fell victim under
such circumstances, there were also waves, "moral panics," in
which large numbers of homosexuals were removed from office.
More often than not, such "purges" took place against a broader
background of political concern and anxiety. As we've already
seen on several occasions, accusations of sexual misconduct of all
sorts are often made against a larger background of political dis-
content. And homosexuals have been among the most prominent victims of such scapegoating. Interestingly, this homophobic
behavior often seems to cross conventional political divisions.
Fascists and communists, American fundamentalists and Cuban

Marxists, all have engaged in the victimization of homosexuals in the search for political orthodoxy and societal purity.

IN THE SERVICE OF THE KAISER

The case I've chosen to focus on in this chapter occurred against the background of just such a purge of homosexuals from the political and military elites of German society in the late nineteenth and early twentieth centuries. Count, later Prince, Phillip zu Eulenburg, one of Kaiser Wilhelm II's closest friends and political allies, was the most prominent of a series of high officials who fell from positions of power and influence because of threats to reveal, or the revelation of, their homosexual behavior.

Phillip zu Eulenburg was born in 1847 to one of Eastern Prussia's oldest aristocratic families. Although the family fortunes were not great at the time of his birth, an inheritance that his mother received as he was just turning twenty made them one of the wealthiest families in Prussia and paved the way to close ties with the country's ruling elite. Phillip initially pursued a military career with some success, but eventually chose to study law and entered the diplomatic service. It was a strange choice for a man who, throughout his life, professed to be more interested in the arts than in politics.

He sang and composed and played the piano. He was charming, had a fine sense of humor, and could converse intelligently (if not always at great depth) on art, architecture, poetry, and theater. Eulenburg was a striking figure and a remarkable personality, tall and handsome, with eyes that captivated some, but that Otto Bismarck said put him off his breakfast. He was an excellent hunter and sportsman and it was at a hunt in 1886 that he first met Crown Prince Wilhelm, the future Kaiser Wilhelm II. The two soon became close friends, indeed, some would say that he was not only Prince Wilhelm's closest friend, but in many senses (his criticisms notwithstanding) he may have been his only friend. Even Eulenburg's enemies conceded that he always acted in what he believed to be Wilhelm's best interest.

The same year he met Wilhelm, Eulenburg came to know Friedrich von Holstein, a privy councilor in the Political Department of the Foreign Office and one of its most powerful figures. Together the three of them, working in coordination, began to wield power, first behind the scenes and then, following Wilhelm's accession to the throne, in public. Although Eulenburg seems to have often served more as a messenger than an instigator, he soon gained a reputation for wielding enormous power. Indeed, together with his allies he played a major role in the appointment of Bernhard von Bulow as foreign secretary and later chancellor. More than anything else, however, he sought to serve what he perceived to be the best interests of Wilhelm.

It should be noted that there is little evidence that Eulenburg's sexual preference affected either his politics or his political performance. As Isabel Hull, who undertook a definitive study of Wilhelm's entourage, noted, the

> vast majority of persons (and there were many) whom Eulenburg caused to be shifted around were not personal friends of his. Most were career civil servants or diplomats whose advancement or relegation to the backwaters Eulenburg felt was beneficial to Wilhelm. Almost all were already candidates for the specific post in question, and Eulenburg merely pushed them over their few competitors.

Eulenburg's rise to power and his eventual disgrace might have been different had he been devoted to and allied with a more stable ruler. While some of his contemporaries viewed Wilhelm as a "most authentic and original genius—with the clearest *bon sens* [good sense]," they were decidedly in the minority. Eulenburg, who knew him as well as anyone, was often one of his harshest critics in private. On one occasion he commented that "His [Wilhelm's] self-esteem has grown with experience—which is no experience." On another he remarked, "He likes to teach others but does not like to be taught. . . . Wilhelm II wants to shine, to do, to decide himself. Unfortunately, what he does himself often turns out wrong. . . . In order to get his approval of an idea, one must act as though it is his own." No one was more skilled than Eulenburg at convincing the Kaiser that the ideas for policies and appointments brought to him were, in fact, his own.

It is no wonder that John C. G. Röhl, one of the foremost experts on Wilhelm II and his period, entitled a chapter "Kaiser Wilhelm II: A Suitable Case for Treatment." Wilhelm was immature, arrogant, and temperamental. He tended to personalize his political relationships and had a remarkable ability for seeing the world not as it was, but as he wished it to be. It may be these latter traits that made it possible for him to be genuinely oblivious to Eulenberg's homosexuality.

For most of a decade Phillip zu Eulenburg's shrewd alliances, excellent intelligence, and friendship with the kaiser enabled him to ex-

ercise incomparable political influence. However, toward the end of
the nineteenth century storm clouds began to appear on the horizon.
In 1897 Phillip's younger brother Friedrich had been divorced by his
wife of twenty years, who charged him not only with cruelty but with
"unnatural passions," namely, homosexuality. Despite "Fredi's" efforts
to convince his fellow officers and his powerful brother to support
him, he was court-martialed and disgraced.[2] Moreover, the kaiser
made it abundantly clear to Phillip that brother or no brother, the verdict had his support. Friendship clearly had its limits.

One year later, the brief marriage of Eulenburg's close friend
Kuno von Moltke collapsed in a similar fashion. Although Lily von
Moltke did not take her concerns about her husband's sexual orientation into court, she did share her suspicions and several letters
exchanged between Moltke and Eulenburg with the journalist
Maximilian Harden. Indeed, she blamed her husband's intimate
friendship with Eulenburg for the failure of her marriage. Small
wonder that as his troubles mounted, Eulenburg destroyed all of
his correspondence with Moltke for fear of "the devilish misinter-
pretation which was then being placed on everything which I and
Moltke had ever written."

From 1901 on, there was a series of attempts to pressure (some
would say blackmail) Eulenburg into resigning. His personal political enemies were one group aligned against him; jealous traditional court elites were certainly another. On January 1, 1900, Eulenburg was raised from the rank of count to that of *fürst* (prince).
While many of his friends warned him against accepting the title,
he ignored their advice. Of course, the accusations against him
could not focus on his new title, but they could mention his attraction to spiritism, including seances, mysticism, and other acts of
the supernatural. Most, however, concentrated on his homosexuality.[3] Despite his previous successes, Eulenburg had little stomach
for political infighting and probably understood the dangers involved in mounting a defense against such attacks. In November of
1902 he was allowed to resign. For the next three years, poor
health kept Eulenburg on the sidelines.

Although Eulenburg's power had been diminished considerably
in the wake of his resignation in 1902, he did not totally exit the

---

2. Friedrich's ex-wife later married the chief of the military court-
martial!

3. The association of "deviant" sexual behavior with "deviant" religios-
ity recurs throughout history.

political stage. By August 1905 he was back at the kaiser's side and even engaged in informal negotiations on his behalf. Although neither this episode nor those that followed in early 1906 really amounted to much, they sounded a warning bell for Eulenburg's enemies in government circles and in the press. His investiture with the Order of the Black Eagle, the highest Prussian order, in 1906 gained him even more enemies.[4] Once again, the fiercest actions against him followed closely upon his receiving high honors. Thus attempts to permanently remove him from the kaiser's entourage were renewed in 1906.

The immediate cause seems to have been his alleged role in the dismissal of his former ally Friedrich von Holstein, one of Germany's most experienced diplomats. Shortly after his resignation was accepted, Holstein expressed his astonishment that "somebody who has as much dirt sticking to him as Phillip Eulenburg, who is open to attack from any side you care to choose," should show so little concern for his own welfare. To Eulenburg himself, he wrote, "Your aim of many years . . . my removal—has now at last been achieved. The filthy attacks against me are also in accord with your wishes. . . . I am now free, I need exercise no restraint, and can treat you as one treats a contemptible with your characteristics."

Eulenburg could have had few illusions as to what awaited him. During a three-year period, courts-martial had convicted twenty officers of homosexuality, and in 1906–1907 six officers committed suicide after being blackmailed over the issue. Eulenburg's enemies probably hoped he would follow the same course.

Eulenburg was arrested in May of 1908 on suspicion of homosexuality. His health had deteriorated so much by this time that he was held in a hospital rather than in a prison. The trial, which began in late June, had to be suspended after eighteen days without a verdict because of his condition. An attempt to resume deliberations in 1909 lasted only a few hours as Eulenburg collapsed yet again. Although the suspension of deliberations meant that he could continue to profess his innocence until the day he died, no one seriously believed him, and his political career was finished.

---

4. Eulenburg was thrilled at receiving the honor and wrote to Wilhelm accordingly, "I saw the brightness of your dear gaze, from which streamed joy at being able to make me joyful." His enemies wondered how "one whose *vita sexualis* [sex life] is . . . [not] healthy" could be given such an honor.

If the case against Eulenburg was so strong, why had his enemies not discredited him earlier? Given the general taboo on public discussions of sexuality in general and homosexuality in particular, bringing charges of this kind was no easy matter. When it happened, as in the case of Eulenburg, it inevitably was a cover for other usually political motives.

Evidence, moreover, was hard if not impossible to come by. Men frequently shared a bed, and to characterize Eulenburg as a homosexual is a bit simplistic. He was almost certainly what we would describe today as bisexual. He not only married, but fathered eight children. He also had numerous adulterous affairs with women.[5]

His long and close ties to the kaiser were doubtless yet another factor. Any charges brought against Eulenburg would certainly reflect on his close friend. The fact that the kaiser had met and even rowed with the fisherman who was the chief witness against Eulenburg had the potential to be a major embarrassment. Thus the Eulenburg-ectomy (the removal of Eulenburg from Wilhelm) had to be undertaken with great care, so as to leave the host body intact.

Once the process was set in motion, it was not so easy to control. The accusations against Eulenburg threatened to cast suspicion over much of the country's leadership. They included Reich Chancellor Bernhard von Bülow and two of his brothers, a son of General Gustav von Kessel, General Kuno von Moltke, Counts Hohenau and von Lynar, Prince Friedrich Heinrich of Prussia, Prince Aribert of Anhalt, and many others. Even the kaiser himself was not above suspicion.

It was an embarrassment on a national scale. Maximilian Harden, one of the instigators of the proceedings, spoke openly of the need to cleanse the national soul through either a war or an abdication. "To clear ourselves of the shame and ridicule, we will have to go to war soon or face the sad necessity of making a change of imperial personnel." As several authorities on the period have noted, the Eulenburg affair and the national crisis it engendered was one of the many factors that paved the way for World War I.

Phillip zu Eulenburg's fall from grace was thus far more than a mere personal tragedy. Even Harden, who devoted himself to deposing Eulenburg, conceded that it might have been one of his gravest

---

5. It is worth noting in this context, and in that of our discussions of their contemporary Charles Parnell, that neither Eulenburg nor any of his contemporaries seem to have been tainted by their numerous heterosexual affairs.

mistakes. This admission came about not because he abandoned his abhorrence of homosexuality, but rather because he came to realize that whatever his sexual orientation, Eulenburg was no worse and perhaps far better than many of those who surrounded Kaiser Wilhelm. Given the structure of the kaiser's government and the personal power he exercised, his people had every reason to worry about the kind of people who surrounded him. However, history teaches us that they would have been better advised to direct their concern to issues of public policy, rather than those of private morality.[6] The former of these were to have a far more damaging effect on the German people in the twentieth century than the latter.

SUGGESTIONS FOR FURTHER READING

Boswell, John. *Same-Sex Unions in Premodern Europe.* New York: Villard Books, 1994.

Hull, Isabel V. *The Entourage of Kaiser Wilhelm II 1888–1918.* Cambridge: Cambridge University Press, 1982.

Katz, Jonathan Ned. "'Homosexual' and 'Heterosexual': Questioning the Terms." Pp. 177–80 in Martin Duberman, ed., *A Queer World: The Center for Gay and Lesbian Studies Reader.* New York: New York University Press, 1997.

Rich, Norman. *Friedrich von Holstein: Politics and Diplomacy in the Era of Bismarck and Wilhelm II.* Vol. 2. Cambridge, England: Cambridge University Press, 1965.

Röhl, John C. G. *The Kaiser and His Court: Wilhelm II and the Government of Germany.* Cambridge, Mass.: Cambridge University Press, 1994.

Rowse, A. L. *Homosexuals in History.* London: Weidenfeld and Nicolson, 1977.

Shephard, Robert. "Sexual Rumours in English Politics: The Cases of Elizabeth I and James I." Pp. 101–22 in Jaqueline Murray and Konrad Eisenbichler, eds., *Desire and Discipline: Sex and Sexuality in the Premodern West.* Toronto: University of Toronto Press, 1996.

Spencer, Colin. *Homosexuality in History.* London: Harcourt Brace, 1995.

---

6. Given the focus of this book, I am unable to discuss in detail either Eulenburg's sympathy for "scientific racism" or Wilhelm's virulent anti-Semitism. The latter is discussed in some detail in Röhl, *The Kaiser and His Court.* The fact that Harden was Jewish made it all the more difficult for some circles to accept the charges he leveled. Although Wilhelm did nothing to defend his friend's honor, he did refer to Harden as a "loathsome, dirty Jewish fiend" and "a poisonous toad out of slime hell, a disgraceful stain upon the Volk." Years later, the Nazis attempted to discredit Harden the Jew's attack on the Prussian aristocrat, Eulenburg. They were, of course, motivated by racist instincts and not by any sympathy for homosexuals.

Eleanor and Franklin: public partners and private affairs

How men hate women in a position of real power!

—Eleanor Roosevelt

Thus far, I've divided this book up into discrete chapters, each of which focuses on a specific theme: sleeping your way to the top, adultery, political marriages, homosexuality. As I've already indicated, there is something rather artificial about such a division. Human relationships are far too complex to be reduced to a single theme, however useful this may be from an analytical point of view.

Accordingly, I've decided to abandon the single-theme format in this chapter and show just how complicated such matters can be. The couple I've chosen to focus on is Franklin and Eleanor Roosevelt. While their relationships with each other and with others may not include all the possible permutations we've seen so far, they offer enough variety that we can see just how complicated things can get.

Although the Roosevelts (along with the Kennedys) are one of the most talked- and written-about "first families" in American history, they're certainly not the only White House couple worth writing about. Although they haven't been around for nearly as long as the royal families of Europe, during the more than two centuries since 1776, American presidents and their families have certainly provided enough stories.

A virtual industry, for example, has grown up around the figure of Abigail Adams, wife of President John Adams and mother of President John Quincy Adams (shades of Barbara Bush!). Although she is nowhere as mysterious as Cleopatra, because she left behind lots of letters, as with the legendary Egyptian, every generation seems to have viewed America's second first lady (if that's not a contradiction!) in a different light. While she may not have been the ardent feminist that some scholars claim, her husband's long absences on political business certainly left her with more responsibility than most women of her time. Similarly, although it may be wishful thinking on the part of authors who depict her as her husband's foremost political adviser, the unusual circumstances of her life placed her in a situation whereby the family "business" was the nation and the issues it confronted in its early years.

Abraham Lincoln and Mary Todd Lincoln could have provided yet another fascinating chapter. Not only had Mary been courted by Lincoln's future political rival Stephen Douglas, but she is reputed to have told him, "I shall become Mrs. President, or I am the victim of false prophets, but it will not be as Mrs. Douglas." It is interesting to note that her decision to accompany her husband to Washington when he was elected to Congress in 1846 was rather unusual. At the time, only about one-third of wives joined their husbands, and these were usually childless women who lived in nearby states. (Today, doubtless the decision *not* to move to Washington would be the subject of comment.) During the presidential years, Mary was, moreover, the subject of a minor scandal because of her close ties with William S. Wood, one of her husband's appointments. Not only was Wood as much her choice as his, their friendship led at least one anonymous correspondent to warn the president of the "scandal of your wife and Wood. If he continues as commissioner, he will stab you in your most vital part."[1] However, all things considered, I still think that the most interesting thing about the Todd–Lincoln union is the way it reflected the shredding of the Union at the time. Not only was Mary Todd's father himself a slaveowner (although one with no particular ideological commitment to the insitution), but eight of her siblings or half siblings supported the Confederate cause. While one of her full brothers sup-

---

1. Baker, *Mary Todd Lincoln: A Biography*, 184.

ported the Union, her other full brother served as a surgeon in a Confederate hospital during the war. One can only imagine the personal nature the political debates of the time held for her.

Yet as fascinating as these couples were, neither of them seems to capture all the aspects of the Roosevelts: political struggles, independent opinions, marital crises, and personal secrets.

FRANKLIN AND ELEANOR AND LUCY

I have the memory of an elephant; I can forgive, but I cannot forget.

—Eleanor Roosevelt

Anna Eleanor Roosevelt was born in New York City on October 11, 1884. Her parents, Elliot and Anna (Hall) Roosevelt, both came from distinguished families who could trace themselves back to colonial America. By all accounts, her father was, despite his history of alcoholism, emotional instability, and infidelity,[2] the one great love of her childhood. His death left a void that was never really filled. Indeed, by the time she was ten, both her parents and a younger brother had died, and she was sent to live with her maternal grandmother. There she found all the stability her parents had failed to provide, but coupled with strict discipline and a distinct lack of warmth.

Owing to their close family ties, Eleanor's father was Franklin's godfather, and Eleanor had known Franklin, literally, all her life. According to family tradition, one of their earliest meetings ended when he carried the two-year-old Eleanor back to the nursery on his shoulders. However, the two only saw each other sporadically over the years. Thus, it was only following Eleanor's return from several years of schooling in London that they reconnected and began to see each other socially. Like his godfather, Franklin was warm, witty, and socially adept. But his widowed mother was so protective that he found it difficult to pursue serious relationships. Eleanor was family, however, and was free to visit whenever she chose. In a short time, she was deeply in love with Franklin, and on March 17, 1905, they married.

As we saw in chapter 6, political marriages were usually designed to promote the fortunes of families and nations. In most

---

2. Her father suffered from serious psychological problems throughout his life and fathered a child by one of the family's maids.

cases, men were the direct beneficiaries of such arrangements, and women, if not always victims, usually profited only indirectly. Obviously, this was not a political marriage, or even an arranged marriage in the traditional sense. Neither of them was *required* to marry the other, nor did the marriage create any diplomatic or political alliances. Indeed, Franklin's mother seems not to have approved of the union and did her best to make the young Eleanor feel like an outsider. Nevertheless, over the course of time, their pairing evolved into a political union that provided the family life and stability Franklin needed to pursue his growing ambitions. This, in turn, offered Eleanor an unprecedented opportunity to place the political causes dear to her on the national political agenda. This was particularly important over the course of time as it became clear just how ill matched the two Roosevelts were in many ways.

Franklin and Eleanor had never been truly compatible when it came to socializing. He was spontaneous, warm, and outgoing, and the parties he organized often left her, by her testimony, feeling like a "spoil-sport and a police woman." As happens with so many couples, the two drifted apart,[3] with her drawing satisfaction from her friends and causes and him finding pleasure with friends and other women. In the fall of 1918, Franklin was stricken with double pneumonia. When Eleanor went to clear out his things, she found among his papers intimate letters from Lucy Mercer, her social secretary, which left no doubt that Lucy and Franklin were having an affair. We can only imagine how devastating this must have been for her. I can't help but wonder if she read *all* the letters, or (as I would have advised her) put them away once she knew what she had to know. Whether she read them all or not, her relationship with Franklin suffered a fatal blow. Whatever hopes she may have harbored for their marriage, as their son James recalled many years later, after the Lucy Mercer affair, Franklin and Eleanor "agreed to go on for the sake of appearances, the children and the future, but as business partners, not as husband and wife. . . . After that, father and mother had an armed truce that endured until the day he died." Things doubtless would have been worse had she known that, contrary to his promises, Franklin continued to see Lucy literally until the day he died.

---

3. On how to avoid such situations, see my recent book prepared with my "Minister of Communications" Pierre Lehu, *Rekindling Romance for Dummies*, Foster City: IDG Books, 2001!

Although Eleanor offered Franklin a divorce, he was not willing to pay the price this would have exacted. To be sure, their children were one major consideration.[4] And his mother's adamant disapproval was another. (Despite his reputation for national leadership, Franklin Roosevelt never managed to free himself from his mother's apron strings.) Both in his life and increasingly in Eleanor's, it became clear that their political goals were more important than any personal problems. While many politicians in the past, and even today, maintain the façade of a happy family life for the sake of political gain, the Roosevelts appear to have added a new twist to this old ruse. In most cases, male politicians have had affairs and their wives remained loyal (see Jackie Kennedy in chapter 10), if not faithful, in order not to lose their status and prestige. Eleanor, however, entered into a bargain that demanded more of her than it did of most political wives, but offered her more as well. Although she could not have known it at the time that she discovered his infidelity, Eleanor would soon be called upon to play an unprecedented public role. In 1921 Franklin was struck with polio, which was to leave him dependent on a wheelchair for the rest of his life. Because of Franklin's infirmity, Eleanor became a sort of roving ambassador, campaigning on his behalf and serving as his eyes as she traveled around the United States. However, her role was not merely limited to representing her husband. Rather, she was given the opportunity to pursue, if not always with FDR's blessing at least with his agreement, her own political causes. This she did with enthusiasm and unbounded energy.

While many people from privileged backgrounds have identified with and devoted themselves to the less fortunate, few have done it so wholeheartedly and with such singular devotion as Eleanor. It is small wonder that she appeared on almost every list of the most admired women of the twentieth century. It is important to note that her deep interest in social justice long preceded either her marriage to Franklin or their marital problems. Indeed, her concern for the downtrodden could be said to be the most constant theme in her life, more so than her husband, her children, or even her most intimate friends. If ever a person can justly be said to have been ahead of her times, it was Eleanor Roosevelt. The causes she championed—women's rights, civil

4. The Roosevelts had six children, five of whom survived infancy. They were to a considerable degree raised by his mother, Sara Roosevelt.

rights, and human rights—are arguably the three great social movements of the second half of the twentieth century.

In the past, Eleanor's political and humanitarian activities, both during her marriage and after, have captured the bulk of the attention of her biographers. Her groundbreaking, almost prophetic role in pushing what were often unpopular causes granted her an almost legendary status, particularly among liberal democratic circles.[5] However, in recent years, in keeping with the trend in modern biography, it is her private life that has garnered the headlines. Suddenly the dowdy, even in some eyes homely, Mrs. Roosevelt has been discovered to have had an enormously rich personal life, which included both men and women.[6] Eleanor may have made many sacrifices for the sake of her marriage and her husband's position, but her private emotional life does not appear to have been one of them.

THE EARL AND THE LADY

In 1929, while Franklin Roosevelt was serving as governor of New York, a problem arose with regard to the security of the state's first lady. Although Eleanor was provided with a limousine and a driver, she insisted on driving her own car. Unable to convince her to budge on the issue, Franklin was able to persuade her to accept a bodyguard. His choice was an athletic thirty-two-year-old state trooper by the name of Earl Miller. Miller, whose credentials included stints as a circus acrobat, boxer, and gymnast, had known the governor since the latter's stint as assistant secretary of the navy.

At first glance, it's hard to imagine a more unlikely pairing than the forty-four-year-old Eleanor and the carefree former naval officer. Perhaps it was a matter of opposites attracting. Whatever the basis, the two developed an intimate friendship that lasted more than thirty years and proved more durable than any of his marriages. Perhaps more than anyone in her life, to quote son James,

> (Earl Miller) encouraged her to take pride in herself, to be herself, to be unafraid of facing the world. He did a lot of good for her. She seemed to draw strength from him when he was by her side, and she

5. While Eleanor certainly had her enemies, they were overwhelmingly *political* enemies.

6. There is, of course, no basis for the widespread prejudice that beauty and sexual passion are linked.

came to rely on him. When she had problems, she sought his help.
. . . Above all, he made her feel that she was a woman.

You don't have to look very far to understand the reasons behind Eleanor's affection for Earl Miller. He was not only handsome
and athletic, but also protective and gallant. His loyalty to her was
unwavering. Although his claim that she would have made a better president than Franklin was not taken seriously by most, he un-
doubtedly meant it. At a time when others wished her to be more
sedate and dignified, he taught her to shoot and dive, coached her
at tennis, and bought a mare for her to ride daily.

Was it more than a friendship? As in many other cases I have
discussed in this book, we will never know for sure. It is, however,
striking to note the extent to which Earl and Eleanor went to keep
the details of their relationship a secret, not only in their lifetimes
but after. Even her relationship with Lorena Hickok (see below) appears remarkably well documented in comparison to her ties with
Earl. While there was, by all accounts, an extensive correspondence between the two for many years, none of their letters have
survived. (Perhaps they had learned a lesson from Franklin's indis-
cretion with Lucy Mercer?) Eleanor's memoir, *This I Remember*,
barely mentions him. Although Earl was more than happy to discuss his failed marriages and other aspects of his life candidly with
biographers, his relationship with ER remained virtually off-limits.

Roosevelt biographer Joseph Lash was convinced that there was
no romance, but ER's son James didn't see it this way, writing: "I
believe there may have been one real romance in mother's life outside of marriage. Mother may have had an affair with Earl Miller."
We will never know for sure. Although many believed Eleanor to
be the mysterious correspondent whose love letters were introduced into evidence in Miller's 1947 divorce proceedings, these
were never made public.

Whatever we may conclude about Eleanor Roosevelt's relationship with Earl Miller, whether we view it as an intimate friendship
or much more than that, it certainly challenges some of the stereo-
types about her and other women like her (if we can really speak
of such a thing). Neither her age nor his comparative youth, her
patrician background nor his taste for the common, his manly good
looks nor her alleged homeliness seem to have prevented the two
from bonding and sharing their lives over several decades. Whatever they may have done together in private, no one can doubt the
depth of their commitment to each other.

JUST GOOD FRIENDS?

If the speculation concerning Eleanor's relationship with Earl Miller came as a surprise to many, recent revelations regarding her connection to the journalist Lorena Hickok have been nothing less than a shock. Doris Faber, the author of *The Life of Lorena Hickok: ER's Friend* and probably the first person to understand the full significance of their connection, was more appalled than excited by her discovery. Faber tried to get the more than 3,000 letters exchanged by the two sealed from the public, and when she couldn't do that, she decided to downplay content that reflected on the relationship. About one particularly romantic passage, she declared that there could be little doubt that "it could not mean what it appears to mean."

Roosevelt and Lorena A. Hickok began their relationship in 1932 during FDR's first campaign for the presidency. Struck by Eleanor's surprising ambivalence to her husband's success, Hick (as everyone called her) suggested to her editors at the Associated Press the then-revolutionary idea that a reporter be assigned to cover the candidate's wife. Hickok, who was already a successful reporter, was not trying to wangle a job for herself, and initially one of her colleagues, Katherine Beebe, was given the assignment. However, when Beebe resigned shortly before the election, Hickok inherited the job. By the time Eleanor had become first lady the two were such close friends that Hickok found it impossible to cover her as a reporter. Their relationship, however, had just begun. They developed an emotional and romantic relationship that peaked in passion and later developed into a friendship that endured until death. Over the course of the next thirty years, they were to exchange over 3,000 letters, many of them not short notes, but epistles that extended over ten or even fifteen pages.

As biographer Blanche Wiesen Cook has noted in the first two volumes of what promises to be for many years the definitive biography of Eleanor Roosevelt, there can be little doubt that after 1920 many of "Eleanor's closest friends were lesbian women. She honored their relationships, and their privacy. She protected their secrets and kept her own."

Does this mean that she and Hick had a lesbian relationship? Paradoxically, some of the strongest evidence for the relationship these two women shared is, as in the case of Earl Miller, the fact that much of their correspondence has been destroyed. Hick herself edited and retyped some letters, and burned others. Her sister Ruby destroyed even more, throwing them in the fireplace, saying,

"This is nobody's business." Nevertheless, many of ER's letters indicate a romantic attachment.

The recent publication of a collection entitled *Empty without You: The Intimate Letters of Eleanor Roosevelt and Lorena Hickok* means that each of us can read the letters and draw our own conclusions. I offer these short excerpts to the thoughtful reader.

March 7, 1933

Hick darling,

All day I've thought of you & another birthday I will be with you, & yet tonite you sounded so far away & formal. Oh! I want to put my arms around you. I ache to hold you close. Your ring is a great comfort to me. I look at it and think she does love me, or I wouldn't be wearing it.

[Date not provided]

[ER to Hick]

I wish I could lie down beside you tonight & take you in my arms.

Only eight more days. . . . Funny how even the dearest face will fade away in time. Most clearly I remember your eyes, with a kind of teasing smile in them, and the feeling of that soft spot just north-east of the corner of your mouth against my lips . . .

Now if this is the sort of material that has survived, we can only speculate as to what sort of material was felt to be too hot to handle! It certainly flies in the face of any assumption that the middle-aged Eleanor (or any other woman for that matter) no longer led a life of romance and passion.

Nevertheless, I must note, in the interest of balance, that several distinguished Roosevelt biographers, while mindful of her intimate relationship with Hickok, do not believe it was ever consummated. Given how progressive Eleanor Roosevelt was in her political and social views, it is easy to forget that she was born and grew to maturity in the last years of the nineteenth century. Ironically, given her later championing of women's issues, she was, in her youth, opposed to granting women the vote! Moreover, at least some of the surviving evidence indicates that her personal sexual attitudes were as conservative as her political views were progressive and liberal.[7] According to the testimony of friends, she expressed revulsion

---

7. Whatever her personal preferences, as we have seen, Eleanor was tolerant and supportive of others regardless of their sexual preferences.

toward homosexuality, and she told her daughter Anna that sex was something to be endured more than enjoyed. Indeed, the same daughter recalled that her mother used to tie her hands to the bars of her crib to keep her from masturbating. By her own testimony, her uncle Eddie's and brother Vallie's drinking and loss of self-control "effectively develop[ed] in me an almost exaggerated idea of the necessity of keeping all of one's desires under complete subjugation." While none of this is conclusive, it is at least a strong caution against *assuming* that Eleanor's intimate relations (or anyone's for that matter) were automatically sexual relationships. Could the woman who wrote such words have been sexually involved with Earl Miller, Lorena Hickock, or both? If so, she would not be the first (or the last) person whose public pronouncements were at odds with her private deeds.

In the final analysis, we may never know the truth about the physical aspects of Eleanor's relationship with either Earl Miller or Lorena Hickok. There appears to be little doubt that both relationships were intimate, erotic, and probably what we would call, for want of a better word, romantic. It is, I suppose, typical of the era we live in that it is the speculation about Eleanor's sex life that has brought her back into the public eye. No doubt she would be appalled—not because of any embarrassment regarding her behavior, but rather because throughout her life her concern for others and for their causes always seemed to be more important to her than her own personal activities. By saying this, I don't go back to the old image of a nurturing woman who denied her own needs to meet the needs of others, but rather I suggest that once again, to quote Eleanor herself, "the most important thing in any relationship is not what you get but what you give."

~

There are several reasons why I decided to put the story of Franklin and Eleanor at the end of this book. Thematically speaking, it would have fit in any one of a number of chapters: political marriages, mistresses, infidelity, lesbianism, etc. However, it is just this diversity and richness that make it such an appropriate story to conclude our journey into the past. Human relationships are never simple and one-dimensional. The Roosevelts provide an excellent example of this. Their story, even if told only from their perspectives, is, in fact, many stories. It is not only theirs, but also Lucy Mercer's, Earl Miller's, Lorena Hickok's, and others'.

Yet another reason for concluding with the Roosevelts is that the "scandals" of their time teach us a great deal about our own. Despite the rumors and speculation, none of these stories ever gained the media status of "scandal." The press (and despite the success of radio, newspapers were still the dominant form of media), to the extent that it was aware of these relationships, was as discreet about them as it was about Franklin's chronic health problems.[8] The norms of their time offered them protection, almost immunity, from public discussion of their private lives. The norms of ours almost guarantee that their private lives will be the most discussed part of any future biographies.

Finally, I have chosen to conclude with the Roosevelts because, as rich as their personal lives may have been, these stories pale in comparison to the roles Franklin and Eleanor played in the history of the twentieth century. Franklin's affair with Lucy Mercer should not blind us to the political legacy he left after more than three terms as president, from the time of the Great Depression to throughout much of World War II. Nor should the speculation about Eleanor lead us to overlook her lifelong devotion to the poor and oppressed.

SUGGESTIONS FOR FURTHER READING

Baker, Jean H. *Mary Todd Lincoln: A Biography*. New York: Norton, 1987.

Beasley, Maurine H. *Eleanor Roosevelt and the Media: A Public Quest for Self-Fulfillment*. Urbana: University of Illinois Press, 1987.

Cook, Blanche Wiesen. *Eleanor Roosevelt 1884–1933*. New York: Viking, 1992.

——. *Eleanor Roosevelt 1933–1938*. New York: Viking, 1999.

Faber, Doris. *The Life of Lorena Hickok: ER's Friend*. New York: W. Morrow, 1980.

Gelles, Edith B. "The Abigail Industry." *William and Mary Quarterly* 45 (1988): 656–83.

Hoff-Wilson, Joan, and Marjorie Lightman, eds. *Without Precedent: The Life and Career of Eleanor Roosevelt*. Bloomington: Indiana University Press, 1984.

Lash, Joseph P. *Eleanor and Franklin*. New York: Norton, 1971.

——. *Love Eleanor: Eleanor Roosevelt and Her Friends*. Garden City, N.Y.: Doubleday, 1982.

Levin, Phyllis Lee. *Abigail Adams: A Biography*. New York: St. Martin's, 1987.

---

8. Earl Miller also played a role in silencing rumors about FDR's health. When several Georgia newspapers questioned whether Roosevelt had the stamina to be president, Earl arranged for a four-mile horse ride in the company of a reporter and photographer from the *Atlanta Journal*.

Roosevelt, Eleanor. *This Is My Story*. New York: Harper & Brothers, 1937.

Roosevelt, Eleanor, and Lorena A. Hickok. *Empty without You: The Intimate Letters of Eleanor Roosevelt and Lorena Hickok*. Edited by Rodger Streitmatter. New York: Free Press, 1998.

Roosevelt, James. *My Parents: A Differing View*. Chicago: Playboy Press, 1976.

http://personalweb.smcvt.edu/smahady/ercover.htm

http://content.gay.com/channels/news/women/eleanor_000301.html

http://www.gaygate.com/media/pages/elanoros.shtml

conclusion

The stories I have discussed here are really only the tip of the iceberg. If I had the time or the space, I could easily include another dozen, just as interesting and thought provoking. But I don't think either my readers or publishers would really tolerate that. So, having considered each of our stories on its own merit, the time has now come for me to attempt to draw some conclusions from this wealth of material.

SEXUAL NORMS: PAST AND PRESENT, NEAR AND FAR

Perhaps the clearest message that emerges from all of this is that the *sexual norms expected of leaders have varied from period to period and from country to country*. A Chinese emperor could have as many wives and concubines as he wished, but it was hoped that he wouldn't care too much for any of them. Being promiscuous was acceptable; deep emotional attachment was not. In many societies, kings and other rulers were *expected* to have mistresses. Indeed, in many places and in many periods, the common folk took pride in the excesses and profligacy of their rulers. Behavior that would have shocked us today was taken as a matter of course or even considered a necessary and positive aspect of the political system. And before we begin to think that this means that we necessarily have the moral upper hand, it should be remembered that divorce, which even a generation or two ago was considered a moral stain, is today not given a second thought by most people in electing their leaders.

Although it has often been claimed that the twentieth century saw a decline in sexual morality, particularly among politicians, there is little historical evidence for such a claim. Indeed, precisely the opposite can be argued. After decades, even centuries, in which political leaders and other powerful people were given a special dispensation and allowed to engage in exceptional behavior, there is now an increasing demand for accountability from our leaders. In other words, I would like to suggest that had rulers from other periods been subjected to the same scrutiny *and* judged by the same standards as our leaders are today, many of them would not have fared very well. In phrasing things this way, I am trying to strike an appropriate balance between those who claim that our current wave of scandals is merely a product of media frenzy (I think that's an exaggeration) and those who believe that there has been a major decline in the actual behavior of our leaders (another rather dubious proposition). Given some of my own experiences, I would hardly deny the role of the media, and I will consider this in some detail below. However, before we turn to this subject, we must do justice to some other trends.

Perhaps the most important of these is the democratization of sexual norms. Over the course of time, with the spread of democratic traditions, *people have increasingly expected their leaders to conduct themselves according to the same standards that they themselves observed or were expected to observe.*

In earlier times, leaders were rarely expected to conform to the same norms of behavior imposed on the average person. This was true in many realms. They dressed differently, ate differently, spoke differently. In many cases, it was almost as if they were a different ("blue blooded") species of person. It should be noted that even the assumption of a separate set of sexual norms for leaders applied differently to different leaders. Secular rulers were given the right to engage in behavior for which commoners would have been publicly condemned.[1] In contrast, in many societies—Catholic Europe was most notable in this respect—spiritual leaders were bound by a different code: one of celibacy and abstinence. Thus a triple standard seems to have applied with rulers, clergy, and common people, each being judged by a different set of norms.

Today, at the dawn of the twenty-first century, these expectations appear to have largely eroded. Viewed from this perspective, I don't think it's accidental that the demand for greater accountability on behalf of politicians and, where they still exist, royalty has come at the same time as increasing calls for the abandonment of celibacy as a norm among the Catholic clergy. Both are indicative of the growing expectation that our leaders should be models of the same type of behavior we expect of ourselves and not bound by either a higher or a lower standard.

I think the theme of democratization is relevant in another crucial respect. One of the things I've been asking myself over and over again is, "Why are we so fascinated by the private lives of powerful figures past and present?" Or to put things another way, if every generation rewrites history to make it meaningful in the present, why are we rewriting the past (and focusing so much in the present) on the sexual behavior of those with power? There are probably an infinite number of possible explanations, but I would like to offer one that I haven't seen mentioned before.

At least in part, it seems to me that our desire, even need, to know about the sex lives, and especially the sexual weaknesses, of our leaders is part of an attempt to humanize them, to bring them closer. If in the past people were happy to be ruled by their superiors, today this is no longer so obviously the case. While we want our leaders to be wise, honest, and effective, on some very deep level, we also want them to be human and approachable. Given the distance that separates us from them, this is not easy to achieve.

One way we try to bridge the gap is by identifying in our leaders the same basic human wants and desires that we have. And sex is about as human a desire as there is! It is interesting in this context to note that we don't limit this exercise to our current rulers or heroes. One of the things I found most surprising in preparing this book is how much interest there is in the private

---

1. As we saw in our discussion of Cleopatra, Egyptian rulers were allowed or even expected to establish "incestuous" marriages in which they married their siblings or other individuals considered off-limits to mere commoners.

lives and sexual behavior of figures from the past. Hardly a month seems to go by without some new revelation about the sex life of some famous politician, artist, or tycoon. Moreover, the Web is overflowing with speculation, debates, and discussions about the personal practices of people who lived not only before *it* was invented, but before the invention of the printing press! As I indicated in my introduction, at times there is so much written about the human failings of great figures that one can easily lose sight of their human triumphs.

While it's easy to dismiss or condemn this demolition of heroes, I'd like to at least suggest that the motives behind it are not totally cynical or destructive. *Sometimes bringing someone down seems to be the only way to bring them closer.* By showing that these people share the same weaknesses and desires as we do, we succeed in a strange, even perverse, way in bringing them closer, in making them more recognizably human. Of course, the terribly unfortunate part of this is, all too often, the only way we seem to be able to bring them closer is to bring them down. If in the past heroes were a symbol of the best humans could attain and celebrated for being exceptional, today they seem to be more representative, if not of the worst, at least of the most common.

SEX AND POLITICS

One of the things we often hear is that a leader's private life is just that, *private*, and it really isn't anyone else's business. One of the biggest surprises for me in writing this book has been the frequency with which sexual relationships had a real impact on political matters. When I started out, I figured that however interesting the stories might be, they were not all that relevant to the politics of the day. In fact, many of the examples studied above have indicated that few leaders have been able to completely preserve the distinction between public and private. Called upon to face what seems to me to be a crucial test, many of the rulers and leaders I looked at seem to have blurred the distinction between their personal lives and their public duties.

Ironically, given her reputation, Catherine the Great generally refused to give her favorites jobs beyond their abilities. While she faltered somewhat in her later years, her reliance on Orlov, Potemkin, and her earlier lovers seems to have been measured and weighed carefully. Similarly, it is hard to see the immediate political relevance of either Franklin or Eleanor Roosevelt's private affairs. However, while Julius Caesar's relationship with Cleopatra does not appear to have had a critical impact on his political judgment, the same cannot be said for Mark Antony. Much like Emperor Xuan's love for his concubine, Antony's devotion to Cleopatra seems to have seriously undermined both his fiscal prudence and political judgment. Parnell's love for Mrs. O'Shea put him and the Irish national cause at the mercy of her unscrupulous husband, and JFK's promiscuity made him vulnerable to political blackmail. While neither Christina nor Elizabeth seems to have fallen victim to such errors of judgment, one relinquished her sex life (at least publicly), creating a potential political crisis, and the other her throne. Juan Perón's delegation of so much power to Evita was certainly a questionable tactic. Indeed, the private businessman Aristotle Onassis seems to have been unusual here in that none of his wives or lovers seem to have had much to say about the way he ran his financial empire. Even here, however, his marriage to a daughter of a business rival shows that the lines were not always clear.

Having acknowledged that the bedroom, the boardroom, and the cabinet room are not easy to separate, I should also point out that *there is very little support in the historical record for drawing a connection between power, people's sex lives, and their political or economic successes.* Despite modern discussions of the personal foibles of politicians that try to draw a connection between their behavior in the bedroom and their public lives—the so-called character issue—the empirical case for this connection is very weak. While it is possible, as we have seen, to point out parallels between Aristotle Onassis's pursuit of women and the way he conducted his business affairs, the *content* of his decisions does not appear to have been shaped by his libido. Moreover, while an older executive or politician married to an attractive younger woman may be trying to convey a message of vitality and success, I've yet to see any studies that indicate that such leaders are more dynamic in their policies or produce larger profits than their counterparts. Similarly, there is, to the best of my knowledge, no data supporting the idea that divorcees lack the character or communication skills to keep a company running smoothly. In fact, there is at least some anecdotal evidence that suggests that the personal experience of a divorce may make an executive more sensitive to his or her employees' lives.

The link between sexual escapades and political success is even more questionable in the case of politicians, kings, and queens. To quote an article that appeared in *Psychology Today* in 1992:

> History shows that libertines have provided the world with some of its best rulers. Take Louis IV or Catherine the Great. Mazarin or Potemkin. Metternich or Talleyrand. Edward VII was an admirable diplomat of tact and wisdom, who kept Europe's powderkeg at peace until his death in 1910. Today, neither Franklin Roosevelt nor David Lloyd-George (known as "the goat" for his libidinous athletics) would have likely been elected, because they had mistresses.[2]

Whatever impact John Kennedy's sexual indiscretions may have had on his effectiveness as president, it is hard to find a clear link between his personal life and political performance. To be sure, some have claimed that JFK's fascination with covert operations and brinkmanship was just another way of proving his manhood. But on the whole Kennedy appears to have been as deliberate and cautious in his formulation of policy as he was reckless and impulsive in pursuing women. He may have admired James Bond, but he rarely seems to have used Ian Fleming's books to formulate his policies.

We may never know the truth about Christina of Sweden's sexual preferences, but there seems to be little question that she guided her country through a difficult period and left it better off than when she assumed the throne. Her ambiguous (at least to us) sexuality finds no echo in her record of decisive political decisions and resolute action.

To look at the other side of the equation, as more than one observer has commented, some of history's most infamous rulers had personal lives that were above reproach. This hardly makes their records of aggression, murder, and even genocide more acceptable. All in all, the "character issue" seems to be a nonstarter at least so far as it posits a link between sexual behavior and political performance.

~

As I noted in the introduction, one of my greatest concerns is that in focusing on the sex lives of wealthy and powerful figures, I may not be doing justice to the richness and complexity of their lives. It has certainly not been my intention to reduce them to one-dimensional

---

2. Simon Sebaf Montefiore, "Royal Scandal: An Insider's Analysis," *Psychology Today* 25, no. 4 (July/August 1992): 36.

characters. In fact, in many cases the impact and consequences of a particular person's personal behavior can only be fully understood in the fuller context of his or her life and times.

What makes the Thomas Jefferson–Sally Hemings controversy so interesting is not so much the personal aspects, but the manner in which it encapsulates the complexity and contradictions of the slaveowner–slave relationship in general and Jefferson's conflicts in particular. It is impossible to read Jefferson's writings on freedom, equality, and slavery without considering the relationship he was engaged in for so much of his life. Charles Parnell's political demise would not have been nearly as poignant and tragic if his long-standing romance with an Englishwoman had not had such grave consequences for the Irish national movement. Elizabeth I's refusal to marry would not have engendered so much controversy had England not suffered through years of upheaval over succession to the throne and the monarchy's relationship to the Catholic Church. Phillip zu Eulenburg's expulsion from Kaiser Wilhelm's inner circle would not be nearly as interesting if it were not so very symptomatic of the time and of the inherent weaknesses in the kaiser's pattern of leadership.

Throughout history, leaders have been forgiven for their personal failings much more readily than for their political or military weaknesses. On the whole, successful, powerful rulers seem to have been able to conduct their personal lives with comparative impunity. The French people may not have approved of the way that Louis XV conducted his private life, but so long as he led his armies to victory, no one seems to have minded very much. High taxes, a shortage of corn, and a disadvantageous peace settlement seem to have caused his and Madame de Pompadour's "drop in the polls" as much as any action on their part. In a similar manner, the criticism that George IV suffered over his treatment of Queen Caroline was in no small measure due to his overall dismal record as a monarch. Julius Caesar may have lost favor with the people and senate of Rome because of his affection for Cleopatra, but it was his dictatorial tendencies that cost him his life. Nor would Antony's devotion to Cleopatra have been viewed quite so seriously had it not been seen to compromise Roman authority and even sovereignty.

I think the case of John Kennedy is interesting to note in this context. Although I haven't carried out systematic research on the topic, it seems to me that attitudes toward his personal life seem to split very closely along political lines. There are plenty of people who admire him politically, and although they don't approve of his personal life, they tend to dismiss it as irrelevant to the larger picture of his career. In contrast, those who oppose or opposed his political agenda seem to view his sexual escapades as a crucial character flaw.

Overall, it's tough to escape the conclusion that most sex scandals teach us a lot more about politics than they do about sex. Often the behaviors for which people were condemned had been going on for years and/or were not that uncommon at the time. Under circumstances of political conflict, crisis, or tension, however, what had previously been tolerated became intolerable or at least the subject of critical scrutiny. Perhaps no one typifies this as much as Elizabeth I, who, as we have seen, was the subject of the harshest criticisms and the most outlandish rumors when her refusal to marry threatened to provoke a political crisis of enormous dimensions.

DOUBLE STANDARDS

Just a moment ago, I commented on the triple standard (royalty, clergy, commoner) that existed in many societies in the past. Now I'd like to comment on a double (gender-based) standard that is still very much with us. *Although norms have tended to vary over time and over space, the sexual norms expected of female leaders are different from those expected of their male counterparts.* This double standard is alive and well. As much as we may like to believe that we live in a more enlightened age, there's little evidence of this when it comes to the judgments made about male and female politicians. Female politicians are held to a different (and usually higher) standard of behavior than their male counterparts.

In part, this has to do with our biases about age as much as our biases about gender. Since the rich and powerful tend to be older than the poor and weak, woman leaders start out at an immediate disadvantage. Catherine's dalliances with men many years her junior were considered scandalous, while similar age gaps between male leaders and their lovers raised nary an eyebrow. We haven't progressed very far on this score. Male business leaders and executives who marry women twenty years their junior are considered vital and dynamic; their female counterparts who would pursue a similar course would be considered slightly ridiculous.

In part this seems to be based on our deep-seated prejudice that men are valued for their achievements and wealth, which accumulate with age, while women are valued for their looks, which follow a different trend. Another part of this equation seems to be some unspoken assumptions about male and female sexuality. Perhaps because men can continue to father children into an advanced age, while women lose their childbearing ability, there seems to be a very mistaken belief that men continue to be interested in sex no matter what their age, while women don't. Although this little bit of folk wisdom flies in the face of most of what is known about the sexual development of men and women, it still has tremendous strength. If a younger woman's sexual desires may be frightening, those of an older woman seem comical.

Whatever the reasons may be, there's little question that powerful women continue to be judged by a different standard. We still don't see many "trophy husbands," and a female politician who conducted a romance with an intern half her age would probably have been committing political suicide.

The survival of the double standard is not limited to the different code of conduct applied to men and women. It is also expressed in the way we interpret different types of behavior. Despite everything we've learned over the past few decades, we still tend to understand many aspects of male–female relations in terms of active males and passive females. The trophy wife, sometimes in contradiction to her own testimony, is assumed to be the prize rather than the hunter. The powerful man *has* a mistress; she doesn't have him.

It's also interesting to see how the double standards can influence historical judgments. In the case of the Turkish harem, even women rulers who were moderately successful seem to have been evaluated negatively. The Chinese concubine Yang Guifei seems to have been blamed for the fall of an entire dynasty, although she had, at best, an indirect impact on government policy. Catherine is best remembered not for her political achievements, but for her legendary sexual exploits and the totally fictitious story of her death. Even Cleopatra, who can be said to have served her country very well through her romances, is remembered more for her relationships than for the politics behind them and is viewed far more critically than either Julius Caesar or Mark Antony.

EVERY STORY IS, IN FACT, SEVERAL STORIES

When I was compiling this book there really was no problem finding plenty of interesting stories. It was, however, much harder to decide what aspect of each story to emphasize. By their very nature, stories of human relations don't break down neatly into single stories with clear unilinear narratives. They are, by their very nature, complex and complicated. Only in the final chapter on Eleanor and

Franklin was I able to begin to do justice to this universal truth. All the others were, by necessity, treated more simply.

The story of Juan and Eva Perón is the story of a powerful man and his mistress/wife and also the story of an ambitious woman's rise to power. The story of Parnell and O'Shea looks very different from Captain O'Shea's perspective, and different again from Kitty's. Although I chose George IV and Caroline as my example of a "political marriage," Louis XV, Catherine the Great, the Turkish harem, and even Elizabeth I also provide us with insight on this phenomenon.

Although the different episodes could have been used to illustrate different themes, the relationships themselves are far more complex than is commonly depicted. In contrast to the often loveless political marriage, many of the "illegitimate" relationships were emotionally rich and enduring. The connections between Louis XV and Madame de Pompadour and between Catherine the Great and Grigory Potemkin transcended the initial sexual basis and developed into deep friendships and, in the case of the Russians, a working partnership. Charles Parnell's relationship with Kitty O'Shea was one that most married couples would have envied, whatever its legal status.

One of the problems with media coverage of today's stories is that much of this richness is lost because of the need to produce a neat one-dimensional narrative. While the "sexy" parts of the story get rehashed ad infinitum, the more complex human elements tend to be lost. Now, I realize this "dumbing down" of the stories is one of the reasons they get so much attention, but it's really a shame that the most complex stories, those about human relationships, get treated this way.

However, there is yet another level to the complexity of these stories. Although some are, at times, truly unusual events detached from the larger context of sexual and social relations in their time, this is the exception rather than the rule. As I have tried to show throughout this book, the stories I have examined in detail are generally representative of larger trends in society and have to be understood in that context.

THE MEDIA

The modern fascination with the sex lives of the rich and powerful is not all that new; however, modern technology and the multiplicity of sources mean that there is quantitatively more material presented.

In George Orwell's futuristic novel *1984*, every feature of an individual's life is open to government scrutiny because *Big Brother Is Watching You!* That novel is still probably the classic expression of the widespread fear that modern technology will enable governments to scrutinize every aspect of individual private lives. Historically, there appears to have been far less concern that the private sector, particularly the media, would overstep its bounds. Perhaps this is because, even to this day, the average citizen is usually not the victim of tabloid headlines, but the consumer of them.

Although the American media was far more respectful in its attitude toward the powerful in some periods of the past, this does not mean that powerful people in all times and places were exempt from scrutiny or even ridicule. Thomas Jefferson had to contend with painful speculation about his relationship with Sally Hemings throughout much of his political life. Contemporary pamphleteers and cartoonists had a field day when George IV tried to divorce Queen Caroline, and even the more serious papers understood that detailed coverage of the hearings could boost their circulation. Elizabeth I was the subject of all sorts of scandalous speculation about her sex life (or lack thereof), and Catherine the Great's sexual appetite appears to have been exceeded only by the exaggerated reports that appeared both at home and abroad.

Although the press often justifies its publication of intimate details of politicians' private lives by claiming the public has a "right to know," this is more than a little self-serving. Few papers and television stations welcome intensive scrutiny of their inner workings, much less the private lives of their reporters and other staff members. Moreover, only a small number of high-quality news outlets are willing to undertake in-depth coverage of a serious scandal unless they think it will bring in viewers or readers.

Polls show that people are highly critical of the press, condemning its preoccupation with sex and scandal. Yet such stories grab high ratings day after day. Perhaps the people who are complaining are not the people who are watching. Or it's a case of the old joke about someone condemning a particular book or movie as pornographic, and saying they hated it every time they watched it.

Of course politicians themselves are not blameless in this respect. To an increasing extent, they have encouraged the blurring of the boundaries between politics and entertainment. Candidates regularly appear on late-night talk shows and politicians often show up in films (*Dave, Contact*) and on sitcoms (*Murphy Brown, Sportsnight,*

Lateline) "playing" themselves and raising the question of how different they are from other celebrities.

Finally, I'd like to say a word about one aspect of the media's treatment of leaders' sex lives that hasn't been considered enough: its relationship to the judicial system. While press coverage of many of the figures I've discussed (Parnell, Eulenburg, George IV) was highly critical and played a major role not only in reflecting the public's perception but in shaping it, it should be noted that it was the judicial system, not the media, that caused them the greatest damage. The press seems to have been largely ignorant of, or to have chosen to ignore, Parnell's unusual domestic arrangement, but the divorce trial made it a matter of public record. Few people could have been ignorant of George IV's shabby treatment of his queen, which had endured for years, but the legal proceedings against her turned their relationship into a media circus. While Eulenburg's downfall may have been instigated by a hostile journalist, it was largely an individual initiative rather than a concerted campaign. His trial, however, could not be ignored, and his perjury doomed him. Put rather simply, in the past the press may have served as accuser and even prosecutor, but rarely as judge and jury.

WHERE ARE WE HEADING?

This is a book about history, not about prophecy. I have no intention of taking on the mantle of Nostradamus, Jeane Dixon, or the people who write the horoscopes in the daily paper. However, I would like to offer some suggestions as to where I think we're heading with all of this.

First, let me say that I see no reason to believe that people are going to become any less interested in the personal lives of the rich and powerful. They've been writing and speculating about it for at least thousands of years, in places as far apart as biblical Israel and ancient China, and I just don't think that's going to change. As long as people are interested, the media—books, movies, television, newspapers, and websites—are going to continue to cater (some would say pander) to the public's thirst for such information.

What seems far less predictable, however, is what we are going to do with such information. I tend to believe (and perhaps this is wishful thinking) that we're slowly evolving toward a situation in which the public attitude toward the private lives of politicians will increasingly resemble the one it takes regarding other "celebrities," like actors, singers, and athletes, all of whom tend to be judged by the "product" they produce rather than by the lives they live.

If there's one area of mass communication I know really well, it's writing and talking about sex. Whatever else we may say about the twentieth century, never has so much reliable, scientifically based information been available to so many people with such ease. And as study after study has shown, the more *information* people have, the more able they are to make *informed* decisions in their lives. I see no reason why this trend shouldn't extend into their judgments about others as well. Sure, there's always going to be the fun and novelty of looking behind closed doors, but there's also going to be an increasing sense of what matters and what doesn't.

One of the reasons media coverage of politicians' personal lives has developed as it has in recent years is that the media itself has been in a period of dramatic expansion and transition. The emergence in the past two decades of both cable television and the Internet has opened up the closed world to mass media in an unprecedented fashion. Now, at the risk of biting the hand that feeds me, it should be noted that the mass media is one area of the modern economy in which competition reduces the quality of the product. Not surprisingly, the world of established journalism has been caught rather flat-footed and often finds itself uncritically following the lead of the newcomers. However, as things shake down, I think we'll see a clearer division of functions (much as we have in the world of magazines) in which all sorts of stories continue to be covered, but not everyone feels compelled to follow every story.

This doesn't mean we've seen the last word on "sex scandals." But I think in the future, the serious press is going to increasingly put such material to a relevance test. That is to say, there's going to be a challenge to prove that there's a real justification for making someone's private life public. We have already seen not only a growing public fatigue with the wall-to-wall coverage of politicians' lives, but also an increasing awareness on the part of the American press and public that this is not the way such matters are handled in many other parts of the world. Some journalists worry that, spurred by the new electronic news services, journalistic standards will continue to descend to the lowest common denominator. However, I think there are some reasons to be a bit more optimistic.

In any event, and whatever the future may hold, I'll be there reading and listening, writing and talking. I hope that many of you will be there with me as well!

index

Potemkin, Grigory Aleksandrovich, 137, 138, 139, 182

power: access to, 43, 48; accumulation, 50, 79; appetite for, 119–20; balance of, 88; concubine as female, xv, 6; different strategies to gain, 37; disdain for women in, 149; double standard, xiv; "extra" women as, 4; harems, 14, 17–22; imbalance of, 4; vs. indiscretions, 113; inherited, 118; judgment on, 106; "normal" women and, 149; Ottoman Empire, 17–18; politics, sex, and lack of relationship with, 177; sacred right, 124; secondhand, 80; sex as access to, xii, xv, xx, xxii, 6, 37; standards, xiii; virgin monarch, 131; women in, xvii–xviii, 64, 49, 131, 148–49; women judged by different standards, 181

pride, 54

princesses, Ottoman, 20n9

prostitutes, 29, 51, 52, 79

Ptolemy XIII, 119, 121

Ptolemy XIV, 121, 121n4, 122

Puritanism, 85

racism, 87

radio, xi, xvi, 77, 171

Radziwill, Lee, 32n7

relationship(s): arranged, 86; balance of power, 88–89; behavioral patterns, 29–30; complications, 161, 181–82; illegitimate, 182; illicit, 73, 75, 98; incestuous, 38; potential for fulfilling, 38

Rice, Tim, 39

rich and famous: confusing celebrities with heroes, xix; double standards, 180; fascination, xi–xii, 175; films,

xxiv; lost coverage in media, 182; ordinary people's media exposure, xix; public knowledge vs. private foibles, xiv. *See also* wealthy

Robin Hood, xixn4

Roosevelt, Eleanor Anna, xiii, xiv, xviii, xxi, xxiv, 163–71, 181–82; humanitarian/political causes, 165–66; intimate vs. sexual relationships, 169–70; lesbian relationships, 168–69; lovers, 166–68; marriage, 163; private emotional life, 166; public role, 164; relationship with Earl Miller, 66–67

Roosevelt, Franklin, xviii, xxi, 181–82; affair with Lucy Mercer, 164; infirmity, 165, 171, 171n8

royalty: alliances between countries, xvi, 61; Catholic Church and, 64–65; children, 65–67, 70–71, 74; corruption, 68–69; divorce, 62; economic situations, 65; failed marriages, 62, 66; heirs, 74; honeymoons, 70; marriages between, 63, 63n3; marriages between commoners and, 62; pawns of, 61; scandals, 63, 64; servants, 67; sexual relations, 61

rulers: divine status, 119; women, 148–49

Ruth (biblical), 38, 47, 54

Salome (biblical), 55n7

Same-Sex Unions in Premodern Europe (Boswell), 153

Samson (biblical), xv, 50–54, 54; as antihero, 50; betrayal of Delilah, 52; complete passivity, 53; destruction, 53; pride, 54; secret of strength, 53; stupidity, 51

scandal(s), 52, 162; age and, 141; Catherine the Great, 135;